Beethoven
String Quartets
Grosse Fuge in B-Flat Major, Op. 133;
Grosse Fuge, Op. 134 (Piano Transcription);
String Quartet in C-Sharp Minor, Op. 131;
String Quartet in F Major, Op. 135

Their Creation, Origins and Reception History
Incorporating
Contextual Accounts of Beethoven and His Contemporaries

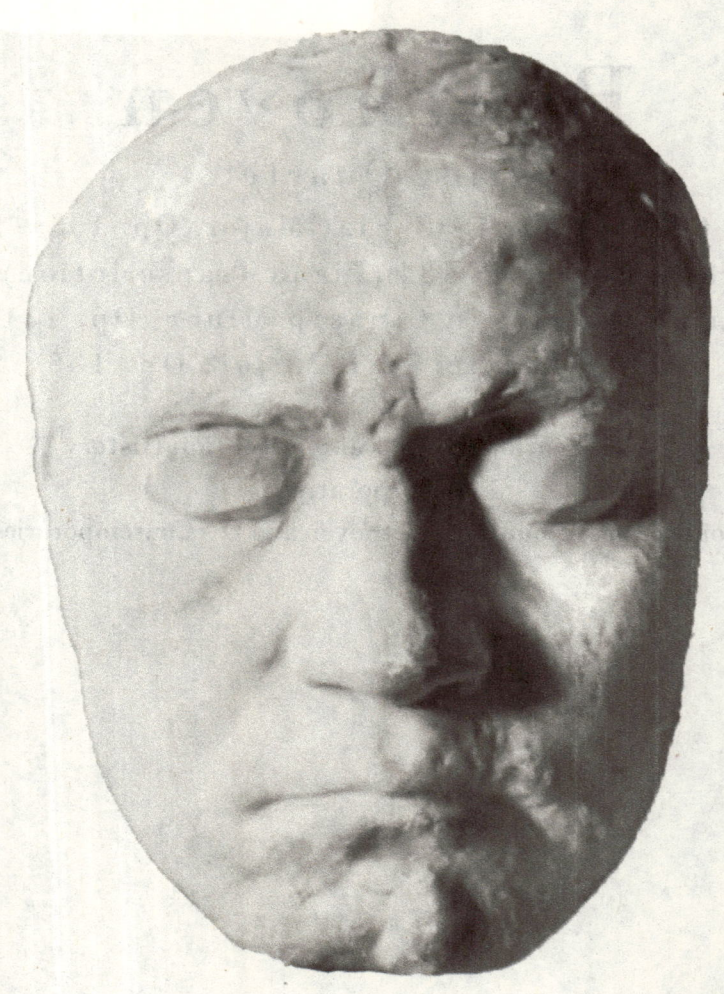

BEETHOVEN
As depicted by the life mask taken by Franz Klein in 1812
(derived from a copy in the author's possession)

BEETHOVEN

STRING QUARTETS

GROSSE FUGE IN B-FLAT MAJOR, OP. 133;
GROSSE FUGE, OP. 134 (PIANO TRANSCRIPTION);
STRING QUARTET IN C-SHARP MINOR, OP. 131;
STRING QUARTET IN F MAJOR, OP. 135

THEIR
CREATION ORIGINS
AND
RECEPTION HISTORY

Incorporating contextual accounts of
Beethoven and his contemporaries

Terence M. Russell

Jelly Bean Books

The right of Terence Russell to be identified as the
Author of the Work has been asserted by him in accordance
with the Copyright, Designs and Patents Act 1988.

Copyright © Terence M. Russell 2022

Published by
Jelly Bean Books
136 Newport Road
Cardiff
CF24 1DJ

ISBN: 978-1-915439-15-4

www.candyjarbooks.co.uk

All rights reserved.
No part of this publication may be reproduced, stored in a
retrieval system, or transmitted at any time or by any means,
electronic, mechanical, photocopying, recording or otherwise
without the prior permission of the copyright holder. This book is
sold subject to the condition that it shall not by way of trade or
otherwise be circulated without the publisher's prior consent in any
form of binding or cover other than that in which it is published.

CONTENTS

AUTHOR'S NOTE	I
INTRODUCTION	IX
EDITORIAL PRINCIPLES	XVII
BEETHOVEN'S FINANCIAL TRANSACTIONS	XXIII
BEETHOVEN STRING QUARTETS, THEIR CREATION ORIGINS AND RECEPTION HISTORY	
Grosse Fuge in B-Flat Major, Op. 133	1
Grosse Fuge Op 134 (Piano transcription)	41
String Quartet in C-Sharp Minor, Op. 131	49
String Quartet in F Major, Op. 135	138
BIBLIOGRAPHY	196
INDEX	231
ABOUT THE AUTHOR	234

AUTHOR'S NOTE

I have cherished the idea of making a study of the life and work of Beethoven for many years. This statement requires a few words of personal reflection. I first encountered Beethoven in my early piano lessons — Minuet in G major, WoO 10, No. 2. At the same time I became acquainted with his piano pupil Carl Czerny — *Book One, Piano Studies*. My heart sank when I discovered the rear cover advertised a further *99* books in the same series — scales, arpeggios studies for the left hand, studies for the right hand — all the way to his Op. 824! By coincidence, my *Czerny Book One* was edited by Alec Rowley — who had the same surname as my music teacher. In my childish innocence, I often wondered why *he himself* never appeared to give me a lesson!

In my teenage years I found myself drawn ever closer to Beethoven's music in the manner that ferromagnetic materials are ineluctably held captive in the sway of a magnetic field. The impulse to which I yielded is well described in words the conductor Bruno Walter gave in one of his rare public addresses: 'It is my belief that young people at that age are more easily impressed by what is heroic and grandiose; that they more easily understand works of art in which passionate feelings are violently uttered in raised accents, and that the lighter sounds of cheerfulness are less impressive to them.' I do indeed recall the stirring effect made on me on first hearing the Overture *Egmont*, the unfolding drama of the Fifth Symphony and the declamatory opening chords of the *Emperor* Piano Concerto.

I resolved to read everything I could about Beethoven, starting with Marion Scott's pioneering English-language study of the composer in the *Master Musicians series*. My father took out a subscription for me for *The Gramophone* magazine, enabling me to read reviews of the new 'LP' recordings — none of which though I could afford! The LP was then — 1950s — beginning to supplant the 78 rpm shellac records, stacks of which could be purchased for as little as six pence each in 'old' money. At this same time I had the privilege of hearing Beethoven's music performed by the *Hallé Orchestra* under the baton of Sir John Barbirolli, and experienced the *Carl Rosa Opera Company* perform the composer's only opera *Fidelio*; I borrowed the piano-reduction score from the City Library to become better acquainted with this moving work — only to find the score's fists full of notes were well beyond my capabilities. Nonetheless, since then *Fidelio's* every note has been woven into my DNA. I also recall the period when the *London Promenade Concerts* were designated 'Friday night is Beethoven night'.

Through these influences I resolved to visit Vienna to see where Beethoven had lived and worked. But how? The support for such travel was beyond the means of my family. Fortunately in my final year at school (1959) an opportunity presented itself. I saw a poster that stated *WUS – World University Service* – required volunteers to work in the Austrian town of Linz to help relocate refugees who were living there in improvised wooden shacks – displaced and dispossessed victims of the Second World War. To those participating all expenses would be paid together with free accommodation – in one of the crumbling wooden shacks! From Linz, I planned to make my way to Vienna.

I applied to *WUS* and, despite being a mere school-leaver, I was accepted. The *WUS* authorities doubtless reasoned the building-trade skills I had acquired during my secondary education in the building department of a technical school would be useful. This proved to be the case. At the refugee camp I dug trenches and was allowed to assist as a bricklayer. All about me were wide-eyed children eager to help but mostly getting in the way. I recall one afternoon when a reporter from *The Observer* newspaper paid a visit to our construction site to gather material for an article he was writing on European post-war recovery – he generously admired my trenches and brickwork!

Of lasting significance was another visit, this time from a Belgian priest. He took a group of us to the nearby *Mauthausen* Concentration Camp, recently opened as a silent and solemn memorial to those who had perished there. It was a deeply moving experience. Years later I learned of the views of the ardent Beethovenian Sir Michael Tippet. After the horrors of the *Holocaust*, he posed the question for mankind: 'What price Beethoven now?' He posited: 'Could we any longer find solace in Beethoven's setting of Schiller's *Ode to Joy* and its utopian vision – "Be embraced you Millions"?'

My refugee contribution duly came to end and Vienna beckoned. On arrival there I found scenes reminiscent of *The Third Man* and *Harry Lime*. I recall, for example, encountering cobblestones piled high in the streets waiting to be replaced after having been disturbed by the heavy armoured vehicles that had so recently passed over them. But Vienna was welcoming. I visited the houses where Beethoven had lived and worked and paused outside others associated with him that were identified by a commemorative plaque and the Austrian flag. A particularly memorable occasion was attending a recital in the great salon within the palace of Beethoven's noble patron Prince Lobkowitz — the very one where the *Eroica* Symphony had been premiered. Ultimately, my steps led me to the composer's first resting place in the *Währinger Ortsfriedhof*. I paid silent homage to the great man and, as I did so, discovered nearby the resting place of Franz Schubert to whom Beethoven was an endless source of admiration and inspiration.

I felt a youthful impulse to discover yet more about Beethoven and his music. But absorption in musicology would have to take second place. My chosen career beckoned in the guise of architecture — 'the mother of the arts' and 'the handmaid of society'. There was room though for Beethoven's music and from that time on it has been my constant companion through attendance at recitals, in concerts and music-making in the home. And at home a reproduction of Franz Kline's 1812 study of the composer has greeted me each day for more than half a century.

On my retirement from a career in architectural practice, research and university teaching, the opportunity finally presented itself for me to devote time to researching Beethoven musicology. Having attained my eightieth year also emboldened me to make progress with my good intentions!

With these autobiographical remarks outlined I will say a few remarks about my working method — see also the comments made in *Editorial Principles*.

As a member of staff of The University of Edinburgh, I had the good fortune to have access to the *Reid Music Library*, formed from a nucleus of books bequeathed by General John Reid and augmented over the years by such custodians as Sir Donald Francis Tovey, sometime *Reid Professor of Music* and renowned Beethoven scholar. Over a period of three years, I made a survey of the many works in the Reid collection. I consulted each item in turn making records on paper slips — many hundreds — that I deemed to be relevant for my researches. I confined my searches to book-publications, as reflected in my accompanying bibliography. All of this was quite some years ago, the cut-off date for my researches being 2007. Beyond this date I have not surveyed any further works. I am mindful though that Beethoven musicology and related publication continue to be a major field of endeavour in the manner of the proverbial 'ever rolling stream'.

In the intervening years since completing my archival researches, personal tribulations associated with family illness and bereavement slowed my progress in giving expression to my projected intentions. Latterly, however, with renewed energy, and more time at my disposal, I have been able to make progress. My studies take the form of a set of monographs. These trace the creation origins and reception history of each of Beethoven's piano sonatas and string quartets. The resulting texts also incorporate contextual accounts of Beethoven and his contemporaries. Also included in my musicological surveys are two related Beethoven anthologies. The set of monographs in question, identified by short title, are:

Beethoven: An anthology of selected writings.
Beethoven: The piano sonatas: An anthology of selected writings.

The Piano Sonatas:
Op. 2—Op. 28
Op. 31—Op. 81A
Op. 90—Op. 111

The String Quartets:
Op. 18, Nos. 1—6
Op. 59, Nos. 1—3 (Razumovsky); Op. 74 (The Harp);
    Op. 95 (Quartetto Serioso)
Op. 127, Op. 132 and Op. 130 (Galitzin)
Op. 131, Op. 135; Grosse Fuge, Op. 133 and Op. 134
    (Fugue transcription)

I provide further information about these studies in the introduction to each individual monograph. Suffice it for me to state here the basic premise upon which my work is founded. I believe it is rewarding, concerning the life of a great artist, to find connections between who he *was* and what he *did*; in Martin Cooper's words 'between his personality, as expressed on the one hand in human relationships, and on the other in artistic creation'. (*Beethoven, The Last Decade*) That is not to say I consider it essential to the enjoyment of Beethoven's music to know this or that fact about it. His music can be enjoyed, as millions do, with — in Robert Simpson's apt phrase —'an innocent ear', for what it is and how it reaches out to us in purely musical terms without any prejudging of its merits based upon extra-musicological facts.

I must make a further point. I am mindful that a scholar who ventures into a field of study that is not rightly his may be regarded with some suspicion. In this regard I can but ask the reader to place his or her trust in me in the following way. I have attempted to bring to my work the care which publishers and their desk editors have required of me in my book writings relating to architecture — listed elsewhere.

As inferred, it is now more than sixty years since I paid homage to Beethoven in Vienna's *Währinger Ortsfriedhof* and my warmth of feeling towards the composer and his music have grown with the passing of the years. My studies are not intended to be propaedeutic — that would be pretentious. However, if in sharing with others what I have to say contributes to their knowledge and understanding of the composer, and thereby increases their own feelings towards him and his works, my own pleasure in bringing my work to completion will be all the more enhanced.

It is perhaps fitting that my studies should appear in Beethoven's 250th Anniversary Year — I must confess more by chance than design!

When Beethoven arrived in Vienna, he was unknown. He was armed though with a note of encouragement from his youthful friend and benefactor Count Ferdinand Waldstein. It contained the often-quoted words: 'Receive Mozart's spirit from Haydn's hands.' Some forty years later Beethoven passed away in the House of the black-robed Spaniards at 200 *Alservorstädter*, the *Glacis* where he had lived since the autumn of 1825. Soldiers had to be called to secure the doors to the inner courtyard of the house from the pressure of onlookers. His body was blessed in the *Alservorsttädt Parish Church*, schools were closed and perhaps as many as 10,000 people formed a funeral procession — an honour ordinarily reserved for monarchs. The *Marcia Funebre* from the composer's Op. 26 Piano Sonata was performed at the funeral ceremony. Franz Grillparzer read the funeral oration. Franz Schubert, who, as remarked in life so admired Beethoven, was one of the pallbearers. The composer's mortal remains were lowered into a simple vault. Beethoven now belonged to history.

Dr Terence M. Russell
Edinburgh 2020

INTRODUCTION

The subjects of this study are the creation origins and reception history of Beethoven's string quartets. It is one of four that broadly correspond with the generally accepted periods into which the composer's compositions are held to conform and which have been described as 'early', 'middle', and 'late' and their counterparts, 'imitative', 'heroic' and 'introspective'. In our first study the string quartets Op. 18, Nos. 1–6 are considered alongside the transcription for string quartet of the Piano Sonata in E major, Op. 14. In the second part are the string quartets Op. 59, Nos. 1–3 (*Razumowsky*), Op. 74 in E-flat major, (*The Harp*) and Op. 95 in F minor (*Quartetto serioso*). In the third part are the string quartets Op. 127, Op. 132, and Op. 130 – the Galitzin Quartets. The fourth part of our study concludes with the string quartets Op. 131, Op. 135 and the *Great Fugue*, Op. 133 together with Beethoven's four-hand keyboard transcription Op. 134.

The collection of writings presented here derives from the string-quartet compositions of Beethoven's so-called third period. They take the form of extended essays that may serve the reader as a source of reference — in the manner of programme notes to a recital. Accordingly, the remarks relating to each string quartet are 'free standing' and can be read independently. That said they are also interlinked by the events unfolding in the composer's life. An attempt has been made, therefore, to interrelate the individual essays so that they may be read as a continuous narrative — in typical book fashion. A summary outline of this narrative is provided in the Index for each individual string quartet. Thereby, the reader is provided not only with a guide to the contents discussed in each quartet-text but also has an over-arching time-line of the principal events bearing on Beethoven's life and work. By way of an introduction to the individual essays in this part of our survey, we provide the following summary-outline bearing upon the compositions to which we make reference.

Beethoven returned to the genre of writing for the string quartet in the spring of 1824. His last essay in the medium had been the String Quartet, Op. 95 that was composed over the period 1810–11 but which was not premiered until 1814. In his remaining years Beethoven devoted his energies exclusively to writing string quartets. They stand alone, distant from the *Choral* Symphony and the *Missa Solemnis*. His renewed interest in the medium may be seen in response to the inner promptings of his developing and changing artistic and emotional outlook. Beethoven, however, was no 'desk' composer. Throughout his career he had composed in response to an external stimulus. Concerning the so-called 'late' quartets we see him creatively stirred primarily by a commission from Prince Galitzin of St. Petersburg for three string quartets. Additionally, circumstances in Vienna in the 1820s favoured the string quartet in public music-making with the advent of the professional string quartet. In this context the return to Vienna of Beethoven's long-term friend the violinist Ignaz Schuppanzigh — and the establishment of the Quartet bearing his name — provided an added incentive to Beethoven to compose quartets. Moreover, Beethoven always composed with performance in mind, even in the case of his most challenging compositions. Last, and by no means least, in an era when composers did not receive performance royalties, Beethoven needed the income for which his compositions were an essential source.

Beethoven worked solely on string-quartet composition from the spring of 1824 until the end of end of 1826 when mortal illness compelled him to lay down his pen. The Quartets in C-sharp minor, Op. 131 and F major, Op. 135 were not composed in response to a commission. In Joseph Kerman's words: 'Beethoven seems to have created these last quartets without any listener in mind but for himself.' They were published after the composer's death from which circumstance they derive their soubriquet *The posthumous Quartets*. To these string compositions should be added the Great Fugue — *Grosse Fuge* — Op. 133 and the composer's own keyboard four-hand arrangement of this Op. 134. The out-of-sequence numbering of these compositions arose from Beethoven negotiating with a number of publishers at the same time, something to which he was prone throughout his career in his business affairs — often setting off one publisher against another.

The Quartet in E-flat major, Op. 127, was largely composed during the second half of 1824, and was completed around February the following year. From then to the midsummer of 1825 Beethoven composed the A-minor Quartet, Op. 132. He worked on the first version of the

Quartet in B-flat major, Op. 130 – including the *Grosse Fuge*, Op. 133 – completing it in November 1825. Composition of the C-sharp minor Quartet, Op. 131 was commenced towards the end of 1825 and was completed in the summer 1826. The string Quartet in F major, Op. 135 and the four-hand piano transcription of the Great Fugue, Op, 134 occupied Beethoven throughout the autumn of 1826 during which period he also wrote an alternative finale for the Quartet Op. 130.

In the late quartets, Beethoven progressively increases the number of movements creating a new formal conception quite unlike anything preceding it. The E-flat major Quartet retains the four-movement sonata form but thereafter the style of musical conception and the number of movements are increased. The A minor Quartet possesses five, the B-flat major Quartet six, and the C-sharp minor has seven movements. Only in the F major Quartet, Op. 135 does he elect to return to the four-movement design. Moreover, in this quartet he reverts to shorter and less discursive movements – a harbinger, perhaps, of new things to come and the onset of a 'fourth' period?

Discussing some of the characteristics of Beethoven late works Maynard Solomon observes: '[Struggle] is sublimated into ecstasy, as in the *Arietta* of the Piano Sonata, Op. 111; chaos strives for lucid formation, as in the transition to the fugue of the *Hammerklavier* Sonata and in the opening of the finale of the Ninth Symphony; victorious conclusions are incessantly sought after and discovered, as in the *Grosse Fuge*, the Piano Sonata Op. 110, and the finale of the Quartet in C-sharp minor, Op. 131.' In support of his contention he quotes from the writings of that pillar of the English musical establishment Sir Charles Hubert Hastings Parry: 'Beethoven had by now found the accepted scheme of organisation which he himself had brought to perfection too constraining and restrictive to the impulse of his thought, and therefore endeavoured to find new types of form to revive sundry earlier types of organisation and combine them in various ways which departed from the essential principles upon which composers had been working for generations.'

Gestated within a few years — in some cases within only a few months — of each other, it is not surprising that the late quartets share thematic and other resemblances — for example a four-note configuration. For many authorities these imply the late quartets share an underlying unity — 'a unified corpus'. Others consider the five last quartets and the Great Fugue to be 'drenched in evocations of the human voice' that are meant to 'sing or to speak instantly to the heart' (Joseph Kerman). By way of illustration, we recall Beethoven's 'wordless recitative' at the beginning of the finale to the Ninth Symphony — where the cellos and bases recall themes heard in the previous movements. The implied meaning is then made evident when the baritone member of the vocal quartet proclaims: 'O friends, not these sounds; let us rather strike up something more seemly, more joyful.'

Assimilation of the late quartets throughout the nineteenth century was slow and protracted. As remarked, neither Op.131 nor Op.135 were performed in Beethoven's lifetime and for several years the companion quartets received only a handful of performances in the composer's native Vienna. They were received more favourably in other musical centres, notably Berlin, Leipzig and Paris. *The Beethoven Quartet Society* was founded in London in 1845 with the express aim of 'honouring Beethoven'. Its founder was Thomas Alsager, a pioneering music critic to *The Times*. One of the aims of the Society was to encourage an understanding of Beethoven's quartets from a study of their scores.

The Society has the distinction of being the first in England to perform the complete cycle of Beethoven's string quartets during the music season of 1845. In Zurich, in 1854, Richard Wagner organised and coached a rehearsal of the C-sharp minor Quartet and contributed analytical notes to the work. More generally, his Centennial Essay of 1870 is recognised for having nurtured a more positive attitude towards, and reception of, Beethoven's late chamber music. William Kinderman remarks: 'Beethoven's deafness, which was previously regarded as the handicap that explained the eccentricities of these works, was seen by Wagner as an enabling factor that had shielded Beethoven from the turmoil of the outer world and enhanced his ability to dwell in the inner-world of the imagination. For Wagner, Beethoven was a deaf "seer" who led the way to new artistic perspectives.'

By the 1870s Beethoven was becoming deified. He was perceived as a near mythic figure, a revolutionary genius without equal and the embodiment of qualities of freedom, inspiration and creativity. His image was reproduced in painting and sculpture with a scowling countenance as if defying fate and adversity. Notwithstanding this celebrity, in 1885 the prominent Viennese music critic Theodore Helm had occasion to write: 'Still today, among all the creations of Beethoven [the late quartets] are the least understood and most in need of a psychological and musical commentary.' He maintained: 'Unlike their predecessors, they were entirely individual, extremely personal, subjective, and wholly divorced from the outside world.' Harold Truscott summarizes the nineteenth century conception – or misconception – of the late quartets: '[They] were regarded reverently as a sort of last will and testament, separate from the rest of his work, regarded awesomely as utterances almost in an unknown tongue, scarcely meant for human ears.'

The dilemma posed by the works in question persisted

into the early years of the twentieth century. For example, the English composer and writer on music Thomas Frederick Dunhill remarked the late quartets 'were little more than imperfectly realized sketches' (*Chamber Music: A Treatise for students*, 1913). In his *Les Quatuors de Beethoven* (Paris, 1925) the French musicologist Joseph de Marliave introduced the late quartets by explaining: 'Lack of comprehension of Beethoven's motive force in the composition of these quartets is the chief reason they are so often thought obscure. The attitude of mind in which people listen to chamber music must undergo a radical change before the listener can understand them.' He elaborates: 'As a rule, the concert-goer is accustomed to notice, especially at the first hearing of a piece, mainly that aspect of it which appeals to the ear — *Aria* and *cantilena* passages, for example, and technical details of theme and melody. The rest he considers an elaborate development of the thematic material, which it is unnecessary to follow with the same close attention as the theme itself, and the ear may rest for a space in order to pick up the return of the subject with revived interest.' De Marliave considered such an attitude to be impossible with the last quartets where, he believed, this type of development to be non-existent — 'Beethoven's thought is linked, bar by bar, from start to finish, into a continuous organic whole, in which all must be grasped or nothing.'

De Marliave's near contemporary, the American musician-musicologist Arthur Shepherd, reflected: 'By reason of their many unique features; their apparent departure from classical procedure; their daring instrumentation; and their generally "problematic" character, much conjectural theorising had grown up around these last quartets. They were long regarded as baffling, experimental, if not indicative of a mental decline on the part of the composer. It became almost axiomatic among musicians, that they were, in many respects, unplayable.' (*The string quartets of Ludwig van Beethoven*, 1935).

Prince Galitzin's words of assurance to Beethoven have proved to be prophetic: 'One might say that your genius is centuries before its time and that there is no listener sufficiently enlightened to appreciate the full beauty of this music. But future generations will honour you and bless your memory more than your contemporaries are able.' (Galitzin to Beethoven, St. Petersburg, 8 April 1824.) It is fitting, therefore, that we conclude our introductory remarks to the composer's final essays in the genre of the string quartet with a selection of aphoristic writings that bear testimony to Galitzin's prediction.

> Writing on the occasion of Beethoven's Death Centenary, the violist Rebecca Clarke reflected: '[The late quartets] are so great that one hesitates to write about them; for the beauty of music lies in the very fact that it postulates itself only and cannot be expressed in any other way.'

Rebecca Clarke *The Beethoven quartets as a player sees them* in: *Musical Times*, Special Issue, 1927, Vol. VIII, No. 2.

> Writing of Beethoven's spiritual development, the Irish mathematician, musicologist and modern-day polymath stated: 'In the last quartets, spiritual experiences are communicated of which it is very difficult to mention even the elements ... And yet it is just this music that moves us and impresses us as containing the profoundest and most valuable experiences that any artist has yet conveyed.'

John William Sullivan, *Beethoven*, 1927.

The pioneering Beethoven German musicologist Paul Bekker perceived the composer's late string quartets to be a thematically unified whole. Of the C-sharp minor Quartet he wrote: 'The spirit of man, illuminated through the anguish of moral conflict and assured of the unity of Will and of Fate, of Freedom and Necessity, returns once more to earth.' He continues:

> 'The same idea which supports the A minor Quartet, Op. 132 and carried to dizzy heights in the B-flat major fugue [String Quartet, Op. 130] now leads it back to face life anew. The three great quartets thus form a tremendous imaginative triptych, the prophet ascends to the mountain top, sees his God face to face and returns to his people with his tables of the law, written and established for all eternity.'

Arthur Shepherd, *The string quartets of Ludwig van Beethoven*, 1935. Originally published in Paul Bekker, *Beethoven*, 1925 and reproduced by Shepherd as an act of homage to Bekker.

> 'With the works immediately following Op. 127, Beethoven passed beyond any semblance of quartet form as it was then understood. For over a century his three greatest quartets, in A minor, Op. 132, B-flat major, Op. 130, and C-sharp minor, Op. 131, remained more or less unsolved enigmas.'

Marion M. Scott, *Beethoven*: (*The Master Musicians*), 1940.

> 'One is carried away, astonished, and ravished by the sheer songfulness of the last quartets — by recitative and aria, lied, hymn, country dance, theme and variations, lyricism in all its manifestations.'

Joseph Kerman, *The Beethoven quartets*, 1967.

> 'It is important to realise ... that these five incomparable masterpieces of chamber music were not Beethoven's intended "last message" to the world. His untimely death came at a point when he was full of new ideas for such things as a Tenth Symphony, a Requiem and a String Quintet. The impression of finality is due to the universal acknowledgement of the quartets as a *summa* of instrumental music.'

Basil Lam, *Beethoven's string quartets*, 1975.

> 'These five works carry not merely the string quartet but the art of music into new regions. Studies of them are innumerable. Like *Hamlet* they will never yield up their last secrets or admit of a "final" solution. They are inexhaustible.'

Gerald Abraham, *Beethoven's chamber music* in: *The Age of Beethoven, The New Oxford History of Music*, Vol. VIII, Gerald Abraham editor, 1988.

> 'At issue for both Beethoven and his listeners, even 200 years afterwards, is the struggle to conceive and transmit the sense of beauty and goodness and the inner struggle with matters of

existential meaning and truth in a way at once general and overarching and also individual and specific to the moment of hearing ... In late Beethoven, the expression aspires to prophecy; to communicate across time and space, to connect the human community through a shared perception of art.'

Leon Botstein, *The patrons and publics of the quartets* in: Robert Winter and Robert Martin editors, *The Beethoven quartet companion*, 1994.

The German philosopher and musicologist Theodor Adorno reflects on the musical challenge posed by aspects of the late quartets: 'I should like to [state] what in purely musical terms, motivates timidity towards late Beethoven, [that is] the feeling of extreme seriousness conveyed by his late work. Listen for example to: the opening of the B-flat major Quartet, Op. 130; first movement, bars 1—4; String Quartet in C-sharp minor, Op. 131; first movement, bars 1—8; String Quartet, in F major, Op. 135, first movement, bars 1—17.' Adorno defines his view of seriousness: 'Something almost overloaded with content ... as if veiled ... It is thus very difficult to indicate what it consists of and, above all, to find out how the content is communicated within the composition.' Adorno asserts that the quartet passages cited conform to Goethe's dictum that 'ageing is a gradual stepping back from appearances ... something like a paring away of the sensuous, a spiritualization'.

Theodor W. Adorno, *Beethoven: the philosophy of music; fragments and texts*, 1998.

'The final five works do have a category of their own, and that category is "late". By then, the music had reached a state which could be called timeless and philosophical, transcending Beethoven's now total deafness and the chaos of his personal life. The first and last of these works do not quite fit the pattern. The first, Op. 127, has links with Op. 74 and Op. 95. The last disentangles itself from the preceding three works, and strides off into the future — except that, in [Beethoven's] quartet terms, there was no future.'

Conrad Wilson, *Notes on Beethoven: 20 crucial works*, 2003.

It is on record that Beethoven's close friend and associate, the violinist Karl Holz, once asked him which of his quartets he considered to be the greatest. He initially replied enigmatically: 'Each in his own way.' Later he confided he thought the String Quartet in C-sharp minor 'was his greatest'. When Franz Schubert heard the Quartet performed, just a few days before his untimely death, the exclaimed: 'What is there left for us to write?'

TMR

EDITORIAL PRINCIPLES

By its very nature a study of this kind draws extensively on the work of others. Every effort has been made to acknowledge this in the text by indicating words quoted or adapted with single quotation marks. Wherever possible, for the sake of consistency, I have retained the orthography of quoted texts making only occasional silent changes of spelling and capitalization. Deleted words are identified by means of three ellipsis points ... and interpolations are encompassed within square brackets [ ]. Quoted words, phrases and longer cited passages of text remain the intellectual property of their copyright holders.

I address the reader in the second person notwithstanding that the work is my own. It follows that I must bear the responsibility for any errors of misunderstanding or misinterpretation for which I ask the reader's forbearance. A collaboration I must acknowledge is the help I received from the librarians of the Reid Music Library at the University of Edinburgh. Over the three-year period it took me to compile my reference sources, they served me with unfailing courtesy, often supplying me with twenty or more books at a time. In converting my manuscript into book format, I wish to thank my editorial coordinator, William Rees, for his support and painstaking care. I would also like to thank Shaun Russell for his work designing the cover for each of the twelve volumes.

My admiration for Beethoven provided the initial impulse to commence this undertaking and has sustained me over the several years it has taken to bring my enterprise to completion. That said, I am no Beethoven idolater. I am mindful of the danger that awaits one who ventures to chronicle the work of a great artist. I believe it was Sigmund Freud who suggested that biographers may become so disposed to their subject, and their emotional involvement with their hero, that their work becomes an exercise in idealisation. In response to such a charge let me say. First, I am no biographer. I do however make occasional reference to Beethoven's personal life and his relationships with his contemporaries. Second, I acknowledge Beethoven has his detractors. Accordingly, I have not shrunk from allowing dissentient voices, critical of Beethoven and his work, to be heard. These, however, are few and are silenced amidst the adulation that awaits the reader in support of the endeavours of one of humanity's great creators and one who courageously showed the way in overcoming personal adversity.

TMR

BEETHOVEN'S FINANCIAL TRANSACTIONS

Beethoven's negotiations with his music publishers make many references to his compositions. Today they are recognised for what they are — enduring works of art — but referred to in his business correspondence they appear almost as though they were mere everyday commodities — for which he required an appropriate remuneration. Beethoven resented the time he had to devote to the business-side of his affairs. He believed an agency should exist, for fellow artists such as himself, from which a reasonable sum could be paid for the work (composition) submitted, leaving more time for creative enterprises. In the event Beethoven, like Mozart before him, had to deal with publishers largely on his own. Beethoven, though, did benefit in his business dealings from the help he received from his younger brother Kasper Karl (Caspar Carl). From

1800, Carl worked as a clerk in Vienna's Department of Finance in which capacity he found time to correspond with publishers to offer his brother's works for sale and — importantly — to secure the best prices he could. In April 1802 Beethoven wrote to the Leipzig publishers Breitkopf & Härtel: '[You] can rely entirely on my brother who, in general, attends to my affairs.' Whilst Carl promoted Beethoven's interests with determination, he appears to have lacked tact and made enemies. For example, Beethoven's piano pupil Ferdinand Ries — who for a while also helped the composer with his business negotiations — is on record as describing Carl as being 'the biggest skinflint in the world'. The currencies most referred to in Beethoven's correspondence are as follows:

- silver gulden and florin: these were interchangeable and had a value of about two English/British shillings
- ducat: 4 1/2 gulden/florins: valued at about nine shillings
- louis d'or: This gold coin was adopted during the Napoleonic wars and the French occupation of Vienna and Austria more widely. It had a value of about two ducats or approximately twenty shillings or one-pound sterling.

Beethoven was never poor — in the romantic sense of 'an artist starving in a garret'. On arriving in Vienna in 1792, he was fortunate to receive financial support from his patron Prince Karl Lichnowsky who conferred on him an annuity of 600 florins that he maintained for several years. Between the months of February and July of 1796, Beethoven undertook a concert tour taking in Prague, Dresden, Leipzig and Berlin. He was well received and wrote to his other younger brother Nikolaus Johann: 'My art is winning me friends and what more do I want? ... I shall make a good deal of money.' Later on, in 1809, Napoleon Bonaparte's youngest brother Jérôme Bonaparte offered Beethoven an appointment at his Court with the promise of an income of 4,000 florins. Alarmed at the prospect of losing Beethoven — now the most celebrated composer in Europe — three of Vienna's most notable citizens, namely, the Archduke Rudolph (Beethoven's only composition pupil), Prince Kinsky and Prince Lobkowitz settled on the composer the same sum of 4,000 florins. Inflation, however, brought about by the Napoleonic wars, soon eroded its value; personal misfortune to Lobkowitz and Kinsky also took its toll.

Beethoven undoubtedly had to work hard to secure a reasonable standard of living. Notwithstanding, despite his occasional straitened circumstances, he contributed generously to the needs of others. For example, he allowed his works to be performed free of charge at charitable concerts; in 1815 his philanthropy earned for him the honour of Bürgerrecht — 'freedom of the City'.

Beethoven earned a great deal of money when his music was performed, to considerable acclaim, at several concerts held in association with the Congress of Vienna (1814-15). He did not though benefit from it personally; he invested it on behalf of his nephew Karl. It is one of the misfortunes of Beethoven's life that in money-matters he was culpably improvident. This is poignantly evident in a letter he wrote on 18 March 1827 to the Philharmonic Society of London just one week before his death; the Society had made him a gift of £100. He sent the Society 'his most heartfelt thanks for their particular sympathy and support'.

TMR

'If Beethoven's enemies find in his last works ... nothing but confusion and contradiction, they must be reminded that even confusion is honourable if it is based on great and noble intentions and carried out by pure means. And it cannot be proved that our master's intentions and means were otherwise. This fact may one day vindicate the works and should encourage the student not to grow weary in his research.'

Anton Felix Schindler, Beethoven as I knew him, edited by Donald W. MacArdle and translated by Constance S. Jolly from the German edition of 1860, (reprint 1966), pp. 308—9.

'A fundamental difference of outlook separates the last quartets from those that preceded them, including the one in F minor, Op. 95, even though it approaches the spirit of the later works in a certain subjective intensity of emotion. Impassioned they may be, these earlier quartets, but they are primarily objective, and the later works are stamped with a profound and undeniable subjectivity; the mind that formed them is now wholly independent of external things for its inspiration, detached from the outside world, and careless of traditional form; the last quartets are essentially the direct expression of Beethoven's most intimate spirit, the channel of inspiration flowing from another sphere.'

Joseph de Marliave, Beethoven's quartets, New York: Dover Publications 1925 (reprint 1961), p. 219.

'In coming to the late quartets we now pass over a period of fourteen years and reach the great last period of Beethoven's work. The deafness that threatened him about the time he began the composition of the first quartets has now become absolute, and his last quartets were never heard by his ears. Cut off as he was from the world of hearing, his thoughts necessarily turned inward and his music became more than ever a thing of the mind. During these last years he found the intimacy of the string quartet the medium in which he could best express himself, and his quartets more and more became to him refuge, consolation, one might almost say testament.'

Rebecca Clarke — writing on the occasion of Beethoven's Death Centenary — The Beethoven quartets as a player sees them in: Musical Times, Special Issue, London: Vol. VIII, No. 2, 1927, pp. 184—90.

'With the passage of time, a consensus has emerged that sees Beethoven's later sonatas and quartets not as wayward productions of a deaf eccentric, as some early critics had seen them, but as some of the richest contributions ever made to musical art. The startling innovations of the last quartets may be said to centre on the musical symbolism in the A minor, paradoxical contrast in the B-flat major, and narrative design in the C-sharp minor ... The last quartets are bold, visionary works that seem to open a new creative period rather than close an old one.'

William Kinderman, Beethoven, Oxford: Oxford University Press, 1997, pp. 323–4.

GROSSE FUGE IN B-FLAT MAJOR, OP. 133

'Even as late as the early part of the twentieth century, Romain Rolland could write: 'The original finale was published separately as Opus 133; it is a terrifically long-drawn fugue and is regarded as almost incomprehensible by even the most ardent admirers of Beethoven's style.'

Rolland, Romain, *Beethoven and Handel*, 1917, p. 189.

'The great B-flat major Quartet contrasts with Beethoven's other quartets, seen as a whole, more a suite-like, free-formation than a strict sonata. That is revealed by the great first movement and the colossal closing movement, the famous so-called *Grosse Fuge*... That the monumental content of the *Grosse Fuge* works better in a full string orchestra than in a string quartet is something that experience has often shown.'

Wilhelm Furtwängler, quoted in: Michael Tanner editor, *Notebooks, 1924–1954: Wilhelm Furtwängler*, 1989, p. 120.

'The conqueror of Fate sees Fate no longer as inimical, but as the only way to greatness. Fate's command, once felt as bitter and fiercely resisted, is now heard as the message of freedom and blends at last with the personal will which once strove against it ... The ideas of Freedom and Necessity are blended by Beethoven in his fugue, upon which he wrote, *Tantôt libre, tantôt recherché* ... The work is one of compelling, almost overwhelming greatness; it is above comparisons save, perhaps, with two other fugues in B-flat major, the finale of Op. 106 and the *Et vitam venturi* of the *Mass* [*Missa Solemnis*]. Even Beethoven could climb no higher.'

Paul Bekker, *Beethoven*, 1925, pp. 332–3.

'One remaining aspect of this amazing work should not be disregarded. It is predominantly the most striking manifestation of the Master's "impulse to abstraction". Its nearest analogy is the fugue in the Piano Sonata Op. 106. In such works Beethoven's monumental architecture was achieved with an almost ruthless, yet superb disregard of essential euphony. Some will always maintain that in the *Grosse Fuge* the intellect is

> served at the experience of the ear. But when all is said and done, these mighty works constitute a challenge to sheer musical understanding and spiritual insight.'

Arthur Shepherd, *The String Quartets of Ludwig van Beethoven*, 1935, pp. 70–1.

> 'Paradox is its essence, the paradox of different forms of the note-set which can be shown to exist in the same sound-world ... The *Great Fugue* burns with its own special flame, pursuing to the point of self-absorption its own retrospective ideal of contrapuntal rigour, and its own proleptic ideal of containing variation ... One would not even want to say that the *Great Fugue* transcends the early parts of the Quartet: it entirely wipes them out ... There is a sense in which this finale trivialises the journey which it means to terminate, and there is also a sense in which the *Great Fugue* orbits upon a private musical sphere of its own, needing no other sounds, needing no other universe.'

Joseph Kerman, *The Beethoven Quartets*, 1967, p. 322.

> 'At eighty I have found new joy in Beethoven, and the *Great Fugue* now seems to me — it was not always so — a perfect miracle. How right Beethoven's friends were when they convinced him to detach it from Op. 130, for it must stand by itself, this absolutely contemporary piece of music will be contemporary for ever.'

Igor Stravinsky and Robert Craft, *Dialogues and a Diary*, 1968, p. 124.

Elsewhere Stravinsky writes:

> 'The *Great Fugue* enlarges the meaning of Beethoven more than any other work ... It breaks all our measurements, too, human no less than musical, especially the sudden sustained, scarcely believable energy, as if from a musical Platformate. The other quartets we can know [but] the *Fugue* is not knowable in the same way. Prejudices as to dimensions and elements must be overcome. When they have been, if they can be, we discover no chain of expectations is built up in us, that the music defies familiarity by being new and different every time.'

Igor Stravinsky, *Themes and Conclusions*, 1972, p. 260.

> '[The] fugue is a lyrical structure; its complexity comes from details spreading from its counterpoint, which itself grows from its melodic content. Beethoven's fugue has drama, it is true, but it is a drama springing from its nature as a fugue, or as a piece in fugue, to be accurate, in spite of the use of certain types of sonata processes in places ... That the fugue remained the proper finale to the work there is no doubt, and today there are far more performances with the fugue than with the alternative finale: more than at any previous time, although the fugue is not even today wholeheartedly accepted. It remains as difficult a movement as ever to bring off, and changes in technique ... have done nothing to alter this.'

Harold Truscott, *Beethoven's Late String Quartets*, 1968, pp. 93—4 and pp. 133—4.

> '*The Grosse Fuge* is unique. The contrapuntal ingenuity of the music, which might suggest an affinity with J. S. Bach's *Kunst der Fuge*, is in reality secondary. What grips the listener is the dramatic experience of forcing — for there is frequently a sense of violence in this mastery — two themes which have, by nature, nothing in common, to breed and produce a race of giants, episodes or variations that have no parallel in musical history.'

Martin Cooper, *Beethoven: the last decade, 1817—1827*, 1970, p. 388.

> 'Artists are praised by historians for their anticipation of later techniques, an element interesting only to connoisseurs of precedence, and meaningless with the passage of time. How shall we praise Beethoven then for inventing a music beyond the historical process? The just word is Stravinsky's — no idle hyperbole but a precise statement of the truth: "This absolutely contemporary piece of music that will be contemporary for ever".'

Basil Lam, *Beethoven string quartets*, 1975, p. 113.

> 'I have heard many a good musician, when listening to Beethoven's *Great Fugue*, cry out: "This sounds like atonal music".'

Arnold Schoenberg quoted in: Leonard Stein editor, *Style and Idea: selected writings of Arnold Schoenberg*, 1975.

> '[in] the *Grosse Fuge*, the fugue's closest analogue is the process of birth, the pain-ridden, exultant struggle for emergence — and the passage through the labyrinth, from darkness to light, from doubt to belief, from suffering to joy, cannot be without its special torments.'

Maynard Solomon, *Beethoven*, 1977, pp. 300–1.

> 'It would be impossible to expect in a work of this size to maintain a strictly fugal texture throughout and the work is best understood if regarded, not as a highly eccentric fugue, but as a kind of symphonic poem consisting of several contrasted but thematically related sections and containing a certain amount of fugal writing ... In no other work did [Beethoven] assemble in a single continuous movement such a variety of incident or show so much resource in developing his material ... When a difficult work is imperfectly known, its more uncompromising features often make at first a disproportionately deep impression, and for many years the rough-edged quality of the first section of the *Grosse Fuge* blinded many musicians to the wonderful beauty of the music that follows it.'

Philip Radcliffe, *Beethoven's String Quartets*, 1978, p. 138, p. 142 and p. 146.

'Occupying almost as many pages of score as the whole of the rest of the work, it is a fugue in three massive stages, a movement in which Beethoven is at his most uncomfortable, whether in his harmony or his often jagged rhythm, his intensive polyphony or his perpetually striving, stretched sonorities.'

Paul Griffiths, *The String Quartet*, 1983, p. 106.

'[Op. 133] amounts to an exhaustive survey of a single subject's rhythmic and fugal possibilities — in Beethoven's words *tantôt libre, tanto recherché*.'

Denis Matthews, *Beethoven*, (*Master Musicians*), 1985, p. 145.

'[At] his sublimest, Beethoven is sometimes at his most problematic: in the case of one famous, discarded finale — Op. 130's first — he burst the bounds of the string quartet altogether, and can only be heard without aural frustration in Furtwängler's self-conducted, string-orchestral arrangement.'

Hans Keller, *The Great Haydn Quartets: their interpretation*, 1986, p. 17.

'The *Grosse Fuge* obviously presents an enormous challenge to any group that attempts to interpret it, string quartet or orchestra. I hate to take an anti-orchestral view of things; I'm not at all of that mind, believe me ... But string-quartet music is like the fine drawing of a master, and the moment you make something grandiose of it you tamper with the spirit.' Michael Tree, violist, quoted in:

David Blum, *The Art of Quartet Playing: the Guarneri Quartet in conversation with David Blum*, 1986, p. 165.

'[My] favourite Beethoven symphony is the Eighth, my favourite movement of all of his sonatas the opening of Op. 101, and, for me, the *Grosse Fuge* is not only the greatest work Beethoven ever wrote but just about the most astonishing piece in musical literature.' Glenn Gould quoted in:

Tim Page editor, *The Glenn Gould Reader*, 1987, p. 102.

'Was [Beethoven] persuaded by the thought of the extra income to be gained by composing a new finale while publishing the old one separately, both in its original form and as an arrangement for piano duet? Or did he himself hold doubts about the viability of the *Grosse Fuge* as a finale for Op. 130? Are both endings equally satisfying, or is one more appropriate than the other? This is a "difficult decision" (Op. 135, *Muss es sein?*) which each listener must make for him- or herself with each hearing.' Nicholas Marston quoted in:

Barry Cooper, *The Beethoven Compendium; a guide to Beethoven's life and music*, 1991, pp. 236–7.

'The resolution of these extraordinary, unprecedented conflicts that the *Grosse Fuge* has posed is surprising and touching — a mixture of the exalted and the humorous that only Beethoven could have invented.'

Michael Steinberg, *The Late Quartets*, in: Robert Winter and Robert Martin editors, *The Beethoven Quartet Companion*, 1994, pp. 240—1.

'There is something Sublime about the form of the *Grosse Fuge*: its sheer size indicates in the analyst a kind of Burkian terror. Faced with such a structure, critics like Marliave, d-Indy, and Mason have simply tabulated the work, since it fits into no pre-existing mould; others describe it as some kind of hybrid — an amalgam of sonata, variation, and fugue, or a "symphonic poem", or a "Baroque suite" — or anything else that is amorphous. Indeed, even its disparateness has been applauded as a resolution of the diversity of the Quartet.'

Daniel K. L. Chua, *The "Galitzin" Quartets of Beethoven: Opp.127, 132, 130*, 1995, p. 225.

'Without the rest of the Quartet ... the *Great Fugue* is effectively orphaned, and the beginning of its elaborate *Overtura* loses point. The *Grosse Fuge* is a finale in search of the work with which it has now, in modern performances, often been reconciled.'

William Kinderman, *Beethoven's Last Quartets* in:

Beethoven, 1997, p. 295.

> '[The] work draws on ... contrapuntal genres, including fugue, fugato, and cantusfirmus variations. In Beethoven's hands, these genres take on an extreme character: while imitative textures normally represent the quintessence of the Quartet's conversational idiom, here they often create the impression of fierce arguments among the members of the ensemble ... What Beethoven created in the *Grosse Fuge* is rather a metagenre in which the canonical types — symphony, sonata, fugue, and so forth — are represented by some, but not all, of their constitutive features ... the "manner" of the Classical sonata, the "tone" of a fugue, the "tendency" of a symphonic work.'

John Daverio, *Manner, Tone, and Tendency in Beethoven's Chamber Music for Strings* in: Glenn Stanley editor, *The Cambridge Companion to Beethoven*, 2000, pp. 162–3.

> 'The original finale, the *Grosse Fuge*, gives a new sense of heightened contrast and climax, in part the natural legacy of fugal movements in the Classical period (in Beethoven's own Op. 59, No 3, the *Hammerklavier* Sonata, Mozart's Quartet in G major, K. 387, Haydn's Op. 50, No. 4 and several symphonies, and any number of masses), more particularly the product of a movement of often obscure erudition and calculated reference back to thematic and tonal concerns from earlier movements.'

David Wyn Jones, *Beethoven and the Viennese Legacy*, in:

Robin Stowell, editor, *The Cambridge Companion to the String Quartet*, 2003, p. 225.

> 'The massive buttress, growing out of a four-note motif with which Beethoven became obsessed while writing these last Quartets, is almost a fifteen-minute quartet in itself and has often been treated as such. Preserving a classical layout, Beethoven here compressed four recognisable movements into one.'

Conrad Wilson, *Notes on Beethoven: 20 crucial works*, 2003, p. 123.

> 'Beethoven seems not to have understood that his audience might find this dense, convoluted work difficult to comprehend, and even today, with our minds used to accommodating complex music, it is hardly easy to listen to.'

Alison Bullock, *Notes to the BBC Radio Three Beethoven Experience*, Friday 10 June 2005, www.bbc.co.uk/radio3/Beethoven

> 'Scholars have been especially concerned with the never-ending controversy over Beethoven's decision to detach the fugue from the Op. 130 Quartet and the writing of a substitute finale. And so they look to the sketches in order to reconstruct Beethoven's intentions regarding the nature of the original finale. Was it initially meant to be a weighty fugue that would counterbalance the powerful opening movement, as Klaus Kropfinger argues [*Das gespaltene Werk*, pp. 313–14]?

> Or was it intended to be of "more modest dimensions" and of a lighter character, as Barry Cooper has asserted [*Beethoven and the Creative Process*, p. 211 and pp. 213—4.]?'

William Caplin, *The Genesis of the Countersubjects for the Grosse Fuge*, in: William Kinderman, editor, *The String Quartets of Beethoven*, 2005, p. 241.

In Beethoven's final years he was repeatedly disposed to giving expression to his musical thoughts through the medium of the fugue and variants on the art of composing in a fugal style. The fugue appears to great effect in the finale of the Cello Sonata No. 2 in D, Op. 102 from 1815. The following year Beethoven adopted the fugal idiom throughout extended passages in the finale of the Piano Sonata in A, Op. 101. In 1818 he wrote a short fugue in D for String Quintet, published later as Op. 137. 1818 also witnessed the appearance of the epochal *Hammerklavier* Piano Sonata, Op. 106, with its challenging fugal finale. In the finale to the Piano Sonata in A flat, Op. 110 he combined a more lyrical style of fugal writing with his well-established variations manner. In the *Missa Solemnis* in D, Op. 123, that occupied Beethoven from 1819 until 1823, there are fugal conclusions to the *Gloria* and *Credo*. Contemporaneous are the 33 Variations in C, Op. 120 on a waltz theme by Diabelli that give prominence to fugal writing at their close. Mention may also be made of the more isolated use of fugatos in the Third, Fifth and Seventh Symphonies and in Symphony No. 9 in D Minor, Op. 125 (1822—4) in which a fugato idiom is adopted in the first movement, a fugal exposition in the second and fugal episodes in the finale. In our previous studies of the Galitzin String Quartets, we have seen Beethoven adopted contrapuntal writing in the *Scher-*

zando vivace of Op. 127 and the *Heiliger Dankgesang* of Op. 132 that was conceived alongside the *Grosse Fuge*.

Of related interest, and indicative of a further impulse that orientated Beethoven towards a fugal-style of writing, was his desire to enshrine in music his homage to J. S. Bach. After reflecting on his achievement he once remarked, in a characteristic play on words, 'not a stream but an ocean' (*bach* meaning brook/steam in German). Beethoven's sketches through 1822–25 reveal him preoccupied with creating a theme on the German musical notation B A C H that was intended to feature in a highly contrapuntal-fugal overture incorporating sonorous passages for three trombones. In the event this did not materialise and found expression only in the short Canon, WoO 191. The spirit of the composer's intentions though infiltrated the *Grosse Fuge*; in Barry Cooper words 'the monumental character of the fugal texture, as well as the key ... were transferred from one work to the other'.[i]

As further evidence of an influence that may have become woven into the fabric and texture of the *Grosse Fuge*, Marion Scott cites inferences from Beethoven's sketchbook for 1815. Amongst other things he was then exploring ideas for a possible opera subject – after *Leonora-Fidelio* this became almost a constant preoccupation. On this occasion, he contemplated a *Bacchus* Opera that would give prominence to *Pan* (Roman equivalent *Faunus*) who in Greek mythology was god of the wild, of nature and mountains and their flock, and a companion of nymphs. Scott suggests that in writing what she call this 'terrifying movement' – the *Grosse Fuge* – Beethoven's thoughts may have arisen once more relating to the Pan myth and, as expressed in the *Grosse Fuge*, 'might well be symbolic of the struggle between body and spirit, and the ultimate triumph of the sprit'.[ii]

Beethoven was well equipped to undertake fugal composition; he was given to saying 'in my youth I wrote hundred of fugues'. As Basil Lam contends: 'Beethoven's knowledge of fugue was not only based on the greatest models, but lay in the depths of his own musical experience.'[iii] Even before he had reached what we now refer to as the teenage years, he had mastered all forty-eight of Bach's *Preludes and Fugues* under the guidance of his teacher Christian Gottlob Neefe — an achievement that places his keyboard powers alongside those of the twelve-year old Franz Liszt who, late in life, was proud to affirm his own similar accomplishment. It is also known Beethoven admired Mozart's severe C minor fugue, K 426 for two pianos. He once copied out the work in full score to gain a better overview of its construction. His manuscript is unusually clear — quite unlike the hasty style he adopted in his compositional sketchbooks — indicative of the care he took.[iv] Moreover, Beethoven had received a thorough grounding in counterpoint from the Austrian composer and theorist Johann Georg Albrechtsberger.

John Daverio believes there is 'compelling logic' in Beethoven's plan to conclude the B-flat major String Quartet with the *Grosse Fuge*. In addition to the impulses we have just cited, he suggests precedents in the quartet repertoire itself may have exerted an added stimulus. By way of illustration, he alludes to Haydn's fugal treatment in his String Quartets Op. 20, Nos. 2, 5 and 6 and to his later Op. 50, No 4 — and we recall that, for a period, Haydn was also one of Beethoven's teachers.[v] Other commentators perceive the *Grosse Fuge* as a direct response to the *Cavatina* in Op. 130. For example, Joseph de Marliave states: 'It seemed as if Beethoven had spent his emotional resources in the agony of the *Cavatina*, and, as he so often felt, strove to sink himself in a *technical tour de force* in working out this massive contrapuntal design, which surpassed in technique anything he had ever achieved before.'[vi] Similarly, Rebecca Clarke: 'One can easily understand how after this outpouring Beethoven felt he must try to cover his emotion and regain his balance by writing a last movement of heroic proportions and contrapuntal grimness; and this he certainly succeeded in doing in his remarkable *Grosse Fuge* which was the original finale to this quartet.'[vii]

Discussing Beethoven's late fugues, Pierre Boulez makes reference to 'their exceptional character' that for him 'makes them such unique, incomparable creations; at the very limits of the possible'. He believed they bear witness to 'the ever-increasing hiatus between those forms which remain as symbols of the strict style, and a harmonic thought which asserts its freedom with growing vehemence'. He concludes: 'When the drama of this hiatus is experienced as keenly as it was by Beethoven, the result is among other things the fugue in Op. 106, and the *Grosse Fuge* for strings.'[viii] When Maynard Solomon reflected on some of the characteristics of Beethoven's late works, he cited the manner in which 'struggle is sublimated into ecstasy', as in the *Arietta* of the Piano Sonata, Op. 111, and how 'chaos strives for lucid formation', as in the transition to the fugue of the *Hammerklavier* Piano Sonata. He makes similar reference to the opening of the finale of the Ninth Symphony, disposing him to generalise 'victorious conclusions are incessantly sought after and discovered, as in the *Grosse Fuge*, the Piano Sonata Op. 110, and the finale of the String Quartet in C-sharp minor, Op. 131'. In his summation he states: 'Beethoven could no longer confront such issues ... with his previous musical vocabulary or procedures.' In support of his contention he quotes from an essay by Sir Hubert Parry: 'Beethoven had by now found "the accepted scheme of organisation which he himself had brought to perfection too constraining and restrictive to the impulse of his thought, and therefore endeavoured to find new types of form to revive sundry earlier types of organisation and combine them in various ways which departed from the essential principles upon which composers had been working for generations".'[ix]

In tracing the creation origins of the *Grosse Fuge*, we recall that on 24 September 1825 Beethoven wrote to his nephew Karl that the third of the Galitzin String Quartets, Op. 130 would be completed 'in ten, at most, twelve days'.[x] As Cooper remarks this was 'a realistic forecast', if the projected finale to Op. 130 had been of typical style and length.[xi] The surviving sketches, however, reveal he was exploring ideas for a final movement for Op. 130 of a more expanded and weighty character. The consequence was that instead of the ten or twelve days, Beethoven worked on what was to become the *Grosse Fuge* for several months. His first inclination was to return to a theme originally considered for the finale of the E-flat major Quartet, Op. 127 that also found expression in the A minor Quartet, Op. 132. It was while working on the finale of Op. 132 that Beethoven made an entry in his sketchbook 'for last movement of the Quartet in B-flat major' including the notation 'fugue'. William Kinderman remarks: 'This evidence implies Beethoven was concerned from an early stage in the genesis of Op. 130, with a complex and ambitious project'[xii]; not least this would culminate in the original expanded great fugal finale.

Paul Bekker characterises the gradual transformations of the fugue theme as being 'more energetic ... more heroic' and no less than 'Destiny calling mankind to action'.[xiii] Discussing the composer's work on the fugue subject, De Marliave pays a characteristically fulsome tribute: 'Beethoven extended the four note phrase into two magnificent pages of working out, another example of his genius for development.'[xiv] Cooper is more measured in his discussion of the manner in which certain of the composer's sketches grew as they evolved in the sketching process: 'By and large, successive drafts tend to be of increasing size, so that the piece represented by the first main sketch is usually smaller — often much smaller — than the final version.' In substantiating this remark he makes the generalization that some compositions extended beyond their original intended length, citing, in particular, the *Eroica* Symphony, the *Waldstein* Piano Sonata, and the *Grosse Fuge*.[xv]

Evidence that Beethoven conceived a fugal string-quartet finale is seen in the de Roda sketchbook that he used from May–September 1825. It derives its name from the Spanish collector Cecilio de Roda who owned it early in the twentieth century and from whose heirs it was acquired in 1962 by the Beethovenhaus; today it consists of 40 leaves.[xvi] The cover of the sketchbook is inscribed: 'Autograph e Louis van Beethoven. Livre d'esquisses des motifs du Quatour/en La Mineur et autre études/L'authenticié en est garantie par Artaria & Co. à Vienne/1847.' Related covers, arising from the later sale of the sketchbook, make reference to 'les ideé pour la *Grande Fugue*.' Ideas for the fugue are worked out on folios 35r–40v passim.[xvii] Amidst the workings-out for the String Quartet Op. 130, Beethoven labelled one section *Fugha*. Other inscriptions in the sketchbook provide evidence he was planning to write string-quartet movements on a more extended scale. At one point he annotates his sketches: 'Letztes Quartett [of the Galitzin set] mit einer ernsthaften und schwergängigen Einleitung' – 'Last Quartet with a serious and weighty introduction.' This he would balance with an even more 'weighty' finale, the *Grosse Fuge*.

In 1846, Beethoven's former secretary and amanuensis Anton Schindler sold a collection of the composer's sketches to the then Berlin Royal Library, today the Berlin

Staatsbibliothek Preussischer Kulturbesitz. Beethoven made use of these from September-November 1825. Under their present-day titles, namely, Autographs 9/1, 9/2, 9/5 and 11/2; they contain extensive sketches for the *Grosse Fuge* alongside ideas for the String Quartets, Op. 127, Op. 132 and Op. 130.[xviii]

From October-November 1825 through to November 1826 Beethoven made use of the so-called Kullak sketchbook that was purchased by Domenico Artaria at the *Nachlass* auction of Beethoven's possession in November 1827. It later came into the possession of the composer Franz Kullak who subsequently bequeathed it to the Berlin Royal Library. By now Beethoven was at work on his last two Quartets, Op. 131 and Op. 135, sketches for which co-exists with advanced ideas for the *Grosse Fuge*.[xix]

With regard to the construction of the *Grosse Fuge*, Barry Cooper draws attention to a phenomenon that becomes an increasingly prominent feature of Beethoven's later music, namely what he describes as 'a tendency to push towards the final movement, and thus for the intellectual or psychological weight of the piece to be shifted from the beginning ... to the end'. He cites the Fifth Symphony and the manner in which its finale 'ends with a blaze of glory' and the Ninth Symphony, whose final-movement cantata 'celebrates the end of serious, orchestral writing'. Of the relevance of this to the Op. 133 he contends: 'The Quartet Op. 130 with the *Grosse Fuge* as finale was intended to have the same effect; but Beethoven substituted for the *Fugue* a much more conventional finale, realizing perhaps that larger performing forces, and not length alone, might be needed for a satisfactory realization of this plan.'[xx] There is perhaps a hint here that Cooper approves of the transcription of the *Grosse Fuge* for string orchestra, to which we make reference later.

Denis Matthews considered the title by which Op. 133 is known to be a misnomer, for reasons that the piece incorporates an introduction, a double-fugue, a slower mildly contrapuntal section, a scherzo, fugal developments, followed by 'a stream of afterthoughts and retrospects'. In his opinion: '[Op. 133] amounts to an exhaustive survey of a single subject's rhythmic and fugal possibilities — in Beethoven's words *tantôt libre, tantôt recherché*.'[xxi] Harold Truscott is succinct: 'The layout of the movement is simple enough. It is Beethoven's own adaptation of the several-fugues-in-one design beloved of the early fugal composers.'[xxii] Scott is fulsome in her praise for Beethoven's construction, describing his intellectual plan as 'almost staggering in its immensity'. She elaborates: 'He begins with an *'Overrtura* in which the fugue motto subject first appears ... [Its] successive guises [forecast] the nature of the three sections in which it will later be developed ... The first section is a complete fugue ... The second part is a short fugue wherein the melodic motto theme ... now becomes the subject ... In the third section both subjects are brought "face to face" and after prolonged conflict the motto theme conquers ... The two [themes] end in a glorious apotheosis where opposition becomes harmonious co-operation.'[xxiii]

Beethoven laid out the *Gross Fugue* in several named sections as follows: *Overtura — Meno mosso e moderato — Allegro molto e con brio — Meno mosso e moderato — Allegro molto e con brio — Allegro*. Contemplating this construction induced Martin Cooper to enthuse: 'It is clear that the ability to conceive such a work argues certain definite psychological traits — a huge fund of aggression, in the first place, and an instinctive resentment of restriction in any form — and a "philosophy of life" ... based on the struggle for self-development on the one hand and self-mastery on the other.' He further reflects: 'In this sense the *Grosse Fuge* is one of the most personally revealing of Beethoven's works; but, as always, he reveals himself in purely musical terms and it is almost as though his "personality", which determined the form and moulded the details, can be withdrawn from the finished work, just as the wooden mould can be withdrawn from the completed arch.'[xxiv] In his evaluation of Beethoven's innovatory constructional procedures, Erwin Stein observes: 'Dissatisfied with traditional resources of form, dynamics and sonorities, Beethoven had initiated a progressive extension of music's entire technical apparatus.' By way of illustration he singles out the composer's 'motivic and thematic work, the way he arranges his characters, his parts and keys, [and how he] develops mere musical shape into musical thought'. Moreover, Stein considers in Op. 133 Beethoven anticipates certain procedures of Schoenberg: 'The rhythmic and melodic changes which the principal theme undergoes betray a similar principal and, above all, have the same significance as Schoenberg's variation technique; a musical idea is, as it were, thought through to the end.'[xxv] In our opening quotations, we have acknowledged Igor Stravinsky's admiration for the *Grosse Fuge* and how modern-sounding he considered it to be. Additionally he comments: 'The vocabulary is itself new, formed in part by an unprecedented use of syncopation, by a new degree of subdivision, and by irregular durations. Beethoven is exploring a region beyond the other late quartets.'[xxvi]

As we have noted, Beethoven provided a clue to the character of the music he had created by heading the score of the *Great Fugue Tantôt libre, tantôt recherché* – that can be interpreted to mean 'sometimes free and sometimes strict'. Bekker reads more into the composer's citation and suggests it implies ideas of 'FREEDOM AND NECESSITY' (Bekker's capitals) are blended by Beethoven in his fugue.

He maintains: 'The inscription is more than a note of form; it is the poetic *programme* of the movement, indicating the reconciliation of the two great opposites of Freedom and Necessity which here finds symbolic expression.' He recalls the movements of the String Quartet, Op. 130 with its sonata-like first movement, the *scherzo-presto* (second movement), the *andante* (third movement], the *danza alla tedesca* (fourth movement), and the *Cavatina* (fifth movement). He likens these to 'a suite, almost a *pot-pourri*, of movements' that are without any 'close psychological interconnection' but which are 'episodic' inasmuch as they prepares for the finale — that is the original ending the *Great Fugue*. Of this he summates: 'The final fugue, however, mighty in form and in range of thought, gathers up all the parts in itself and makes unity of the work, portraying the changing aspects of life as revelations of a single will which is seen in unveiled majesty at the close.'[xxvii] In his estimation of the character of the *Great Fugue*, Joseph Kerman also calls to mind Op. 133: 'The *Fugue* seems to strive fantastically to make up for the fantastic discontinuities of the earlier movements ... But if anything it confirms, rather than resolves, the previous dynamic of disruption — with its violent system of shocks joining the various great sections, and its cryptic *Overtura* and concluding section.'[xxviii]

The challenges posed by the *Great Fugue*, both technical and musical, were evident from the moment of its inception. On 3 January 1826 the B-flat major String Quartet was rehearsed in Beethoven's apartment, complete with the *Great Fugue* as the finale. It soon became the subject of discussion. Entries in the composer's Conversation Books reveal the violinist Karl Holtz, then acting as Beethoven's assistant and confident, sought to reassure him 'everything will go easily, except for the fugue', This, he suggested, required practice by the players in their own homes and accordingly they were allowed to take their parts with them. The players in question were the members of Ignaz Schuppanzigh's String Quartet. Subjects of discussion centred on 'bowing, clarity, and ensemble of the sections in swift tempo involving triplets and leaps in register'.[xxix]

The first public performance of the String Quartet in B-flat major, Op. 130, complete with the *Grosse Fuge*, took place on 21 March 1826. The second and fourth movements were so well received they had to be repeated. However, the challenge, to both performers and audience, proved to be the concluding fugue. Cooper comments: '[The] finale, a massive fugue of 741 bars, was inevitably bewildering; for Beethoven, following his principle that difficulty and greatness are closely connected, seems to have set out to make the movement extremely taxing both to performers and listeners to comprehend.'[xxx] The correspondent for the Leipzig *Allgemeine musikalische Zeitung* wrote pointedly about the fugue: '[The] critic does not dare to interpret the meaning behind the fugal finale: for him it was incomprehensible, like Chinese. When the instruments in the regions of the South and North Poles have to battle with immense difficulties, when one plays different motifs and the musical lines cross each other per transitum irregularem in a host of dissonances, when the players mistrust themselves, are not able to play properly in tune, I declare the Babylon-like confusion is then complete; then there is a concert which can only be enjoyed by the Moroccans.'[xxxi] Even Anton Schindler, Beethoven's most ardent admirer, amanuensis and biographer, categorised the *Grosse Fuge* as *Monstrum aller Quartett-Muisk* and was disposed to expostulate: '[To] crown everything, the finale in the form of a fugue! This composition seems to be an anachronism. It should belong to that grey future when the relationship of notes will be determined by mathematical computation.

Unquestionably such combinations must be regarded as the extreme limit of speculative intellect, and its effect will always remain one of Babelic confusion. We cannot speak here of darkness in contrast to light.'[xxxii]

At the close of the first performance, Karl Holtz wasted no time in searching out Beethoven who had not been present at the concert; he was waiting for a report of the unfolding events in a nearby tavern. Holtz drew attention to the warm reception of the *Alla danza tedesca* and the *Cavatina* and how they had been encored. Beethoven appears to have been unimpressed, dismissing these movements as 'mere delicacies'. 'Why not the Fugue?' he snapped. When Holtz conveyed the audience's response, it provoked Beethoven to the rejoinder: 'Cattle! Asses! Beethoven's younger brother Johann tried to put a gloss on the event, declaring 'the "whole city" was delighted with the work'. More soberly, and truthfully, a number of the composer's closest friends and associates argued that the fugue had not been understood but added, reassuringly, that objections to it 'would vanish with repeated hearings'. Others, more candidly, suggested that the fugue should be removed from the Quartet and be published as a separate work — with a new and lighter finale to replace it. These, significantly, included the publisher Matthias Artaria who had already secured the publication rights for the Op. 130 Quartet.[xxxiii] According to Holtz's account: '[Artaria] charged me with the terrible and difficult mission of convincing Beethoven to compose a new finale, which would be more accessible to the listeners as well as the instrumentalists.' He later suggested to Beethoven that the fugue so departed from the ordinary and surpassed even the last quartets in originality that it should be published as a separate work and that it merited its own designation as a separate opus.'[xxxiv] To his surprise, and relief, Holtz relates Beethoven said he would reflect on the proposal. Evidently he quickly did so and sent a letter to Holtz giving his consent.[xxxv]

Schindler's account conveys something of the feelings stirred by the first performance of the Op. 130 Quartet and its fugue. '[It] was the publisher Matthias Artaria who, as purchaser of the manuscript, took the initiative. He offered to buy the fugue as a separate work if Beethoven would compose another finale in free style to put in its place. The Master complied with this condition and wrote the movement that appears in the published version. This was his very last composition, and was written in November 1826.'[xxxvi]

'In January 1826, Beethoven sent Prince Galitzin corrected copies of a set of parts of the String Quartet, Op. 130 as it was originally conceived with the *Grosse Fuge* as the last movement.[xxxvii] The *Grosse Fuge* was subsequently published as a separate work with the following Title Page: 'Grande Fugue / tantôt libre, tantôt recherché / pour 2 violons, Alte et Violoncelle, Op. 133 / de Louis van Beethoven / dédiée avec la plus profunde veneration à son / Altesse Impériale et Royal Eminentissime / Monseigneur le Cardinal Rodolphe / Archiduc d'Austriche, Prince de Hongrie et de Bohôme / Prince-Archevêque d'Olimütz, Gde. Croix de l'ordre hongrois de St. Étienne, etc., etc., / et arrangée pour le pianoforte à quatre mains / par l'Auteur Même, Œuvre 134 / Propriété de l'Éditeur, Maths. Artaria, Kohlmarkt 258, Vienne.' By way of interest, this text was published at the head of the score of a two-piano transcription of the *Great Fugue* undertaken by Harold Bauer. This was published by G. Schirmer Inc., New York in 1927 and was first performed by Harold Bauer and Arthur Loesser in the Music Hall of the Library of Congress in October 1929.[xxxviii]

As can be seen from the Title Page, Beethoven dedicated Op. 133 to his patron, friend and composition pupil

His Imperial Highness the Archduke Rudolph. In so doing he was consolidating a long list of dedications to Rudolph that included the *Emperor* Concerto — Rudolph was pianist of considerable ability — the *Archduke* Trio, the *Farewell*, *Hammerklavier*, and Op. 111 Piano Sonatas, and the *Missa Solemnis*.

One of Beethoven's final business transactions involved the negotiation of the sale of the publication rights in France of the *Grosse Fuge* and other of his last Quartets. On 24 January 1827 he signed a contract to this effect with Ignaz Pleyel & Sons. The original, in French and signed by Beethoven, reads in translation: 'I the undersigned Louis van Beethoven declare, in the presence of a notary, that I have sold, as entirely their property for the full extent of the kingdom of France, to Messieurs Ignace Pleyel & Elder Son in Paris, my three compositions as follows: Op. 130 ... being the third Quartet dedicated to Prince Nicolas de Galitzin; Op. 133, *Grosse Fugue* in B flat ... dedicated to Archduke Rudolph of Austria; [and] Op. 134. The same *Grosse Fugue* in B flat arranged for piano, four hands by myself.' As witness, Beethoven enlisted Mathias Artaria, who held the Viennese publication rights to these works, as well as the music publisher-dealer Johann Traeg.[xxix]

In his estimation of the *Grosse Fuge*, Phillip Radcliffe describes it as 'a work of the utmost complexity, containing within itself all the contrasting elements that are characteristic of a full-length symphonic work ... showing a structural power of unprecedented monumentality'. He considers these to be the very qualities that make the piece 'so impressive and satisfying as a separate work'. He adds: 'In some ways the *Grosse Fuge*, with its enormous dimensions and elaborate thematic transformations, comes nearer to Wagner than anything else in the quartets.'[xl] For Matthews, as a sequel to the *Cavatina* of Op. 130, 'the *Great Fugue*, with its stupendous renewal of energy, was the most dramatic continuation possible' and which makes 'superhuman demands on the players comparable with the strenuous vocal climaxes in the Ninth'.[xli] Scott also considered the *Grosse Fuge* embodies Beethoven's ideas, relating to fugal writing, that are to be found in other of his symphonic work: 'The "two opposing principles" of his early poetic period, the linking of variation form with fugue (as once in the *Eroica*) and his final belief that a poetical element must be introduced into the traditional form of fugue – all are here.'[xlii] The celebrated interpreter of Beethoven's symphonies Otto Klemperer also found parallels in the composer's symphonic writing and that in Op. 133. In the prefatory notes to his 1961 complete recordings of the Beethoven Symphonies, he states: 'Beethoven's language attained ever-greater heights with the passage of the years, becoming more difficult and idiosyncratic.' Turning to his writing for the medium of the string quartet he continues: 'At the head of his *Grosse Fuge*, Op. 133 Beethoven wrote *tantôt libre tantôt recherché*. These words might equally be applied to the last movement of the Ninth Symphony, with its formal dissolution and absence of sonata movement, rondo and fugue — yet from this chrysalis there emerged something new, a sort of euphoria.'[xliii]

In Allison Bullock's estimation: 'The *Grosse Fuge* puts the complexities and questions arising from the earlier movements of the Quartet [Op. 130] in the shade – it is a truly heroic effort.'[xliv] Robert Simpson is content to reflect: 'The *Grosse Fuge* is clearly part of a grand design ...'.[xlv] In composing the *Great Fugue*, Pierre Boulez describes Beethoven as 'a great innovator'.[xlvi] Igor Stravinsky was given to calling the music in question '*die sehr Grosse Fuge*'.[xlvii] He considered: 'The fugue lacks ancestors and inheritors alike ... parts of the fugue might have been incubated in a satellite

...'.[xlviii] In his eightieth year he praised the *Great Fugue* as 'the most perfect miracle in music', adding 'it is also the most absolutely contemporary piece of music I know and will be contemporary for ever ... Hardly birth-marked by its age. The *Great Fugue* is, in rhythm alone, more subtle than any music of my own century ... I love it beyond everything'.[xlix]

There is agreement amongst authorities that the *Grosse Fuge* poses challenges to both performers and listeners. '[In] pieces like the *Hammerklavier Sonata* and the *Grosse Fuge*, the sense of strain or difficulty placed on the performer and listener alike appears almost to be a calculated part of the aesthetic effect: the music seems at times almost to court incomprehensibility.'[l] The English composer and musicologist Christopher Headington acknowledged Beethoven's debt to Bach in his fugal writing, although at the same time recognising it is 'world's away from Bach'. As with others, he finds close associations between the mood of the *Grosse Fuge* and that of the 'awe-inspiring striving' of the finale of the *Hammerklavier* Piano Sonata. He enthuses: 'It is literally aggressive, with its shrilling trills and melodic leaps, in spite of a gentle interlude a little beyond the halfway point which offers a brief respite from the conflict.'[li]

According to Ivan Mahaim in his *Beethoven: Naissance et Renaissance des Derniers Quatuors* (1964), the *Grosse Fuge* had to await almost thirty years before it received a second hearing in public — a measure of the caution with which it was approached by both quartet players and recital impresarios. Even Louis Spohr (1784—1859) despite being, like Beethoven, a bridge between Classicism and Romanticism, pronounced the *Grosse Fuge* to be 'an indecipherable, uncorrected horror'. A more favourable estimation of the *Great Fugue* derives from a performance of the work rendered by the Joseph Hellmesberger Quartet. Founded in 1849 it was recognised for its 'unabashedly subjective and emotional manner of delivery'. After hearing a performance of the Hellmesberger Quartet in 1859, the music critic of the *Neue Zeitschrift für Musik* (issue 26) wrote: 'The masterworks of [Beethoven's] last period, the C-sharp minor, Op. 131 and E-flat major, Op. 127 Quartets, as well as the first performance here of the *Grosse Fuge*, Op. 133 [were featured].' The critic in question continued: 'It is Hellmesberger's great service to have made this prophetic and progressive artist so popular among us ... The crowning contribution of the Quartet [is] that even a many-faceted structure, Beethoven's Quartet fugue, was listed to so attentively by the entire audience and after its completion greeted so warmly and with so much applause.' The reviewer ended, however, with words of caution: '[Even] the very practised score-reader will require many repetitions to grasp this musical pyramid.'[lii]

An entry from the Diary of Cosima Wagner from 15 February 1871 reveals that the technical challenges posed by the *Great Fuge* continued to defeat even an ensemble of accomplished musicians. She recorded: 'Around four o'clock our musicians arrive; we start on the so-called *Grosse Fuge*, respectfully acknowledged that it can be interpreted correctly only by the greatest virtuosos and only after long study.' However, the attempt failed and the performance was abandoned. Instead the ensemble performed the Op. 130 Quartet with Beethoven's revised ending. This disposed Cosima to suggest to Wagner that the *scherzo* of the Quartet reminded her of Haydn and the finale of Mozart. To which he responded: 'Yes, it is like with children, when we suddenly see unfulfilled volitions planted by Nature in our ancestors putting in an appearance, thus bringing to light the wonderful resemblances between succeeding generations; it is like that here.'[liii]

Franz Liszt's correspondence provides insights into

orchestral music-making in Europe in the late nineteenth century and of the still cautious reception of the Op. 133 into the repertoire. On 2 December 1883 he wrote to one of his many women admirers, Princess Carolyne. He described a Beethoven concert given by the Meiningen orchestra under the direction of Hans von Bülow. He first praised the orchestra for its 'precision ... rendition of the subtlest and most appropriate rhythm,' and its capacity to 'perform prodigies'. Turning to the concert he enthused: 'Here's something astonishing! Beethoven's most difficult work for quartet — the last *Great Fugue* Op.133 which, because of its complexities, never appears in programmes — is performed by the Meiningen orchestra with a perfect ensemble of all the stringed instruments, more than thirty players. This is, up to now, a unique achievement, before which every musician must raise his hat.'[liv]

In 1905 the English composer, pianist, and writer on music Ernest Walker published a monograph on Beethoven and felt obliged to describe the *Grosse Fuge* 'as quite beyond the pale' and likewise the fugue in the C-sharp minor Quartet as 'a mystery'.[lv] Some twenty years later the fortunes of the *Great Fugue* were in the ascendant as is evident from the concert repertoire of the German conductor Herman Scherchen. Known for his championing of twentieth-century music, he once directed an orchestral performance of the *Grosse Fuge* at the Bauhaus, celebrated for its advocacy of modernism in the arts and crafts.[lvi]

Arnold Schoenberg describes how, as a child he, wrote several string quartets each of which adopted the style of a particular composer. He relates how one day he purchased some second-hand Beethoven scores that included two of the *Razumovsky* String Quartets and the *Great Fugue*, Op. 133. He states: 'From this minute, I was possessed by an urge to write string quartets.'[lvii] 'The fugue and fugato occupy a prominent role in Bartók's writing for string quartet. In his study of the composer's writing for the medium he singles out for particular mention the First, Third and Fifth String Quartets in which he states 'Bartók unequivocally follows the example of Beethoven'.[lviii]

In 1906 Felix Weingartner transcribed the *Grosse Fuge* for string orchestra; as we have seen, from our Franz Liszt anecdote, others had done so before. In Weingartner's adaptation he added double basses occasionally to give added resonance to the cellos. This calls to mind an occasion when Fritz Reiner gave a performance of this orchestral version. For a period, during his stay in Philadelphia Reiner trained and conducted the student Curtis Symphony Orchestra. He had a reputation for being a hard taskmaster who insisted on nothing less than high standards. This was evident on the occasion when he was preparing the orchestra to perform the *Great Fugue*. To impart Weingartner's further sonority, he added a double bass part but found the playing of the individual in question to be unsatisfactory. He proceed to try a succession of other bassists, declared them all to be below standard and so resigned himself to performing the work without any bass part.[lix]

The legitimacy of transcribing the *Grosse Fuge* for string orchestra has divided both music critics and performers alike. Radcliffe is amongst the adherents stating: 'The extreme technical difficulty of the first section of the *Grosse Fuge* undoubtedly imposes a strain on both performers and listeners; this is much less felt when it is played on a string orchestra.' He does, however, acknowledge that some take the contrary view that 'the music loses some of its essential character when transferred to a smoother [less challenging] medium'.[lx] Hans Keller, never one to mine words, opined: '[At] his sublimest, Beethoven is sometimes at his most problematic: in the case of one famous, discarded finale — Op. 130's first — he burst the bounds of the string quartet altogether, and can only be heard without aural frustration in Furtwängler's self-conducted, string-orchestral arrangement.'[lxi]

On 26 May 1947, Neville Cardus heard a rendering of the *Great Fuge* performed by the Philharmonic Orchestra under the direction of Otto Klemperer. In his subsequent review in the *Manchester Guardian* he justified the transcription: 'A string-orchestra version is justifiable for the voltage of the music strains painfully at the tone and capacity of four fiddlers only.' He continued: 'And out of the giant strength came a certain poignancy, as though the music were aware that for all its efforts it was trying to express something beyond the scope of music to express at all. We could no doubt make out a case supporting the view that in this colossal movement Beethoven was occupied mainly with tonal, textural, and rhythmical problems; but Klemperer's treatment of it dismissed such a conjecture as flippant, not to say sacrilegious.' He concluded by reaffirming his personal conviction: 'That the monumental content of the *Grosse Fuge* works better in a full string orchestra than a string quartet is something that experience has often shown.'[lxii]

The question of performing the *Grosse Fuge* in an orchestral version, as opposed to rendering it as Beethoven intended for four voices only, divided the members of the Guarneri Quartet as became apparent on the occasion they were interviewed by David Blum. Violist Michael Tree argued: 'When the *Grosse Fugue* is played by a string quartet, its like scaling a mountain peak. At times it sounds rather strident — even unpleasant — deliberately slow.' He asked: 'What's wrong with that?' He contended: 'By adding player upon player, by smoothing the edges and making it more agreeable, you eliminate the immediacy of the confrontation. When four players are solely responsible for maintaining their parts in a work of that magnitude, there has to be a greater sense of responsibility. There's also more room for spontaneity, for the unexpected ... thirty or sixty string players cannot react like four. It's a different view.' Cellist David Soyer responded: 'I agree. A great deal is sacrificed when that sense of struggle is lacking.' He concluded: 'I don't believe the *Grosse Fuge* was intended for orchestral performance.' Second violin John Dalley raised his dissentient voice: 'My view may be considered heretical, but I'm not sure that Beethoven's concept of writing the *Grosse Fugue* for the quartet medium is successful.' He acknowledged: 'Yes, from the players' point of view there's a Herculean struggle, and that's most impressive. But I think that the material is ideally suited to a large mass of strings, particularly if the basses are used with discretion. I prefer something that sounds better, even if it's not totally authentic.'[lxiii]

We have seen Beethoven opens the *Grosse Fuge* with an introduction that he titled *Overtura*, the constituent parts of which we have identified. In Conrad Wilson's estimation the *Overtura* is no less than 'five tiny disjointed overtures, each of them just a handful of notes' out of which the four-note motif is heard from which the fugue, in due course, evolves.[lxiv] Bekker likens the *Overtura* to 'a short prelude' that provides a 'fantasia-like summary' of the sections of the movement that follows.[lxv] Solomon describes this terse, concentrated movement as a 'prefiguration of the [anticipated] action' that represents itself as 'a labyrinthian process, a set of apparent dead ends, with each segment apparently in search of a beginning, a path to the fugue'. He characterises the various motifs and themes that are heard as 'disparate' and whose elaboration and musical interconnections will only become apparent later in the movement.

Quoting Joseph Kerman, he likens Beethoven's artifice as though he were 'hurling all the thematic versions at the listener's head like a handful of rocks'.[lxvi] Stravinsky takes issue with Kerman for characterising the *Overtura* in this manner. He dismisses his imagery for being too 'Davidic' – a reference, presumably, to David slaying Goliath with stones from his sling. He elaborates his own estimation of the *Overtura* as being 'a thematic index that identifies the different versions of the subject as well as prognosticating and priming the larger components of the form.' He proceeds to elaborate how each thematic version in the music that is to follow 'is endowed with its own distinctive secondary attributes such as pitch, rhythm, trill and *appoggiatura*'.[lxvii]

As the movement opens, the Op. 130 Quartet is recalled through Beethoven's adoption of the key of G major: '[The] emphatic octaves on G that launch the *Overtura* represent a drastic reinterpretation of the gentle, lingering, fading G heard as the highest pitch at the close of the moving, lyric *Cavatina* in E-flat major.' Kinderman, whom we have quoted, contends 'this G has more to do with the *Cavatina* than with the *Fugue*.'[lxviii] Robert Simpson is more questioning: 'When the *Grosse Fuge* is played as a separate piece, its opening can hardly be said to make sense; it was conceived as the transition from the E flat of the *Cavatina*.'[lxix]

The serenity of the *Cavatina* is left behind as the opening bars create 'a vivid atmosphere of suspense, presenting a kind of preview of the various shapes in which the main theme will appear'.[lxx] Discussing the genesis of the *Grosse Fuge*, William Caplin draws attention to what he considers to be one of its primary characteristics, namely 'its persistent leaping motion'. As he further remarks: 'Within the tonal space of an octave, the melody regularly skips between the lower and upper regions.'[lxxi] A double fugue unfolds in dramatically leaping tones, the four instruments of the quartet bursting out in triplets, dotted figures, and cross-rhythms. Michael Steinberg considers the feeling Beethoven intended to convey in his heading to the *Grosse Fuge – Tantôt libre tantôt recherché* – is soon made evident: 'In its thirty measures it changes tempo twice and character more often than that. In music of extreme disjunction, its gestures separated by unmeasured pauses, Beethoven hurls scraps of material about.'[lxxii] Martin Cooper intriguingly likens the manner in which Beethoven presents the character of the music that is to unfold, to a 'cinematic trailer of coming events'. He compares this to the similar procedure Beethoven adopted in the lead up to the finale of the Ninth Symphony, when the melodies of the movements that have gone before are briefly reviewed.[lxxiii] Daverio compares what he describes as the movement's 'thematic reminiscences' to dramatic procedures typical of operatic genres, the purpose of which he maintains is 'to help to unify the whole sprawling structure'.[lxxiv]

Barry Cooper suggests the overall structure of the *Great Fugue* may be compared to the three movements of a sonata, namely, an allegro, a slower movement, and a lively concluding one all of which are unified by the fugal theme.[lxxv] The main melody, anticipated five times in the *Overtura*, is heard in the fugue proper on the viola whilst the first violin 'proclaims its spikily countermelody'.[lxxvi] To quote Cooper once more: '[The] fugue theme is accompanied first by incessant repetitions of a dotted rhythm, which is combined with large leaps to provide daunting, forbidding sound ... Throughout this section, the combination of repetitions, dense textures, angular melodic lines, and incessantly loud dynamic level, creates a monolithic jaggedness that intensifies the music's impenetrability.'[lxxvii]

Bekker characterises the first energetic exposition of the

fugue as 'the fate theme'.[lxxviii] Arthur Shepherd regarded the entire first episode to be devoted to what he describes as 'the joyous idea [implicit] in a complete fugue', with its several entries, episodes, and exposition in altered rhythm, the last exposition guiding the fugue to the tonality of G-flat major.[lxxix] To quote him once more 'and now the battle begins!' In this long second section Beethoven never lets the volume level fall below *forte* with 'sharp accents lending even more power to the frenzied music'.[lxxx] In the third and longest fugal section, Beethoven subjects the music to 'a great variety of dynamic levels, keys ... note lengths, and textures'. He also manifests his own accomplishments in 'the art of fugue' through such devices as 'stretto, augmentation, inversion ... counterbalanced by passages of greater textual simplicity such as one- or two-part writing, or grand unisons, and trills become a prominent feature that is extensively developed'.[lxxxi] Shepherd describes this section as a contest between the fugue's two principal subjects 'accompanied by capricious twists and turns [and] twenty-two bars of uneasy hesitation ... shedding its garb of gloom'.[lxxxii] Bekker describes the third great phase of the fugal movement as 'an exposition of the "Will" theme' leading on to 'an expression of world-embracing might'.[lxxxiii]

With the commencement of the *Meno mosso e moderato* a gentler version of the fugue is heard in running semiquavers. The music is quieter, more flowing and provides respite — for both performers and listeners — from the animated intensity of the *Overtura*. Bekker describes this short passage as 'a tender, dreamy G-flat major episode'. To him it suggests 'the self-consecration of the "Will" of the combatant', while the *fate* motif of the fugue theme 'loses its inimical aspect and is freely and joyfully accepted by the "Will".'[lxxxiv] Radcliffe is equally expressive and avows the *Meno mosso e moderato* 'brings with it a sense of blissful relaxation' the effect of which he suggests is comparable to that found in the D major episode in the finale of the Piano Sonata Op. 106. He also draws attention to the episode's quietly flowing melody that he describes as 'weaving a texture of the most ethereal kind, far removed from the tumult of the first section [*Overtura*]'. He maintains the music now has 'an entirely changed personality ... its chromatic contours give a gentle edge to the music ... for the most part the *pianissimo* is as sustained as was the *fortissimo* of the first section'.[lxxxv]

With the *Allegro molto e con brio*, the music becomes progressively more agitated and angular in its figuration: 'The disjunctions, the violence of the leaps, also surpass anything we have heard up to now ... There are many interruptions as well as reappearances of earlier passages.' Michael Steinberg, whom we have quoted, considers these manifestations to be 'so startling that you could almost think you were dealing with a copyist's error'. To underline the drama, Beethoven marks *forte* on every single beat.[lxxxvi] The music is 'defiant' (Bekker) and possessed of 'nervous energy' (Wilson). This section functions as a *scherzo* augmented by a dance-like rhythm. Perhaps its most significant feature is the prominence of the trill to which we have made reference. 'The trill becomes longer and more menacing, often lasting for several bars and recalling certain passages in the finale of the Piano Sonata, Op. 106 ... [Eventually] the trills are left for a few moments in sole possession, echoing each other and producing an atmosphere of sullen suspense.'[lxxxvii]

The music continues without interruption to the *Meno mosso e moderato* in which two fugues intertwine, one in the high register and the other in the lower. As it proceeds to what Bekker describes as its 'joyful and confident ... *stretta* apotheosis', it becomes more fragmented with changes of mood. Pauses, and thereby silence, also play there part —

as though Beethoven himself were reflecting over his manuscript score.

In the penultimate *Allegro molto e con brio*, the fugue resumes its jaunty progress, only to be slowed occasionally with further meaningful silences.

The final *Allegro* draws this majestic work to a close, opening with a declamatory reminiscence of the fugal theme. Beethoven brings his full musical vocabulary to bear including unison chords, trills and pauses whilst allowing the first violin to hover, lie a song-bird in flight, in its highest register. He has said all that can be said and the *Grosse Fugue* closes unceremoniously with a few bars of 'matter-of-fact tonic and dominant' (Radcliffe). We can imagine Beethoven setting down his quill pen and laconically exclaiming — 'That's that!'

---

[i] Barry Cooper, 1990, p 68 and 1991, p. 85 and pp. 276–7.

[ii] Marion M. Scott, 1940, p. 270.

[iii] Basil Lam, 1975, p. 107.

[iv] See: Beethoven House Digital Archives, Library Document BH 83.

[v] John Daverio, *Manner, tone, and tendency in Beethoven's chamber music for strings* in: Glenn Stanley editor, *The Cambridge companion to Beethoven*, 2000, pp. 162–3.

[vi] Joseph de Marliave, 1925 (reprint 1961), p. 286.

[vii] Rebecca Clarke *The Beethoven quartets as a player sees them* in: *Musical Times*, Special Issue, Vol. VIII, No. 2, 1927, pp. 184–90.

[viii] From an original essay *Aupres et au Loin* — 'Near and Far', 1954, reproduced in: Pierre Boulez, 1991, pp. 150–1.

[ix] Maynard Solomon, 1977, pp. 294. Parry's essay, to which Solomon refers, is contained in: C. H. H. Parry, *Style in Musical Art*, 1911, p. 95.

[x] Emily Anderson, editor and translator, 1961, Vol. 3, letter No. 1416, pp. 1237–8. For a facsimile reproduction of this letter see: Beethoven House, Digital Archives, Document BH 29. For a discussion of related contextual matters, see also: Elliot Forbes editor, *Thayer's life of Beethoven*, 1967, 2000, p. 970.

[xi] Barry Cooper, 2000, pp. 332–3.

[xii] William Kinderman, 1997, p. 295.

[xiii] Paul Bekker, 1925, p. 332.

[xiv] Joseph de Marliave, 1925 (reprint 1961), pp. 213–4.

[xv] Barry Cooper, 1990, p. 127.

[xvi] For a facsimile reproduction of the de Roda sketchbook see: Beethoven House, Digital Archives, Library Document, NE 47a and H. C. Bodmer, HCB Mh 101.

[xvii] Douglas Porter Johnson, editor, 1985, pp. 306–7, pp. 309–10, p. 313, p. 317,

pp. 426–9, and pp. 432–7.
[xviii] *Ibid.*
[xix] *Ibid.*
[xx] Barry Cooper, 1991, p. 207.
[xxi] Denis Matthews, 1985, p. 145.
[xxii] Harold Truscott, 1968, p. 94.
[xxiii] Marion M. Scott, 1940, p. 270.
[xxiv] Martin Cooper, 1970, pp. 388–9.
[xxv] Erwin Stein, 1953, pp. 90–3.
[xxvi] Igor Stravinsky, 1972, pp. 261–2.
[xxvii] Paul Bekker, 1925, pp. 331–2.
[xxviii] Joseph Kerman, 1967, p. 322.
[xxix] William Kinderman, 1997, p. 301. See also: Thayer-Forbes, 1967, pp. 975–6.
[xxx] Barry Cooper, 2000, p. 337.
[xxxi] As quoted in: Beethoven House, Digital Archives, Library Document, H. C. Bodmer, HCB Mh 104.
[xxxii] Anton Felix Schindler, *Beethoven as I knew him*, edited by Donald W. MacArdle and translated by Constance S. Jolly from the German edition of 1860, 1966, p. 307.
[xxxiii] Thayer-Forbes, 1967, pp. 975–6.
[xxxiv] Maynard Solomon, 1977. Originally derived from Thayer-Dieters-Riemann, Vol. V, p. 298.
[xxxv] This letter has not survived.
[xxxvi] Anton Felix Schindler, *Beethoven as I knew him*, edited by Donald W. MacArdle and translated by Constance S. Jolly from the German edition of 1860, 1966, p. 308.
[xxxvii] For a facsimile copy of the violin part bearing the dedication to Prince Galitzin, see: Beethoven House, Digital Archives, Library Document, BH 90.
[xxxviii] For facsimile reproductions of various fist editions of the *Great Fugue* see: Beethoven House, Digital Archives, Library Documents: C 133/1; C 133/2; C 133/7; C 134/1; H. C. Bodmer, HCB C Md 53, 9; H. C. Bodmer, HCB C Md 79, 12; and Sammlung Helferich 64 d.
[xxxix] Theodore Albrecht, editor and translator, 1996, Vol. 3 Letter No. 458, pp. 176–7.
[xl] Philip Radcliffe, 1978, p. 123, p. 177 and p. 183.
[xli] Denis Matthews, 1985, pp. 144–5.
[xlii] Marion M. Scott, 1940, p. 270.
[xliii] Martin Anderson editor, *Klemperer on music: shavings from a musician's workbench*, 1986, pp. 97–9.
[xliv] Alison Bullock, *Notes to the BBC Radio Three Beethoven experience*, Friday 10 June 2005, www.bbc.co.uk/radio3/Beethoven
[xlv] Robert Simpson, *The chamber music for strings* in: Denis Arnold and Nigel Fortune editors, *The Beethoven companion*, 1973, p. 273.
[xlvi] Pierre Boulez, 1991, p. 225.
[xlvii] As quoted by Michael Steinberg, *The late quartets*, in: Robert Winter and Robert Martin editors, *The Beethoven quartet companion*, 1994, p. 239.
[xlviii] Igor Stravinsky, 1972, pp. 260–1.
[xlix] Igor Stravinsky, *The Observer*, 17 June 1962, cited in: William Kinderman editor, *The string quartets of Beethoven*, 2005, p. 279.

[i] Barry Cooper, 1991, p. 64.
[ii] Christopher Headington, 1974, p. 173.
[iii] Derived from Robert Winter, *Performing the Beethoven quartets in their first century* in: Robert Winter and Robert Martin editors, *The Beethoven quartet companion*, 1994, pp. 41–3 and p. 52.
[iv] Gregor-Dellin and Dietrich Mack editors, *Cosima Wagner's diaries: Vol. 1, 1869 - 1877*, 1978–80, pp. 337–8.
[v] Adrian Williams, editor and translator, 1998, pp. 906–7.
[vi] As quoted by Philip Radcliffe, 1978, Chapter 10 passim.
[vii] See: Glenn Watkins, 1994, p. 320.
[viii] As recalled in: Joseph Henry Auner, *A Schoenberg reader: documents of a life*, 2003, pp. 12–3.
[ix] János Kárpáti, 1994, p. 27.
[x] Kenneth Morgan, 2005, pp. 76–7.
[xi] Philip Radcliffe, 1978, p. 140.
[xii] Hans Keller, 1986, p. 17.
[xiii] Michael Tanner editor, 1989, p. 120.
[xiv] David Blum, *The art of quartet playing: the Guarneri Quartet in conversation with David Blum*, 1986, pp. 164–5.
[xv] Conrad Wilson, 2003, p. 123.
[xvi] Paul Bekker, 1925, p. 333.
[xvii] Maynard Solomon, 2003, pp. 240–1.
[xviii] Igor Stravinsky, 1972, pp. 261.
[xix] William Kinderman, 1997, p. 303.
[xx] Robert Simpson, *The chamber music for strings* in: Denis Arnold and Nigel Fortune editors, *The Beethoven companion*, 1973, p. 299.
[xxi] Philip Radcliffe, 1978, p. 140.
[xxii] William Caplin, *The genesis of the countersubjects for the 'Grosse Fuge'*, in: William Kinderman editor, *The string quartets of Beethoven*, 2005, p. 237.
[xxiii] Michael Steinberg, *The late quartets*, in: Robert Winter and Robert Martin editors, *The Beethoven quartet companion*, 1994, p. 239.
[xxiv] Martin Cooper, 1970, p. 381.
[xxv] John Daverio, *Manner, tone, and tendency in Beethoven's chamber music for strings* in: Glenn Stanley editor, *The Cambridge companion to Beethoven*, 2000, pp. 162–3.
[xxvi] Barry Cooper, 2000, pp. 337–8.
[xxvii] Alison Bullock, *Notes to the BBC Radio Three Beethoven experience*, Friday 10 June 2005, www.bbc.co.uk/radio3/Beethoven
[xxviii] Barry Cooper, 2000, pp. 337–8.
[xxix] Paul Bekker, 1925, p. 333.
[xxx] Arthur Shepherd, 1935, pp. 71–2.
[xxxi] Alison Bullock, *Notes to the BBC Radio Three Beethoven experience*, Friday 10 June 2005, www.bbc.co.uk/radio3/Beethoven
[xxxii] Barry Cooper, 2000, pp. 337–8.
[xxxiii] Arthur Shepherd, 1935, pp. 71–2.
[xxxiv] Paul Bekker, 1925, p. 333.
[xxxv] *Ibid*.
[xxxvi] Philip Radcliffe, 1978, p. 141.
[xxxvii] Michael Steinberg, *The late quartets*, in: Robert Winter and Robert Martin

editors, *The Beethoven quartet companion*, 1994, pp. 242—4.
[lxxxvii] Philip Radcliffe, 1978, pp. 142—4.

GROSSE FUGE, OP. 134 (PIANO TRANSCRIPTION)

> 'The duet version is all but impossibly difficult,
> but it is also marvellously illuminating in the ways
> it sorts out strands of polyphony and dynamics.'

Michael Steinberg, *The Late Quartets* in: Robert Winter and Robert Martin editors, *The Beethoven Quartet Companion*, 1994, p. 239.

We reserve our opening remarks to recall the circumstances whereby the transcription of the *Grosse Fuge* for four hands came about.

The first public performance of the String Quartet in B-flat major, Op. 130, complete with the *Grosse Fuge*, took place on 21 March 1826. The second and fourth movements were so well received they had to be repeated.

However, the challenge, to both performers and audience, proved to be the concluding fugue. The correspondent for the Leipzig *Allgemeine musikalische Zeitung* wrote pointedly about the fugue: '[The] critic does not dare to interpret the meaning behind the fugal finale: for him it was incomprehensible, like Chinese. When the instruments in the regions of the South and North Poles have to battle with immense difficulties, when one plays different motifs and the musical lines cross each other per transitum irregularem in a host of dissonances, when the players mistrust themselves, are not able to play properly in tune, I declare the Babylon-like confusion is then complete; then there is a concert which can only be enjoyed by the Moroccans.'[i] Even Anton Schindler, Beethoven's most ardent admirer, amanuensis and biographer, categorised the *Grosse Fuge* as *Monstrum aller Quartett-Muisk* and was disposed to expostulate: '[To] crown everything, the finale in the form of a fugue! This composition seems to be an anachronism. It should belong to that grey future when the relationship of notes will be determined by mathematical computation. Unquestionably such combinations must be regarded as the extreme limit of speculative intellect, and its effect will always remain one of Babelic confusion. We cannot speak here of darkness in contrast to light.'[ii]

At this period the violinist Karl Holz was acting as Beethoven's assistant and confident. At the close of the performance he wasted no time in searching out the composer who had not been present at the concert; he was waiting for a report of the unfolding events in a nearby tavern. Holtz drew attention to the warm reception of the *Alla danza tedesca* and the *Cavatina* and how they had been encored. Beethoven appears to have been unimpressed, dismissing these movements as 'mere delicacies'. 'Why not the Fugue?' he snapped. When Holtz conveyed the audience's response, it provoked Beethoven to the rejoinder: 'Cattle! Asses! Beethoven's younger brother Johann tried to put a gloss on the event, declaring 'the "whole city" was delighted with the work'. More soberly, and truthfully, a number of the composer's closest friends and associates argued that the fugue had not been understood but added, reassuringly, that objections to it 'would vanish with repeated hearings'. Others, more candidly, suggested that the fugue should be removed from the Quartet and be published as a separate work — with a new and lighter finale to replace it. These, significantly, included the publisher Matthias Artaria who had already secured the publication rights for the Op. 130 Quartet.[iii] According to Holtz's account: '[Artaria] charged me with the terrible and difficult mission of convincing Beethoven to compose a new finale, which would be more accessible to the listeners as well as the instrumentalists. I maintained that this fugue, which departed from the ordinary and surpassed even the last quartets in originality, should be published as a separate work and that it merited a designation as a separate opus.'[iv] To his surprise, and relief, Holtz relates Beethoven said he would reflect on the proposal. Evidently he quickly did so and sent a letter to Holtz giving his consent.[v] As we have seen in our previous account, the *Grosse Fuge* was subsequently published as the Composer's Op. 133.

Sometime in April 1826 Beethoven visited Artaria's premises as is evident from entries in his Conversation Book (No. 108). Artaria wrote: 'There has been a great deal of demand for a pianoforte arrangement for four hands of the fugue. Would you allow me to publish it?'[vi] Beethoven appears to have asked 'what kind of an edition?' to which the publisher responded: 'Score in parts. The four-handed fugue arranged by yourself to be published at once.' Beethoven appears to have warmed to the suggestion — at least in principle. In the past he had made a number of transcriptions of his own compositions, including: Piano Trio, Op. 1, No. 1 – as String Quintet, Op. 104; Piano Sonata in E, Op. 14, No. 2 – as String Quartet in F; Piano Quintet, Op. 16 – as Piano Quartet; Septet, Op. 20 – as Piano Trio, Op. 18; Symphony No. 2, Op. 36 – as Piano Trio; Violin Concerto, Op. 61 – as Piano Concerto, Op. 61 a; and a partial transcription for piano of the Symphony No. 7, Op. 92.[vii] On this occasion, however, Beethoven declined to undertake the transcription himself; instead he nominated the composer and pianist Anton Halm to make the arrangement.

Beethoven made Halm's acquaintance in 1815 and the following year accepted the dedication of one of his own piano sonatas. Moreover, Halm was an early enthusiast of Beethoven's works for piano; for example he performed the third Piano Concerto at a concert in Graz (1814) and took on the piano part in the Choral Fantasia (1817). Halm visited Beethoven on 16 April 1826 to discuss the arrangement with him – in particular to learn his views on the keyboard setting required for the various voices. Halm appears to have set about his task diligently since on 24 April he wrote to Beethoven: 'I have finished your Fugue which I have the honour of sending along, with the greatest possible diligence and care! At every bar, I was amazed at your power of harmony and its flow, as well as the musical motives that you have used and their development to the point of exhaustion!' He then raised a point of difficulty that he had experienced in making the transcription that was to give Beethoven cause for concern. He states: 'Concerning the arrangement, it was unfortunately not possibly always to keep the *subjects* in their original shape; rather more frequently they had to be broken.' He exonerated himself: 'Otherwise it is so brilliant, so advantageously playable and, as I hope, still intelligible enough, that your most devoted most elevated masterwork will be acknowledged as that which it is.'[viii]

Notwithstanding Halm's care and precautions in discussing what was to be undertaken with Beethoven, the resulting transcription was not to his satisfaction. He considered Halm had divided the parts too much so as to avoid the crossing of hands — the transcription being for four hands at *one* piano. In addition Beethoven took exception to Halm having given passages to the right hand which should logically have been given to the left.[ix] On 12 May Artaria honourably paid Halm the fee of 40 gulden (100 florins) for his arrangement despite its rejection by the composer. Word of the latter circumstance eventually reached Halm as is revealed in an entry in Beethoven's Conversation book for 9 June. In this Holtz has written: 'Halm seems to notice that you are not satisfied; he dares not come near you!'[x]

Beethoven had initially considered that his former piano pupil Carl Czerny should undertake the required transcription. Years earlier he had trusted him to make a piano reduction of the score of his opera *Fidelio* but on this occasion he appears to have had a change of mind in favour of Halm. Dissatisfied with the latters efforts, and overcoming his initial objections, he decided to undertake the transcription himself. However, as he revealed in a letter to Holtzt, the undertaking gave him no pleasure and caused him considerable trouble. He states: 'Here is the pianoforte arrangement for four hands — for Herr Matthias [Artaria], and may God decide him to take it — The latter will realize that it was impossible for me to waste so much time to no purpose.'[xi] Beethoven made it clear to Holz that he should inform Artaria that he now regarded his four-hand transcription of the *Grosse Fuge* to be a *new* composition for which he requested payment of 12 gold ducats.

Realizing his request would incur Artaria additional

expense, he wrote once more to Holtz on 26 September: '[I] request you to tell Herr Matthias Artaria that I do not wish in any way to compel him to take my pianoforte arrangement. Therefore I am sending you Halm's pianoforte arrangement so that when mine is returned to you, you may immediately deliver Halm's to Matthias Artaria.'[xii] As Emily Anderson explains in the commentary to her translation of this letter: 'Despite Artaria's additional financial expense incurred in paying Beethoven an additional fee, he doubtless preferred the composer's transcription for reasons of its inherent musicological merits and, more significantly, he probably reasoned a transcription by the composer would win over more adherents — and sales — than one from a relatively little known musician.'[xiii] Artaria reconciled himself to paying twice for the transcription and paid Beethoven his fee on 5 September — but not before having to endure a typical Beethovenian prod in the form of a Canon (WoO 197) to which he appended the text: '*Da ist das Werk, sorgt für das Geld?*' — 'Here is the work, give me the money?'[xiv]

One of Beethoven's final business transactions involved the negotiation of the sale of the publication rights in France of the *Grosse Fuge* and other of his last Quartets. On 24 January 1827 he signed a contract to this effect with Ignaz Pleyel & Sons. The original, in French and signed by Beethoven, reads: 'I the undersigned Louis van Beethoven declare, in the presence of a notary, that I have sold, as entirely their property for the full extent of the kingdom of France, to Messieurs Ignace Pleyel & Elder Son in Paris, my three compositions as follows: Op. 130 ... being the third Quartet dedicated to Prince Nicolas de Galitzin; Op. 133, *Grosse Fugue* in B flat ... dedicated to Archduke Rudolph of Austria; [and] Op. 134. The same *Grosse Fugue* in B flat arranged for piano, four hands by myself.' As witness, Beethoven enlisted Mathias Artaria, who held the Viennese publication rights to these works, as well as the music publisher-dealer Johann Traeg.[xv]

Artaria published Beethoven's four-hand transcription of the *Grosse Fuge* on 10 May 1827, some two months after the composer's death. The Title page bore the dedication to his former patron and only composition pupil His Imperial Highness the Archduke Rudolph.

For many years it was considered Beethoven's Autograph Score was lost. The only known surviving text was a fragment consisting of the last seventeen bars of the fugue. Authorities believed Beethoven may have removed this from the Autograph that he then replaced with an amended version before sending the final score to Artaria.[xvi] The manuscript was listed in an 1890 catalogue and sold at an auction in Berlin to William Howard Doane, a Cincinnati industrialist. In 1952 his daughter gave this, and other manuscripts, to the Palmer Theological Seminary. Beethoven's manuscript languished in the basement of the Seminary until its discovery in 2005 by the Seminary's Librarian Heather Carbo. It later sold at auction for £1, 128,000.

The manuscript consists of 80 heavily worked pages that bear testimony to the effort Beethoven expended on the task — whilst on his deathbed — and illustrate why he was dissatisfied with Anton Halm's version. When *The Times* Arts Correspondent Dalya Alberge was invited to consult the manuscript she reported: 'It is covered with the composer's feverish amendments and deletions in ink, pencil and red crayon, some so deep that they puncture the paper ... The passion and struggle are much in evidence. Smudges indicate how in the rush to get the music down, Beethoven wiped ink away while it was still wet. In places he rubbed the paper through leaving small holes.'[xvii] Beethoven's indomitability of spirit clearly persisted to the end.

i As quoted in: Beethoven House, Digital Archives, Library Document, H. C. Bodmer, HCB Mh 104.
ii Anton Felix Schindler, *Beethoven as I knew him*, edited by Donald W. MacArdle and translated by Constance S. Jolly from the German edition of 1860, 1966, p. 307.
iii Thayer-Forbes, 1967, pp. 975–6.
iv Maynard Solomon, 1977. Originally derived from Thayer-Dieters-Riemann, Vol. V, p. 298. Schindler's account conveys something of the feelings stirred by the first performance of the Op. 130 Quartet and its fugue. '[It] was the publisher Matthias Artaria who, as purchaser of the manuscript, took the initiative. He offered to buy the fugue as a separate work if Beethoven would compose another finale in free style to put in its place. The Master complied with this condition and wrote the movement that appears in the published version. This was his very last composition, and was written in November 1826.' Anton Felix Schindler, *Beethoven as I knew him*, edited by Donald W. MacArdle and translated by Constance S. Jolly from the German edition of 1860, 1966, p. 308.
v This letter has not survived.
vi Beethoven House Digital Archives, Library Document H. C. Bodmer, HCB Mh 25.
vii With acknowledgement to Barry Cooper, *Beethoven and the creative process*, 1990.
viii Theodore Albrecht, translator and editor, 1996, Vol. 2 Letter No. 431, pp. 137–8.
ix *Ibid*.
x *Ibid*.
xi Emily Anderson, editor and translator, 1961, Vol. 3, Letter No. 1500, p. 1296.
xii *Ibid*, Vol. 3, Letter No. 1529, pp. 1310–11.
xiii *Ibid*, footnote.
xiv Beethoven House, Digital Archives: *Grosse Fuge*, Op. 133.
xv Theodore Albrecht, translator and editor, 1996, Vol. 3 Letter No. 458, pp. 176–7. For a facsimile reproduction of the Contract between Beethoven and Pleyel, see: Beethoven House, Digital Archives, Library Document H. C. Bodmer, HCB Br 289.
xvi See text to: Beethoven House Digital Archives, Library Document H. C. Bodmer, HCB Mh 25.
xvii Dalya Alberge, *The Times*, 2 December 2005.

STRING QUARTET IN C-SHARP MINOR, OP. 131

'The higher the great geniuses soar, the further out of reach of those who claim they are created for them. This is especially so in music and dramatic literature. The other day I heard one of Beethoven's last quartets. M. Baillot [Pierre Baillot, professor of violin at the Conservatoire de Paris] introduced it at one of his evenings. I was intensely curious to see what effect this extraordinary work would have on the audience. There were nearly three hundred there, and precisely six of us half dead with emotion — we were the only ones who did not find the work absurd, incomprehensible, barbarous. [Beethoven] soared into regions where one breathes with difficulty. He was deaf when he wrote this Quartet, Op. 131. For him, as for Homer, "the universe was clasped within his mighty soul". It is music for him alone, or for those who have followed this incalculable progress of his genius.'

Hector Berlioz, *The Making of an Artist*, volume one, 1829, p. 311. Reproduced in: Martin Geck, *Beethoven*, 2003, p. 125.

'It is one of the beauties of the C-sharp minor Quartet that moments of hesitation, of reflection, if not altogether absent, are confined to short *intermezzi*, short connecting movements numbered separately, which, since the main line of development ascends steadily throughout the work, are merely bridge passages from the emotional sphere of one main movement to that of the next.'

Paul Bekker, *Beethoven*, 1925, p. 334.

'This quartet is generally recognised to be musically the finest of them all, and undoubtedly reaches the highest point ever attained in quartet literature. Here one finds a rich flowering of all the qualities that mark the later works; originality and freedom of form, which is nevertheless always a strictly logical and supple technique; and intellectual and imaginative conception of an idea, of each note, and of each bar of development. As in many of the later works, there is also to be noticed the working out of a continuous psychological idea. A great soul rises above the trials of

> human suffering, out of the darkness of irreparable grief to a spiritual strength and power, vigour, vitality, and triumph over the hosts of evil, over the bitterness of fate, to inner peace and reconciliation.'

Joseph de Marliave, *Beethoven's quartets*, 1925 (reprint 1961), pp. 295–6.

> 'The Quartet in C-sharp minor, Op. 131, is held by most people to be the greatest of all Beethoven's quartets, and he himself is said to have considered it so. It is a work of gigantic power, which, compared to the very personal Quartet in B-flat major, seems to transcend personality, and voice the feelings of all mankind ... The seven movements are played without a break, and although each differs so much in character from the others they seem welded together by one central idea. They are stupendous, almost overpowering, to play.'

Rebecca Clarke, *The Beethoven quartets as a player sees them* in: *Musical Times*, Special Issue — Beethoven's Death Centenary, Vol. VIII, No. 2, 1927, pp. 184–90.

The pioneering Beethoven German musicologist Paul Bekker perceived the composer's late string quartets to be a thematically unified whole. Of the C-sharp minor Quartet he wrote: 'The spirit of man, illuminated through the anguish of moral conflict and assured of the unity of Will and of Fate, of Freedom and Necessity, returns once more to earth.' He continues: 'The same idea which supports the A minor Quartet, Op. 132 and carried to dizzy heights in the B-flat major fugue [String Quartet, Op. 130] now leads it back to face life anew. The three great quartets thus form a tremendous imaginative triptych, the prophet ascends to the mountain top, sees his God face to face and returns to his people with his tables of the law, written and established for all eternity.'

Originally published in Paul Bekker, *Beethoven*, 1925 and reproduced as an act of homage by Arthur Shepherd in, *The string quartets of Ludwig van Beethoven*, 1935, p. 61.

> 'Here indeed is the Palestrina style, miraculously translated into the language of instruments, not human voices ... I think Wagner's explanation of the nature of Palestrina's music "where rhythm is only perceptible through changes in the harmonic succession of chords", gives some real assistance.'

Marion M. Scott, Beethoven: The master musicians, 1940, p. 272.

> 'In his last quartets, which were long regarded as the productions of an insane and deaf man, there seems to be some padding until you study them thoroughly. But ask someone who is familiar with these works, say, a member of a quartet who has performed them frequently, if there is anything superfluous in the C-sharp minor Quartet. Unless he is an old-fashioned musician brought up on Haydn, he will be horrified at the thought of abbreviating or cutting any part of it.'

Peter Ilitch Tchaikovsky, from a notebook entry of 1888

quoted by Ferruccio Bonavia, *Musicians on music*, 1956, p. 262.

Alongside his love and understanding of music, the British broadcaster and music critic Alec Robertson was possessed of a deep religious conviction. This is evident in the passing reference he makes to Beethoven's String Quartet, Op. 131:

> 'I do not know what thoughts are left in the mind of a man profoundly moved by the *St. Matthew Passion* or Beethoven's C-sharp minor Quartet who does not believe in God, and it is none of my business. I am concerned with those who feel, with Edgar Allen Poe, that "It is at once by poetry and through poetry, by music and through music that the soul divines what splendours shine beyond the tomb", and if we *feel* — it cannot be proved — that music, this great angel of God, opens Heaven to us then we can be sure that it is one of the ways to Him which we can simply and trustingly follow.'

Alec Robertson, *More than music*, 1961, p. 227.

> 'When Schotts, the publishers, received the score of Beethoven's C-sharp minor Quartet they were alarmed to find he had written on it: "Cribbed together variously from this and that." They wrote asking for an explanation. Beethoven passed it off, the phrase, as a joke. But was it? I think it was a perfectly accurate statement for the work, thematically, has a good many quotations from is own earlier works.'

Harold Truscott, *Beethoven's late string quartets*, 1968, p. 100.

> 'Original and novel the C-sharp minor Quartet most certainly is, in every detail as well as in general conception, but quite without the *nimiety* and the sense of strain that could be felt in the *Grosse Fuge* of Op. 130 and even, perhaps, in a different sense in the deliberate austerity of the *Heiliger Dankgesang* in Op. 132.'

Martin Cooper, *Beethoven: the last decade, 1817–1827*, 1970, p. 391.

> 'Everything in this masterpiece is perfect, inevitable, unalterable. It is beyond the impudence of praise, too (partly because of difficulties with vocabulary in that service); if not quite beyond criticism, which can be overstated, however, and is destined to disappear in context.'

Igor Stravinsky, *Themes and conclusions*, 1972, p. 262.

> 'The C-sharp minor Quartet has a perfection that is perhaps beyond controversy. Beethoven himself thought it his finest, and no one of any consequence has disagreed with him ... The unity of this mighty conception, from the profound contemplation of the fugue to the magnificently conclusive statement of the finale, is so clear, so utterly convincing, so completely original, that it defeats all attempts at criticism, rendering them impertinent. The work has the clarity of the

simplest classical quartet, and a power beyond that of any other composer's mightiest symphonies.'

Robert Simpson, *The Chamber music for strings* in, Denis Arnold and Nigel Fortune, editors, *The Beethoven companion*, 1973, pp. 274—5.

'Perhaps Beethoven considered this quartet [Op. 131] a summary work, ending the exploration of the set of musical problems to which the late quartets (and perhaps all late works) were devoted; and this may explain what appear to be numerous references to other works — from the ... similarity of the opening fugue to themes from Op. 132 and the Fugue of Op. 130, to what I hear as conscious recollections of the *Heiliger Dankgesang* in the fourth variation of the *Andante* (bars 1—4), and of the main theme of the opening *Allegro* of Op. 132 in the third variation (bars 1—2, 9—10). The raging, victorious finale is surely the *Grosse Fuge* revisited — and conquered ... A continuity of rhythmic design adds to the feeling that this is one of the most completely integrated of Beethoven's works.'

Maynard Solomon, *Beethoven*, 1977, p. 325.

'Certainly it would be hard to find in any other work of [Beethoven's] containing so wide a range of mood. Its plan might have seemed more unconventional in 1827 than forty years earlier, when composers were writing divertimenti and similar works in which the order of the move-

> ments was decidedly variable ... It my be that the C-sharp minor Quartet contains nothing that makes quite as overwhelming an impact as the *Cavatina* from Op. 130. But taken as a whole, it may be said to be at the same time the more varied and the more closely unified of the two quartets.'

Philip Radcliffe, *Beethoven's string quartets*, 1978, p. 164.

On hearing a performance of the C-sharp minor Quartet, Bernhard Shaw took the opportunity in his revue of the recital in question to polish his irony:

> 'The great attraction for me at this concert was Beethoven's posthumous quartet in C-sharp minor. Why should I be asked to listen to the intellectualities, profundities, theatrical fits and starts, and wayward caprices of self-conscious genius which make up those features of the middle period Beethovenism of which we all speak so very seriously, when I much prefer these beautiful, simple, straightforward, unpretentious, perfectly intelligible posthumous quartets? Are they to be always avoided because the professors once pronounced them obscure and impossible?'

Originally published in *The World*, 21 February, 1894 and quoted in:

Dan H. Laurence, editor, *Shaw's music: the complete musical criticism in three volumes*, 1981.

> 'The view of Op. 131 as a pinnacle of Beethoven's achievement was fully developed by

> Theodor Helm. He wrote that "the novelty, freedom and spirituality of the nevertheless lucid and strictly logical form, the speaking soulfulness of the content into every note, every measure, finds its purest embodiment in the C-sharp minor Quartet, [wherein] as in few string quartets the unfolding of a definite psychological idea is undeniable".'

William Kinderman, *Beethoven*, 1997, p. 9. (Kinderman is quoting from Theodor Helm, *Beethovens Streichquartette*, Leipzig, 1885, p. 223.)

> 'Opus 131 occupies a unique place even among the greatest of Beethoven's works ... Playing it is an awesome experience. It's the longest nonstop work in our repertoire. Not only does one have to sustain the highest degree of concentration for forty minutes, but it's no small matter to maintain good intonation on instruments which over that length of time are bound to go out of tune, especially when we have to contend with a very warm stage. And all four instruments can go out of tune in different ways. We somehow have to cope with that.'

Michael Tree, viola member of the Guarneri Quartet, recollected by David Blum in: *The art of quartet playing: the Guarneri Quartet in conversation with David Blum*, 1986, p. 171.

Claude Debussy's estimation of Beethoven was ambivalent — he frequently referred to him disrespectfully as 'The old deaf one'. He could also at times be dismissive of his music as we detect in a letter he wrote on 23 February 1895 to his friend the poet and writer Pierre Louÿs:

> 'Beethoven's fourteenth quartet is without question one long practical joke, in spite of what these young metaphysicians say in *L'art et la vie*. [a short lived journal 1892—97]. People should stop lumbering us with old furniture which hasn't even retained its period smell.'

Reproduced in: François Lesure, and Roger Nichols, editors, *Debussy, letters*, 1987, p. 77.

> 'Just as the Quartet, Op. 131 forms a cycle of human experience, so it is a kind of microcosm of European musical history. The drama of the sonata principle is resolved back into its elements: first into operatic aria and recitative — with no longer any direct suggestion of the theatre — out of which the interior drama of sonata has grown; then into the rediscovered unity of song variation and fugue.'

Alec Harman with Anthony Milner and Wilfrid Mellers, *Man and his music: the story of musical experience in the West*, 1988, p. 655.

> 'Every new work by Beethoven — even as he retreated further and further into his obscure, introverted, deaf world — was eagerly awaited by his contemporaries, whom he still managed to involve despite his handicaps. The C-sharp minor Quartet was difficult to approach in 1826, and still is; but his contemporaries knew it, as we

> know it now, to be a most remarkable manifestation of the human spirit.'

Thomas P. Lewis, editor, *Raymond Leppard on music: an anthology of critical and personal writings*, 1993, p. 17.

> 'Romanticism may have given Beethoven licence to represent the forbidden and the boundless; but his will to form — his classicism if you like — enabled him to set boundaries upon the infinite to portray disorder in the process of its metamorphosis into order, to transform suffering, tragedy, and death into healing, hope, and affirmation, and to do so this by shear aesthetic power.'

Maynard Solomon writing in response to the C-sharp minor string quartet in *Beethoven: Beyond Classicism*, in: Robert Winter and Robert Martin, editors, *The Beethoven quartet companion*, 1994, p. 74.

> 'The Quartet in C-sharp minor is perhaps the most fully realized of all Beethoven's intrinsically musical narrative designs. In Op. 131 he merges tendencies from some of his earlier works to forge a unique seven-movement sequence without any real breaks between movements. The large-scale rhythmic continuity is only one aspect of the integrated network of relationships that holds together these seven movements, which are explicitly numbered in the score.'

William Kinderman, *Beethoven*, 1997, p. 308.

> 'Today there was ... a concert that gripped me

> right to my soul. They played a string quartet by
> Beethoven, one of his last works where he didn't
> care at all any more whether people would like
> it, and instead expressed his innermost life in
> music ... Would that there were a little bit more
> of the great soul in me too, I thought as I listened
> to it!'

Leoš Janáček writing to his wife Zdenka in February 1880. As recalled by John Tyrrell editor and translator, *My life with Janácek: the memoirs of Zdenka Janácková*, 1998.

> 'The C-sharp minor Quartet is one of his most
> tightly integrated compositions; indeed, for many
> critics it represents the apogee of Beethoven's
> achievement in the genre.'

John Daverio, *Manner, tone, and tendency in Beethoven's chamber music for strings* in: Glenn Stanley, editor, *The Cambridge companion to Beethoven*, 2000, p. 159.

> 'As concert halls became bigger and audiences
> became larger, music became gradually more and
> more difficult to understand at first hearing. That
> paradox is essential to the history of modern
> culture. Mozart was already difficult for his
> contemporaries who were distressed by unintelli-
> gible modulations and over-complicated textures.
> Beethoven was much harder than Mozart, and
> polemic about the insanity of his late conceptions
> continued literally until the end of the nineteenth
> century ... The music that survives is the music
> that musicians want to play. They perform it until
> it finds an audience.'

Charles Rosen, *Critical entertainments: music old and new*, 2000.

> 'Musically speaking the Quartet in C sharp minor represents the highest development of Beethoven's new style. It contains elements of innovation, extraordinary for his time. The selection of the key itself was unusual if not unprecedented. The quartet has seven movements, linked so that there is no distinct separation between the component parts, but a liquid transition from one mood to another.'

Nicolas Slonimsky, *The great composers and their works*: edited by Electra Slonimsky Yourke, 2 Vols., 2000, p. 167.

> 'Beethoven's String Quartet in C sharp minor, Op. 131 is a unique piece. It begins with an *Adagio* ... It begins with a fugue. Its movements run continuously ... more ... unique this is a minor-mode composition destined to end unassertively ... Most commentators say it ends tragically. Most seem to sense a deep sadness in the opening fugue — "the saddest thing ever said in notes", according to Wagner — and then a rich kaleidoscope of lighter experiences in major keys, some of them not only light but humorous and quirky. The sadness deepens into tragedy when the piece reverts at last to the minor.'

Joseph Kerman, *Op. 131 and the uncanny* in: William Kinderman editor, *The string quartets of Beethoven,* 2005, p. 275.

> 'With its rich and manifold structure, the whole quartet derives a rather rhapsodic expression so to say, from the fact that all the movements are to be played consecutively and without intermission, as well as from the interpolation of the short and rather improvisatory introductory movements [3 and 6], and from the frequent change of theme and tempo in the variations.'

Preface to the Philharmonia Miniature score, Wiener Philharmonischer Verlag, Wien, anon and undated.

The reader will recall, from our previous accounts of the period when Beethoven was working on the Galitzin Quartets, the violinist Karl Holz had become a close friend and confident of the composer. Moreover, he had temporarily supplanted Anton Schindler as Beethoven's amanuensis, copyist and secretary-assistant. Years later he shared his recollections of this period with the German music scholar Ludwig Nohl — now perhaps best remembered in Beethoven musicology for his discovery of the manuscript of *Für Elise*. What Holz related to Nohl makes a fitting introduction to the creation origins of Beethoven's last two string quartets.

Holz states: 'While composing the three quartets requested by Prince Galitzin, such a wealth of new quartet ideas flowed from Beethoven's inexhaustible imagination that he virtually had to write the quartets in C-sharp minor and F major involuntarily.' Holz recalls how, when the pair were out walking together, Beethoven would say jocularly — his eyes glistening: 'My dear fellow, I've just had another idea' and would write down a few notes in his sketchbook. It is also from Holz that we learn he once remarked to

Beethoven that in his opinion the quartet in B-flat major was the greatest of the three quartets Opp. 127, 130 and 132 to which the composer allegedly replied: 'Each in its own way. Art demands of us that we shall not stand still.' On further reflection Holz states Beethoven considered the C-sharp minor Op. 131 Quartet 'to be his greatest'.[i]

A phrase from the writings of William Kinderman — Beethoven scholar and acknowledged interpreter of his keyboard music — endorses the spirit of Holz's remarks bearing on the composer's compositional prowess. Based upon his study of the sketches for the late quartets, Kinderman believes these compositions share particular affinities bearing upon their extension of the conventional classical framework of four movements. He avers: 'Thus, in writing each of these works, Beethoven conceived material that spilled over beyond the composition immediately at hand. His fertility of invention refused to be contained within the boundaries of the singular work.' We have seen Beethoven's original intention was to conceive the formal design of the Quartet Op. 127 to include perhaps as many as six movements. Although he eventually retained the four-movement form, in Kinderman's phrase 'his flirtation with such an expansion of the narrative chain of movements bore fruit in the following trilogy of quartets in A minor, Op. 132, B-flat major Op. 130 and C-sharp minor, Op. 131'.[ii]

Michael Steinberg reminds us that in his piano-sonata writing, Beethoven had frequently questioned the primacy of the three and four-movement design.[iii] For example, from 1804 we have the two-movement F major Piano Sonata and from 1821–22 the mighty C minor Piano Sonata, Op. 111 — his last, and similarly constructed, essay in the medium.

Paul Bekker considered the A minor, B-flat major and C-sharp minor quartets form a triptych preceded by — and differing markedly from — the E-flat major Quartet and followed by — and also differing markedly from — the last quartet in the set of five, namely the quartet in F major.[iv] We recall, when considering Op. 132, that its opus number does not correspond with its date of completion; it was actually finished before Op. 130 and Op. 131. These three compositions were conceived in close proximity to each other and while Beethoven was working on the B-flat major Quartet he began studies for the C-sharp minor Quartet — testimony, as we shall in due course remark, to their thematic interrelatedness. Discussing the compositional interrelationships to be found between the late quartets, Marion Scott states: 'Simultaneously with the A minor Quartet, Beethoven was evolving the great B-flat major ... This relation went deeper than Beethoven's habit of working on several things at the same time; the two works are thematically joined ... While still in the midst of the B-flat major Quartet he began to work on the C-sharp minor.'[v]

Denis Matthews considered the C-sharp minor Quartet constitutes 'a vast single span' insofar as its seven movements are linked by the expression *attacca* indicating they are to be played without a break — or at least with only a moment's pause.[vi] Barry Cooper's observations here are of interest regarding the listener's concept of time as the C-sharp minor Quartet unfolds. He maintains: 'By a variety of techniques ... Beethoven breaks down the concept of "movement" ... and makes the work as a whole the artistic unit of measurement.' He argues this means 'taking in much larger stretches of music at a time'. As he further observes, Op. 131 does not appreciably exceed the performance time of some of the Op. 18 quartets — notably the F major, A major and B-flat major which can approach thirty minutes in a spacious rendering. What is significant in the case of the C-sharp minor Quartet is the manner in which '[Beethoven] takes the listener on a long and varied journey through a variety of keys, moods and textures'.[vii]

To cite Cooper once more, he draws attention to Beethoven's preoccupation with ways of linking consecutive movements in a multi-movement work. He quotes the Piano Sonata *Quasi una fantasia*, Op. 27, No. 1 from 1801 in which the movements are unified and in which material from the slow movement is recalled in the finale. Cooper observes: 'From here it was only a short step to the song cycle *An die ferne Geliebte*, where [most of the songs] are linked to the next by a modulatory passage.' He concludes how such procedures led ultimately 'to the extraordinary relationships in the Quartet Op. 131 — relationships that were to be created only through a lifetime's experience in developing composition along these lines'.[viii]

With regard to the character of the C-sharp minor Quartet it is salutary to recall how the nature of string-quartet writing — brought about by Beethoven — had changed from the classical era so well exemplified in the works of his teacher Haydn. The string quartet was no longer a polite musical dialogue between four voices. In Reginald Barrett-Ayers' words: '[The] later quartets of Beethoven are more like debates to be had in public, in which many speakers have their say, some serious, some humorous, but all related to a central theme.'[ix] The life-affirming nature of the C-sharp minor Quartet was not lost to the American composer-musicologist Arthur Shepherd who proselytised: 'The idea of a reawakening to the joy of life is expressed both in the general plan and in the particular sequence of the succeeding movements. In contrast to the kaleidoscopic changes presented in the B-flat major Quartet, those of the C-sharp minor Quartet represent a steadily ascending line. Even external interruptions by pauses between the individual movements is avoided.'[x] We have noted how Beethoven regarded his Op. 131 as being no less than *primus inter pares* – 'first among equals'. More generally, later in life, he was also given to saying: 'Thank God there is lass lack of imagination [regarding the medium of the string quartet] than ever before.'[xi]

Worthy of recollection is that Beethoven's writing for the medium of the string quartet was in part stimulated by the development of the professional string-quartet ensemble. As we have previously noted, this owed much to the pioneering efforts of Ignaz Schuppanzigh whose quartet premiered many of Beethoven's string quartets – in particular the late string quartets. His return to Vienna in 1823, after a six-year sojourn in St. Petersburg, had doubtless come to the attention of Prince Galitzin who we have previously seen commissioned the string quartets, Opp. 127, 132, and 130. As Tully Potter writes: 'The knowledge that this faithful servant was once again available was undoubtedly a stimulus to Beethoven, who always had performance in mind for even his most advanced music.'[xii]

An additional stimulus to Beethoven writing string quartets at the period under consideration was the growing interest in the genre on behalf of music publishers and the musically minded public. For example, on 22 April 1826 Beethoven wrote to his publisher Moritz Schlesinger, based in Paris, 'quartets are now in demand everywhere and it really seems that our age is taking a step forward'.[xiii] Beethoven consequently realised there was serious money to made from the sale of string quartets. After selling the first of the Galitzin Quartets Op. 127 to the publisher Schotts for 50 ducats he raised the price for the next two, Opp. 132 and 130, to 80 ducats (360 florins). This was a considerable sum, almost as much as he had been paid for his last three piano sonatas and not far short of the annual salary of a rank-and-file musician toiling at the Opera.[xiv] On completion of the Galitzin Quartets, therefore, Beethoven had every incentive to write additional compositions secure in the belief they would find a publisher eager to secure them.

Beethoven's choice of key for the Op. 131 Quartet is of particular interest. He had not had recourse to this key in a major composition since as far back as 1801 when he had composed the Piano Sonata Op. 27, No. 2 — *The Moonlight*. His mind appears to have turned to the potentialities of the key of C-sharp minor during the composition of the *Missa Solemnis* by which time he was already considering the writing of another Mass — subsequently forestalled by his untimely death. Notwithstanding, it has been suggested that the properties of this unusual key lingered in his mind and found expression in his Op. 131.[xv] The philosopher-musicologist Theodor Adorno characterises the key of C-sharp minor as an *archaic* key whose effect upon us he describes as 'difficult to fathom'.[xvi] Beethoven's interest in archaic-sounding music, as typified by the old modes, had been roused during his composition of the *Missa Solemnis* — and of course in the *Lydian Hymn* of the *Adagio* to the String Quartet Op. 132.

In considering Beethoven's harmonic language, as expressed in the late quartets, the music critic Paul Griffiths refers to the 'key landscape' that he believes characterise these works stating: 'It has often been observed that there are sub-thematic links among the late quartets, and particularly the three vaster ones, Opp. 130–132 ... that contributes much to the harmonic colour of these quartets ... [and] contributes to the sense that Opp. 130–132 are a trilogy.' He adds words of caution though that there is no conclusive evidence that Beethoven planned his quartets with this in mind but he is unequivocal 'there is no doubt that his awareness of the extent and range of harmonic landscapes was without peer in the whole history of music, and it is not too much to suppose that he instinctively found a way to make Opp. 130–132 complimentary'.[xvii] Shepherd also remarks on the 'unifying element' to be found in the late quartets. He cites the 'unifying function' of the four-note motif found in the B-flat major Quartet, Op. 130, namely, G sharp, A, F, and E. He imaginatively likens these 'jostling and shifting ideas' to a family trait that may be discerned in a line of children that becomes 'more and more refractory' as it progresses through the generations.[xviii]

In Joseph Kerman's words the C-sharp minor Quartet is 'the most deeply integrated of all Beethoven's compositions'.[xix] Perhaps being mindful of the innovatory nature of the work, he lists all the movements in a numbered sequence as follows: I – *Adagio, ma non troppo e molto espressivo*; II – *Allegro molto vivace*; III – *Allegro moderato*; IV – *Andante, ma non troppo e molto cantabile – Andante moderato e lusinghiero – Adagio – Allegretto – Adagio, ma non troppo e semplice – Allegretto*; V – *Presto – Molto poco adagio (scherzo)*; VI – *Adagio quasi un poco andante*; and VII – *Allegro*. This numbered sequence prompted Marion Scott, in her pioneering study of the composer, to discern a metaphysical dimension in the quartet's construction: 'So here we have *seven* (the perfect number in the lore of numbers), forming a circle (which is a symbol of eternity), and the motto fugal theme [of the first movement] (probably symbolizing Life) all combined by Beethoven.'[xx]

In his praise of the C-sharp minor Quartet, Maynard Solomon asserts: '[There] are many pressures toward discontinuity at work in this Quartet: six distinct main keys, thirty-one changes of tempo (ten more than in Op. 130), a variety of textures, and a diversity of forms within the movements – fugue, recitative, variation, scherzo, aria, and sonata form – which makes the achievement of unity all the more miraculous.'[xxi]

The many surviving sketches for Op. 131 (see later) suggest Beethoven may initially have envisioned an even greater composition in eight movements.[xxii] As remarked, the existing seven movements are linked *attacca* conveying the impression of a work that unfolds in one great sequence of events; moreover, in the opinion of some authorities, a resemblance to an improvisation is also conveyed.[xxiii] Notwithstanding the grandeur of Beethoven's conception, the sequence of movements in Op. 131 remains close to the traditional string-quartet format, with only the *Adagio-Fugue* in C-sharp minor and the *Allegro molto vivace* in D major departing from the norm.[xxiv] If No. 3 (an eleven-bar recitative-like transition) and No. 6 (a slow introduction to the finale in the form of a twelve-bar tune with repeats) are accepted for what in fact they are — primarily short pieces that serve as a brief introduction to what follows — then the Quartet assumes the proportions of a five-movement work as in the case of the Quartet Op. 132. In the estimation of David Wyn Jones: '[Broad] characteristics of the Quartet are the familiar ones of making a slow movement in variation form the core of the work (movement 4) and providing a mix of movement types that promote continuity.'[xxv] Kerman remarks pragmatically: 'To be quite precise about it, the players are required to move in strict rhythm from No. 2 to 3, 3 to 4, and 6 to 7. There must be no break of attention, no catching of breath, no coughs or turning of legs.'[xxvi] Shepherd is more eloquent, as befitting this great work: 'Beethoven had life-long propensity for exploring every nook and cranny of *tone-structure* and for bringing the various traditional designs — fugue, sonata, suite, variation and rondo — into new relationships. In his hands they are all, perforce, subjected to a metamorphosis, but they are all suffused in the end by the transfiguring power of his imagination; they all become as satellites that move in their orbits around the sun of his indomitable will.'[xxvii]

Before proceeding directly with our discussion of the creation origins of the C-sharp minor Quartet, we pause for moment to gain insights into Beethoven's personal circumstances and how others perceived him at the period under consideration.

We have an account of Beethoven from Johann Reinhold Schultz when he visited the composer sometime in September 1823 — he was seeking the English publication rights to various compositions. He recalled his meeting the following year in the London periodical *The Harmonicon*. Schultz describes his day with the composer as his *dies faustus* — 'happy days' As a consequence of the composer's deafness Schultz records 'when he plays the pianoforte, it is at the expense of some twenty or thirty strings'. Beethoven's nephew Karl was then residing with Beethoven whom Schulz describes as 'a fine young man of about eighteen' and observed Beethoven's 'goodness of heart' towards him. Beethoven expressed his admiration for Handel who by then had supplanted Mozart as his idol. He was given to saying: 'Handel is the greatest composer that ever lived.' He spoke with reverence of the *Messiah* and of its composer he remarked: 'I would uncover me head, and kneel down on his tomb!' Schultz had previously met Beethoven in 1816 prompting him to remark upon his changed (aged) appearance: 'The portrait you see of him in the music shops is not now like him, but may have been so eight or ten years ago.'[xxviii]

Beethoven's respect for his contemporary Carl Maria von Weber did not approach that for Cherubini — whom he held in high regard. However, the sensational success of *Der Freischütz* led him to study the score that considerably influenced and changed his opinion. When Weber went to Vienna to attend the rehearsals and the first performance there of his opera *Euryanthe* (25 October 1823), Beethoven sent an invitation to call on him at Baden where he was spending the early autumn; this was a rare privilege since Beethoven guarded his privacy resolutely. Weber later wrote to his wife of the encounter: '[Beethoven] received me with the most touching affection; he embraced me at least six or seven times in the heartiest fashion, full of enthusiasm ... We spent the noon hour together, very merrily and happily.' Later in life Weber's son Max recalled his father telling him how he had entered a bare, almost poverty-stricken room: 'The chamber was in the greatest disorder. Music, money, articles of clothing lay on the floor ... the grand piano, which was open, was thick with dust'. Weber likened Beethoven in appearance to King Lear: 'His hair was thick, grey and bristly, here and there altogether white ... like in his [later] portraits ... beneath the bushy eyebrows ... small radiant eyes beamed mildly out'. Weber, like Beethoven, was small in stature but he describes how the eminent composer 'towered cyclopean' above him'.[xxix]

To these pen-portraits of Beethoven we can make reference to a painterly likeness. In January 1823, the publisher Gottfried Georg Härtel wrote to Ferdinand Georg Waldmüller requesting he should make a portrait of Beethoven. Doubtless this was to form the basis for a subsequent engraving with which to adorn one of his forthcoming sets of musical works, as was then the custom. Waldmüller was a respected genre and portrait painter and on 18 April he responded to Härtel's request, undertaking to attend on the composer in this capacity 'with the greatest pleasure'. Although Beethoven subsequently promised Waldmüller several sittings, in the event the artist had to make do with only one hurried session. Under these circumstances it can be assumed Waldmüller had time only to portray Beethoven's face, adding the details of his clothes retrospectively. Anton Schindler disliked Waldmüller's study condemning it for being 'further from the truth than any other'. At a later date, Waldmüller prepared a more carefully considered version of his original study, this time for the Leipzig publisher Friedrich Kistner. In Alessandra Commi's study *The Changing Face of Beethoven* (New York, 1987), contrary to Schindler's opinion, she defends Waldmüller's study 'for its accuracy'.[xxx]

Returning now to our survey of the creation origins of the C-sharp minor Quartet, we consider Beethoven's various negotiations with his publishers and others associated with its gestation.

We learn of the putative progress Beethoven alleges he was making with the C-sharp minor Quartet from a letter he wrote in August 1825 to the Leipzig-based publisher Carl Peters. On 18 May 1822, Peters had introduced himself to Beethoven and enthused how long he had 'zealously endeavoured to issue [his] excellent works in good printings'. He stated that whatever the composer could send him would be welcome 'for I seek your association not from self interest, but rather from honour'.[xxxi] In his rather tardy reply, Beethoven endeavoured to rekindle Peters' enthusiasm for publishing his works by informing him 'a quartet — and what is more a grand one' is waiting for him. This is a reference to the String Quartet Op. 132. For this composition he requested 360 gulden or 80 ducats. He remarks: 'My compositions are now being paid for at higher rates than ever.'[xxxii] He adds this is as good a work as he could give to his best friend. Of particular relevance, however, is that Beethoven tempted Peters with the prospect of receiving a further quartet on which he had started work — taken to be a reference to Op. 131. Doubtless with the intention of putting a little pressure on Peters — Beethoven was not averse to playing one publisher off against another — he intimated that Moritz Schlesinger, of the Paris branch of the music firm, was then in Vienna and was potentially interested in purchasing his newest quartet compositions. Notwithstanding Peters' expressed enthusiasm, in the event nothing came of his good intentions — he considered Beethoven's prices to be beyond his means.

Confirmation that Beethoven was indeed at work on the C-sharp minor Quartet — or was at least turning his mind in its direction — comes from an entry in a Conversation Book from the close of the year; by then Beethoven's loss of hearing was such that he had to request visitors to communicate with him in writing. In the midst of remarks about New Year's greetings, Beethoven inscribed a melody concerning which the pioneering Beethoven authority Alexander Wheelock Thayer remarks: 'It is very interesting that the opening idea for the Quartet in C-sharp minor should appear before the close of 1825.' Below the melody Beethoven had written one of his characteristic aphorisms: 'Only the praise of one who has enjoyed praise can give pleasure.'[xxxiii]

The composition of the String Quartet Op. 131 belongs to 1826 and it is to this period we now direct our account. In Thayer's words: 'The year 1826 was a year of awful happenings and great achievements; a year of startling contradictions, in which the most grievous blows which an inscrutable Providence dealt the composer as if to crush him to earth, were met by a display of creative energy which was amazing not only in its puissance but also in its exposition of transfigured emotion and imagination ... The year which witnessed the last of Beethoven's completed labours, and by what by general consent might be set down as the greatest of his string quartets, that in C-sharp minor, Op. 131.'[xxxiv]

The grievous blows to which Thayer makes reference were primarily those inflicted by the conduct of his adopted nephew Karl. Having failed in his university studies he made an attempt on his life — the oppressive demands made upon him by Beethoven may also have been a contributing factor. Beethoven's troubled relationship with his nephew lies outside the scope of our discussion but we shall have cause to make further reference to this in due course.

Also bearing down upon Beethoven were bodily ills of several kinds that he endured through January until March. Anton Schindler, Beethoven's long-term amanuensis, was now more-or-less returned to favour and, reflecting on the composer's misfortunes, was disposed to quote from Homer's *Odyssey*: 'For quickly doth misfortune make men old.' He elaborates: 'One could see in the master's stooped posture his deep grief over the public infamy that had once more befallen his name. The once sturdy, vigorous body now stood before us like an old man of nearly seventy'.[xxxv] To quote Thayer once more: 'That [Beethoven] could continue to write amidst all the disturbing circumstances of this year in the higher and purer regions of chamber music was a source of admiration and wonder to his friends ... the little community of stringed instruments is become more than ever his *colporteur* — confident, comforter and oracle.'

A hint of the progress Beethoven was making with Op. 131 is contained in a letter he sent to the publisher Bernhard Schotts on 28 March 1826. His primary reason was to supply Schotts [more correctly Schotts and Son] with the metronome markings for the Ninth Symphony, the *Missa Solemnis*, and the F major String Quartet, Op. 127; as we have seen in our discussion of the Galitzin Quartets, Beethoven was now placing reliance on Mälzel's metronome for the adoption of the correct tempo indications in the performance of his compositions. Concerning the C-sharp minor Quartet, he remarks: 'I should perhaps be able to produce a new quartet.' Concerning the price for such an undertaking he comments: '[Now] I receive *for a quartet of this kind* [Beethoven's italics] at least 80 gold ducats.' He adds: 'Although I certainly do not compose merely for the sake of the fee, yet my circumstances demand that I give some consideration *to this matter*.'[xxxvi] [Beethoven's italics]

On 20 May, Beethoven wrote once more to Schotts. He complained of being overwhelmed with business affairs and of constantly being dogged by ill health. He intimated the C-sharp minor Quartet was finished although not yet ready to be dispatched. He was unwilling to reduce his requested fee of 80 ducats. With this in mind, and mindful of the high fee he was charging, he suggested that Schotts should pay him in two instalments of 40 ducats. He promised the required metronome markings would be sent within the week — which proved to be over-optimistic.[xxxvii]

While waiting for a response from Schotts, on 3 June Beethoven wrote to Heinrich Albert Probst another Leipzig publisher; this is indicative of his disposition to negotiate with a number of publishers simultaneously. He informed Probst: 'I am offering you an absolutely new quartet for two violins viola and violincello [Op. 131]. But you must not be surprised if for this I ask for eighty gold ducats. I can assure you on my honour that this sum has already been paid to me for several quartets.'[xxxviii] Nothing came of Beethoven's proposal to Probst. However, Probst later collaborated with Carl Czerny in the publication of the latter's four-hand arrangements of the composer's nine symphonies that were published after Beethoven's death over the period 1827–9.[xxxix]

From a further letter Beethoven sent to Schotts on 12 July, it appears the publisher had not only agreed to purchase the C-sharp minor Quartet for 80 ducats but had also agreed to pay for the work, as requested, in two instalments. Beethoven repeated his reassurance, 'I must tell you that the work is finished and ready for delivery'.[xl] He had still not prepared the required metronome markings though as he confessed in a further latter (29 July) but assured Schotts he would receive them shortly. He explains he would have sent them sooner 'if my anxiety to send you this work absolutely correct and ready for engraving had not decided me to check it again most carefully'.[xli]

Beethoven's tardiness in completing the C-sharp minor Quartet may in part be explained by the pressure he had placed himself under in composing — more correctly transcribing — a four hand arrangement of the *Grosse Fuge*. From our earlier account of the origins of this composition, we have seen that Beethoven had initially trusted Anton Halm with the undertaking but was dissatisfied with the outcome. Consequently, Beethoven diverted his own energies to the project — it is known he had little enthusiasm for making transcriptions of his own compositions. The enterprise occupied him well into August.

On the 19th of that month Beethoven was in a position to inform Schotts he was sending the manuscript copy of the Op. 131 String Quartet to them via his agents Franck & Co in exchange for the agreed payment. Meanwhile, the composer's pervasive sense of humour had been the cause of a misunderstanding between himself and Schotts. He had written in the score that the Quartet had been 'cobbled together with filched bits of this and that' ('zusammengestohlen aus verschiedenem diesem und jenen').[xlii] Although intended as a joke, the publishers had taken Beethoven's words at their face value and made it known to him 'that they had contracted for an original work!' In his letter Beethoven informed Schotts he was hurt by having his joke so misunderstood and assured him the composition really was *brand new* (Beethoven's italics). He explained he still could not provide the music's required metronome markings as a consequence 'of a great misfortune' — a reference to the attempted suicide of his nephew Karl.[xliii]

At the close of September, Beethoven sought Schotts' reassurance that the Quartet was now safely in their hands and, mindful of the unusual key in which the work was set, remarked: 'Don't be frightened at the four sharps.'[xliv] By way of further reassurance he informed Schotts he anticipated the piece would be performed at a future date in Vienna — which was good for publicity and Schotts' future sales.

The following month Schotts confirmed the manuscript of Op. 131 was indeed safely with them and expressed their (his firm's) intention to make progress with the engraving. This was, however, subject to receiving the metronome markings that they were still awaiting; Beethoven had not been able to send the required information since his metronome was broken. Of interest, and confirmation of Beethoven's capacity — and propensity — to work on a number of compositions at once, are other remarks in Schotts' letter. His firm was at this time preparing for publication both the *Missa Solemnis* and the Ninth Symphony for which metronome markings were also needed. In this letter Schotts makes reference to wishing to oblige Beethoven by adopting the Archduke Rudolph's coat of arms in the Title Page of the forthcoming *Missa Solemnis* so that it could be presented as 'beautifully as possible'.[xlv]

Beethoven eventually (13 October) provided Schotts with the metronome indications for the Ninth Symphony but was still not in a position to provide those for the *Missa Solemnis* or the Quartet. But he took the opportunity to raise a subject close to his heart, namely, the publication of a complete edition of his works — in the event this did not come about in his lifetime.[xlvi]

On 18 December Beethoven wrote to Schotts again, once more raising the matter of the Quartet's metronome markings. He urged: 'Do wait for them. In our country such indications are certainly necessary. We can scarcely have *tempi ordinari* any longer since one must fall into line with the ideas of unfettered genius.' He also gave an undertaking to provide the name of the Quartet's dedicatee. Beethoven closes by regretting his confinement to his sickbed and trusts that 'God will help him get up again'.[xlvii] This was not to be. He was in his final illness that consumed him a few months later.

A measure of the discomfort Beethoven had to endure in his last weeks is provided by the recollections of Gerhard von Breuning, the son of Beethoven's lifelong friend Stephan. Gerhard — who studied medicine — attended upon the composer in his last illness and left the following account. He tells how Beethoven became disillusioned by the daily visits of his physician Professor Wawruch who insisted his patient should drink a great many daily concoctions. According to Breuning, Beethoven's housekeeper Sali had to regularly return 80 six-ounce bottles to the dispensary. Excess fluid accumulated to such an extent that in order to provide relief the Chief Surgeon, Johann Seibert of the Vienna General Hospital, was called to puncture the composer's abdomen. Altogether Seibert attended Beethoven on four such occasions to relieve dropsy; Beethoven is said to have born his painful adversity 'like a knight'.[xlviii]

Such was Beethoven's standing that news of the composer's illness reached Schotts in Leipzig. An indication of the esteem felt by the publishers for him is they wrote solicitously: 'We send you the friendliest greetings ... on the occasion of the upcoming New Year, requesting the continuation of your valued friendship, and wish you not only a long life, but also health, and everything else that can bring satisfaction and pleasure to your life.'[xlix] For the reasons, stated none of this came to pass.

In the New Year, Beethoven turned his mind to the question of the dedicatee for the C-sharp minor Quartet that we have seen Schotts required in order to engrave the Title Page. Beethoven's intention had been to confer this honour on Johann Nepomuk Wolfmayer, a wealthy Viennese cloth merchant. He was an enthusiastic lover of music and early recognised and admired Beethoven's genius. In 1818 Wolfmayer had tried to induce Beethoven to compose a requiem with the offer of 100 gulden but nothing came of this. Wolfmayer had attended the first performance of the String Quartet, Op. 132; the effect of the *Adagio* upon him was such that it was said he had 'wept like a child'. Wolfmayer was at Beethoven's bedside just before he died and left the sick room exclaiming: 'The great man! Alas, alas!' His final act of homage to the composer was to serve as a pallbearer at his funeral.[i]

Beethoven informed Schotts on 22 February that Wolfmayer was to receive the dedication to the Op. 131 Quartet. Poignantly he asked Schotts to secure for him some good Rhine wine that he could not obtain in Vienna. His doctor had prescribed it partly in the belief it would help to restore his health but, more particularly, since he was aware of his patient's fondness for it.[ii] On 1 March Beethoven repeated his request '*for some old white Rhine wine or some Moselle wine*' emphasising the urgency of his request with underling. He made reference to his fourth operation adding, prophetically: 'Even so I cannot yet hope for a complete recovery and cure.'[iii]

We pause here in our narrative for a moment and make reference to the following. Despite his preoccupation with the Quartets Opp. 131 and 135, Beethoven found the time and energy to consider other matters close to his heart. On 28 February he had occasion to write to Carl Gottlieb von Tucher. He was the son of the mayor of Nuremberg who had a fondness for Renascence and Baroque music. In 1824 Tucher travelled through Italy collecting early church music. On his return to Nuremberg, in 1825, he sent a two-volume collection of music by Palestrina and his School to Beethoven's publisher Artaria in Vienna. Tucher requested Beethoven's consent to have the volumes dedicated to him to which the composer readily agreed. Beethoven's willingness to accept the dedication is taken as testimony to his identification with the ecclesiastical music of the past, the spirit of which infiltrates his last compositions.[liii]

Solicitous of Beethoven's wellbeing, on 8 March Schotts informed Beethoven of the measures they were taking to send him a case of choice Rhine wine combined with herbs specially medicated to assist the dropsy then afflicting him. According to Thayer, Schotts put in hand the delivery of a case of twelve bottles of Rüdesheimer Berg of the 1806 vintage to be sent via Frankfurt. He records: '[But] in order that [Beethoven] might receive a slight refreshment, they had sent that day four bottles of the same wine, two pure and two mixed with herbs, to be used as medicine which had been prescribed for his disease.'[liv]

Turning to business matters, the publisher confirmed: 'The C sharp minor is already finished, and will likewise be [ready] in Paris soon. Have the kindness to issue a certificate about this Quartet, and send it immediately with the key and the opus number, and transferring to us the exclusive property rights not only in Mainz but in Paris and all other places where we think it appropriate to produce [it] in engraving as our property.' Schotts urged the need for circumspection to protect him from rival publishers as such as Maurice Schlesinger with whom Beethoven also had been negotiating. As a further indication of his sympathy for the composer's plight he appended to his letter a remedy for dropsy.[lv]

On 20 March Beethoven responded to Schott's request — his letter is one of the very last of the composer's formal business transactions. It was written by Anton Schindler and signed by Beethoven. The text reads: 'By virtue of this declaration I herewith transfer to the publishing firm of Bernhard Schotts Söhne at Mainz the sole ownership also the sole copyright of my latest quartet in C-sharp minor, Op. 131.' He adds that as it is their property: 'They are empowered to publish engraved copies of it both in Paris and at Mainz and also in all centres which the aforesaid publishing firm may consider advisable.'[lvi]

The following week Beethoven wrote once more to Schotts — in faltering pencil. He states: 'According to my letter [of 22 February] the Quartet was to be dedicated to someone whose name I had already sent you [Johann Wolfmayer].' He continues: 'But something has happened which has decided me to make an alteration in this respect.' He states: 'The Quartet must now be dedicated to Lieutenant Field-Marshall, Baron Joseph von Stutterheim to whom I am indebted for many kindnesses.' He pleaded 'for Heaven's sake alter it' and promised to bear the cost of having the Title Page re-engraved if necessary.[lvii] The circumstance that brought about this last-minute change of mind was that von Stutterheim, to the composer's great relief, had assisted in the rehabilitation of his nephew Karl. He admitted him to his regiment, then stationed in Moravia.[lviii] Karl would, in due course, acquit himself well and rose to the rank of officer.[lix] Wolmayer's solicitude towards Beethoven did not go unrecognised. In due course the String Quartet in F major, Op. 135 appeared posthumously with the dedication 'à son ami Jean Wolfmeier [sic]'.

On 29 March Bernhard Schotts Söhne expressed regret on not receiving any news of improvement to Beethoven's health. He confirmed the Op. 131 Quartet would be dedicated as requested to Baron von Stutterheim. Unwittingly Schotts took leave with friendly greetings and heart-felt wishes for improvements to the composer's condition unaware he had died three days previously.[ix] The promised fine wine had in fact reached Beethoven before his passing but of which he had only been able to take meagre sips administered with a spoon.

On 12 April Anton Schindler explained the circumstances of Beethoven's passing to Schotts and gave a moving account of the composer's last hours. He alleges Beethoven whispered to the few gathered about his death-bed 'Plaudite amici, commoedia finite est!' He requested thanks should be expressed to the Philharmonic Society of London for their generous gift of one hundred pounds, sent previously to alleviate his financial circumstances. Schindler was obliged to make reference to business matters. He requested three copies of the C-sharp minor Quartet be printed on fine paper that would be sent to the work's dedicatee von Stutterheim. Schindler confirmed the composition's opus number, as requested by Schotts, was Op. 131 and that the Quartet in F major was intended for the publisher Schlesinger and was to be designated Op. 135.[lxi]

On 23 April 1827, almost a month to the day following Beethoven's death, the C-sharp minor Quartet was announced in the *Intelligenzblatt der Caecilla* (Annual Series VII, No. 25), as being available from Bernhard Schott's Söhne: 'With pride we can inform the public that Beethoven's last Quartet [sic] ... has been published by us and forwarded to all music warehouses of note, as well as the score of this masterpiece.'[lxii] There was some confusion as this stage as to both the composition's chronological sequence – it was not in fact his last – and Schotts had designated the work as Op. 129.

The error of the Quartet's opus number was subsequently rectified before published copies were circulated. The Title Page duly proclaimed: 'Grand Quatuor pour deux Violins Alto et Violoncelle composé et dédié à Son Excellence Monsieur Le Baron de Stutterheim, Lieutenant-Maréchal de Camp Impérial et Royal d'Autriche. Conseiller aulique actuel de Guerre, Commandeur de l'ordre miltaire de Marie Thérèse et de l'ordre de Leopold d'Autriche. Chevalier de l'ordre Impériale de Wladimir de Russie de la 3me Classe. Grand-Croix de l'ordre Royal de Sardaigne de Maurice et Lazare, et de l'ordre Royal miltaire de St. George de la Réunion de Sicile, deuxième propriétaire du 8me Regiment d'Infanterie de ligne Impériale et Royal par Louis van Beethoven Oeuvre 131. Propriété des Editeurs. Mayence chez les fils de R. Schott à Paris, rue de Bourbon No. 17, à Anvers, chez A. Schott.'[lxiii] The Quartet was first published in parts with the work appearing in full score later in June.

Given Beethoven's close connection with Ignaz Moscheles (see our pervious writings), on 14 September 1827 Schindler sent him a remembrance of his friend. He writes: 'The [enclosed] is one of those noteworthy pocket books in which Beethoven wrote his sketches, usually in the open air, and then [copied] at home in score. I was fortunate enough to rescue several of these that have the greatest interest for me. No one will be able to decipher it unless he knows the child of which it is the embryo. This one here contains the sketch of one of his last quartets and if you ever hear these quartets you will surely know to which one it belongs. A few of his thoughts are very clearly written out.'[lxiv] The work in question was the C-sharp minor Quartet. Of related interest is that Schindler sent Moscheles a lithograph copy of Joseph Karl Stieler's portrait of Beethoven depicting him working on his *Missa Solemnis*; Schindler considered this was 'the best' and that all others were 'worthless'.[lxv]

In 1828 a reflective article appeared in the *Allgemeine musikalische Zeitung in* which the author, Friedrich Rochlitz, outlined his views on the nature of the string quartet. He acknowledged it was 'difficult and hazardous to write about Beethoven's last great works', even though by then fifteen months had elapsed since the composer's death — by which time the musically minded public had some experience of them and opportunities for their assimilation. Rochlitz set out the case in favour of artistic tolerance whether it be of new music or of music from an earlier time. He divided the musical public into two groups: those 'who expect nothing more from music than amusement' and, with the C-sharp minor Quartet in mind, those 'who see it as the key to an inner spiritual life'.[lxvi] Rochlitz acknowledged the C-sharp minor Quartet posed formidable, though not insurmountable, challenges to ready comprehension through its recourse to what he considered to be its 'whimsical fragmentation' (*zerstücken*) and 'hide-and seek'.[lxvii]

Rochlitz was not alone, amongst Beethoven's early critic-admirers, to be perplexed by his late music. The Belgian musicologist, composer and teacher François-Joseph Fétis likewise found these works challenged musical orthodoxy in ways he found discomforting. Writing in the 27 June 1834 issue of the *Revue musicale*, he speaks of 'the caprice which mars the admirable qualities of Beethoven's last works'. Of Op. 131 and Op. 135 he writes: 'In the two last quartets by this celebrated musician ... there is much to occasion surprise; it is difficult to imagine how so powerful an inspiration could be linked with so much sheer extravagance.'[lxviii]

Public performances of the late quartets were rare at this time. Amongst the earliest on record is one given in Vienna in 1835 by the Leopold Jansa Quartet. Jansa was a Bohemian violinist, composer, and teacher and from 1834 to

1850 he participated in various string quartets. He took over from Ignaz Schuppanzigh with Karl Holz (second violin), Joseph Linke (cello) from the Schuppanzigh Quartet, adding Karl Traugott Queisser (viola).[lxix]

One who was not fazed by Beethoven's 'whimsical fragmentation' or his 'sheer extravagance' was the archmodernist Hector Berlioz, one of France's foremost early champions of the composer's music. He once described the String Quartet, Op. 131 as 'a heavenly inspiration that took material shape'.[lxx] Not surprisingly, the majority of his fellow countrymen, even those seriously musically inclined, did not share his views. This is evident from an account Berlioz has left of a performance of Op. 131 before what turned out to be a hostile audience. He describes how, after about two minutes into the concert, the audience grew restless: 'People began to talk, each telling his neighbour of his discomfort and boredom.' Unable to stand 'such weariness of spirit' Berlioz relates how nine tenths of the audience left complaining aloud that the music 'was unbearable, incomprehensible, ridiculous — the work of a madman defying common sense'. Silence was requested by the remaining few and the Quartet was duly concluded. Notwithstanding, the leader of the string quartet, Pierre Baillot, was accused of making fools of the audience by 'presenting extravagant nonsense'. Some exclaimed: 'What a pity that such a great man should have produced deformities after all his masterpieces'. Berlioz himself had taken the precaution of sitting amongst a handful of known Beethoven admirers so as not to be unduly disturbed by the disorder they had anticipated. He concluded his account laconically: 'Here is music, then, which repels almost all those who hear it and which, among a few, produces sensations wholly out of the ordinary.'[lxxi]

As the nineteenth century progressed, the merits of the C-sharp minor Quartet came to be more widely acknowledged. This is evident in a recollection concerning the ardent Beethovenian Anton Bruckner. It derives from the writings of August Stradal, a Bohemian virtuoso pianist, arranger, music teacher, and pupil of Franz Liszt. From him we learn of Bruckner's improvisations at the Court Chapel — Bruckner being one of the greatest organists of his day. Stradel recalls: 'At such times, once the hymns were over, he would take one of their themes as a basis; once he chose a theme from Beethoven's C-sharp minor Quartet and composed a splendid fantasy which lasted almost half an hour.'[lxxii]

Our reference to Bruckner provides a convenient link with Richard Wagner whom he admired at least as much as, if not more than, Beethoven. In his study of the composer and his music Kinderman states: 'Serious engagement with Beethoven's later music had gained acceptance by the 1850s ... fuelled not by changing views about Beethoven's deafness but by the novelty and power of the works themselves.' He attributes a major factor in their acceptance to their sheer novelty that had originally so often provoked initial resistance. He continues: 'By the 1850s, the progressive features of Beethoven's later musical language were seen as urgently relevant to new developments in composition.' He illustrates his assertion by citing Wagner's own enthusiasm at this time for the C-sharp minor Quartet, Op. 131. He informs: 'At Zurich in 1854, he organized and coached a performance of this work, and also contributed analytical notes to the piece.'[lxxiii]

We linger in the 1850s to make reference to the pioneering String Quartet of Joseph Hellmesberger. Founded in 1849, it was celebrated for performing 'in an unabashedly subjective and emotional manner' that seemed, to the audiences of the period, to have been especially well suited to Beethoven's late quartets. Reflecting on the repertoire of the Hellmesberger Quartet in 1859, the music critic of the *Neue Zeitschrift für Musik* (issue 26) relates that the C-sharp minor Quartet, Op. 131 and the E-flat major Quartet, Op. 127 were both played as well as a first performance of the *Grosse Fuge*, Op. 133. Concerning the Quartet's interpretation, the critic in question enthused: 'It is Hellmesberger's great service to have made this prophetic and progressive artist so popular among us ... The crowning contribution of the Quartet [is] that even a many-faceted structure, Beethoven's Quartet *Fuge*, was listened to so attentively by the entire audience and after its completion greeted so warmly and with so much applause.'[xxiv]

In his role as Director of Vienna's Philharmonic Concerts, Gustav Mahler conceived the daring idea of including in its 1899 season a performance of Beethoven's String Quartet in C-sharp minor — to be performed by the entire string section of the orchestra. According to the music critic Eduard Hanslick, Mahler justified his actions on the grounds that when a string quartet was performed in a large hall its intimacy was lost; the four parts being so weakened as not to reach the listener with the strength envisaged by the composer. Mahler reasoned: 'I give them this strength by reinforcing each part.' Mahler added double basses in his orchestration. He was convinced the inherent intimacy of the quartet medium could be preserved if the sound-volume was adapted to the dimensions of the hall.

Mahler's controversial views inevitably divided opinion amongst the musical cognoscente. From the recollections of Mahler's devoted friend, the violist Natalie Bauer-Lechner, we learn the following. From the start of the concert some of the audience booed and others applauded. Natalie herself considered that in the most expressive passages of the music, Mahler obtained 'a discreet piano' and a 'magical sound which could not have been bettered by a single string instrument'. Mahler's detractors did not agree; some continued to boo so incessantly that he had to have them removed. Others sat 'in deathly silence'. At the close of the finale the audience's reaction was 'very cool'. Mahler was apparently unrepentant but 'very angry'.[lxv]

Mahler's approach to Beethoven string-quartet performance calls to mind a modern-day incident of a similar nature. The Greek born writer Helena Matheopoulos remembers an occasion in London in May 1979 when Leonard Bernstein gave a press conference — he was due to conduct the London Symphony Orchestra. She recalls how he enthused about his reading of the C-sharp minor Quartet with full strings because he felt 'It didn't work as a quartet!' At the time Matheopoulos felt 'highly incensed' at what she took to be 'an unbearably arrogant statement'. Giving her cause not to reach too hasty a judgement was a remembrance of Bernstein performing the Op. 131 Quartet in 1977, this time with the string sections of the Vienna Philharmonic Orchestra. The venue was the Herodes Atticus Theatre, Athens. Matheopoulos writes: 'I admitted that it sounded good but that it didn't calm my misgivings.'[lxvi]

Our citation of the views relating to the C-sharp minor Quartet, deriving from modern-day sources, leads us to an anecdote concerning the philosopher Ludwig Wittgenstein. It derives from an occasion in the 1930s when he was in conversation with fellow philosopher John King. King recounts how the two of them listened to a gramophone recording of the second, third and fourth movements of the C-sharp minor, String Quartet. (Could this have been a recording made by the celebrated Busch String Quartet?) According to King, Wittgenstein was 'rapt with attention and most excited at the end of the playing'. He describes how Wittgenstein jumped up from his seat as if something had suddenly struck him and said: 'How easy it is to think that you understand what Beethoven is saying.' At which he seized a pencil and piece of paper and, drawing two-thirds of a circle, exclaimed 'How you think you have understood the projection'. Then he added a bulge exclaiming: 'You realize that you haven't understood anything at all.'[lxxvii]

Reflecting on Wittgenstein's response to the Op. 131 Quartet, Robert Martin and Robert Winter comment: 'Beethoven's discourse in the quartets cannot be corrupted or invalidated by repetition and familiarity. Their inexhaustibility and uncompromised vitality have confronted past auditors and modern listeners alike.'[lxxviii]

We draw our prefatory remarks to the C-sharp minor String Quartet to a close by returning to the year following Beethoven's death. By then the life of Franz Schubert, who had so much admired the composer, was nearing its untimely end. The circumstance in question bears upon one of the most poignant moments in all musicology.

Schubert had taken a keen interest in Beethoven's musical development throughout his short life. He followed him, not as the crow follows the farmer's plough — to pick up this or that — but to draw inspiration for his own music. To paraphrase words of Alfred Einstein, the after-effect of learning from Beethoven's music later infiltrated into his own and its subsequent fermentation lifted his creations to a higher plane. Not surprising then that, despite his waning energies, he should want to hear a performance of the recently published C-sharp minor Quartet. This was duly arranged for Schubert by a small circle of friends in November 1828 — just five days before his death. The leader of the group that performed the work was Karl Holtz. Schubert's friends later testified to the state of deep emotion and excitement that hearing the work created in him. Schubert himself is said to have remarked: 'After this what is there left for us to write?' With Schubert's passing, Holtz is said to have remarked: 'The king of Harmony had sent the King of Song a friendly bidding to the crossing.'[lxxix][lxxx]

The C-sharp minor String Quartet did not fall effortlessly from the composer's pen, it was the product of considerable and sustained endeavour as attested to by the many surviving sketches involved in its creation. It is to a survey of these to which now direct our attention. We confine our remarks to a summary-overview mindful this is the province of the Beethoven musicologist proper. In this context may be mentioned the scholarly researches of: Robert Winter, *Plans for the structure of the String Quartet in C-sharp Minor, Op. 131*, in: Alan Tyson editor, *Beethoven studies 2*, 1977, pp. 106–37 and Winter's additional, expanded text, *Compositional origins of Beethoven's Opus 131*, 1982; Douglas Porte Johnson editor, *The Beethoven sketchbooks: history, reconstruction, inventory*, 1985; and Nicholas Marston, *Biographical and musical source material* in: Barry Cooper, *The Beethoven compendium: a guide to Beethoven's life and music*, 1991, pp. 186–7 – to which should be added the many scholarly commentaries to Beethoven's sketches by Cooper himself. It is primarily to these sources the present writer is indebted in the passages that follow. Other related sources are cited in the endnotes.

The sketch sources are of three types: those found in pre-bound sketchbooks conforming to a standard format; collections of leaves bound by Beethoven himself to form pocket sketchbooks – mostly pencil sketches that today present a challenge to decipher; and extended drafts in quartet score – evolved in the composer's last years. Through these can be traced Beethoven's early and developing ideas for the string quartets Op. 131 and Op. 135. These sketchbooks follow each other in chronological sequence with the emphasis being work on the C-sharp minor String Quartet; The F major String Quartet makes an appearance in the last of the set in late August 1826. The sketchbooks share the same physical characteristics measuring about 15 by 26 centimetres so as to fit into a (large) coat pocket when Beethoven was outdoors on his rambles in the countryside. The sheets were pre-ruled both recto (r) and verso (v).

The Berlin Staatsbibliothek Preussischer Kulturbesitz possesses a number of sketchbooks that were purchased by Domenico Artaria at the *Nachlass* auction of Beethoven's effects in November 1827. One of these came into the possession of the collector Franz Kullak – pianist, composer and pedagogue – who later donated it to the Berlin, Royal Library (Berlin, Staatsbibliothek – Berlin, State Library). It consists of 62 leaves that Beethoven worked on between November 1825 and November of the following year. Kullak probably purchased the sketchbook from the publisher and music dealer Artaria & Co. who secured some twenty-six sets of sketches and sketchbooks from the fifty or so on sale. When Artaria sold the sketchbook in 1847, he inscribed the cover as follows: 'Autographs de/Louis van Beethoven / Livre d'esquisses / contenant / les / idées / pour / le grande fugue [Op. 133] ... / et pour differents Quators / L'authenticité / est guarantie par les soussinges / Artaria & Co. à Vienne / 1847.' Sketches for the C-sharp minor Quartet are found at folios 10r–12v, 14r–v, and 15v–17r.

Beethoven used a pocket sketchbook, Autograph 9/1A from November 1825 to early 1826. Ideas for Op. 131 are combined with sketches for the *Grosse Fuge*, Op. 133, as the finale to the String Quartet Op. 130. Authorities consider this source reveals Beethoven was actively turning his mind to the C-sharp minor Quartet by December 1825.

From February to March 1826, Beethoven used a set of sketch leaves that later came into the possession of the collector H. C. Bodmer.[lxxxi] It was from these that, as we have remarked, Schindler gave a selection (sixteen leaves) to Ignaz Moscheles as a keepsake in recognition of his close association with Beethoven. Moscheles did not keep his bundle intact. When the Beethoven memorial was being erected in 1845, Moscheles removed a leaf and gave it to Ernst Julius Hähnel, the sculptor who designed the statue. Moscheles inscribed a dedication: 'Beethoven's manuscript. To H. Professor Hähnel in memory of the unveiling of the monument in Bonn, which awoke the greatest admiration in me for the perfect manner in which it had captured the immortal master. August 1845. I. Moscheles.' This leaf is now in possession of the Beethoven House, Bonn. In 1856 Schindler sold the rest of the sketchbook to the Berlin Royal Library, today the Staatsbibliothek Preussischer Kulturbesitz.[lxxii] The C-sharp minor Quartet is represented in this source as follows: first movement (pp. 1, 2, 5); second movement (pp. 1–3, 5, 15, 23–6); third movement (p. 24); and fourth movement (pp. 1, 4, 6–8, 10–14, 22).

Between April–May, 1826 Beethoven made use of Autograph 9/3 that now consists of 28 leaves. These are devoted largely to the fourth movement of Op. 131 and include sketches for the variations that found their way into the final version of the Quartet. Ides for further variations are also indicated but which Beethoven subsequently discarded. He also appears to have contemplated a further movement, alternately as a scherzo and a finale.

By late spring, Beethoven used a further 21 leaves known as Autograph 9/4. These reveal his exclusive preoccupation with Op. 131. Much of the book is taken up with developing ideas for the fourth movement (1r–15r). Ideas for other movements are explored as follows: second movement (19r); fifth movement, (15r, 16v, 18r, 19v); and sixth and seventh movements (15r–16r, 18r–21v). These sketches also contain ideas for the rejected scherzo.

By the early summer of 1826, Beethoven made use of a further set of 16 leaves, Autograph 10/1, previously owned by Anton Schindler and sold, with others, to the Berlin Royal Library in 1846. The composer reserved these exclusively for Op. 131 with the emphasis being on the last three movements: fourth movement (1v, 18r, 14v); fifth movement (1r–13v); sixth movement (6v–8r, 13v, 15r); and seventh movement (8v–9r, 13r–16r).

Between Late June/July – August 1826, Beethoven compiled a set of leaves now known as Artaria 205, Bundle 3. The first part of the sketchbook is devoted to Op. 131 and the second part reveals Beethoven turning his mind to ideas for the String Quartet, Op. 135. The C-sharp minor Quartet is explored as follows: fourth movement (pp. 18–22); fifth movement (p. 10, p.15); sixth movement (p, 3, p.8, p. 9); and seventh movement (pp. 1–12, pp. 22–5).

In his work on the late string quartets, Beethoven introduced an innovation into his sketching procedures. He made use of manuscript paper that was ruled in the form of quartet score-sheets. These enabled him to set down more extended compositional drafts encompassing all four instruments — doubtless prompted, in part, by the challenges posed by the growing contrapuntal complexity of the music evolving in his mind.[lxxxiii] As Barry Cooper remarks, the composer's 'limitless aspirations' required a new method of composing. He elaborates: '[Beethoven] began making frequent use of sketching in open score on four staves, instead of merely on one or two as before.' This was to assist with what Beethoven himself described as 'a new kind of part writing'. Cooper continues: 'The score sketches did not supplant other types of sketching, but ran in parallel with them.'[lxxxiv] Beethoven authority Douglas Porter Johnson remarks that Beethoven rarely worked in full score prior to working on the autograph of the work under consideration.

Consistent with what we have just said he states: 'The enormous body of such [full score] sketches from the years 1824–26, when he was occupied almost exclusively with the late quartets, must therefore reflect an important development in Beethoven's compositional process.'

Porter's researches, and those of others, reveal the paper Beethoven used for these late score-sketches is similar to that found in the sketchbooks and autographs. These take the form of oblong-format leaves with 10, 12, 14, or 16 staves to a page, usually pre-ruled but sometimes lined by Beethoven himself. Unlike the sketchbooks, Beethoven left the score sketches loose. At his death about 350 of these leaves were purchased by the music publisher Domenico Artaria. These were acquired by the Berlin State Library in 1901, catalogued as Artaria 206 MS. Another hundred or so such leaves were gifted over time by an unknown benefactor to the Gesellschaft der Musikfreunde, catalogued as MSS A51 and A55. Their sheer number is testimony to the effort Beethoven expended in the creation of the late quartets.[lxxxv]

The score sketches for Op. 131 are preserved in greater numbers – over 200 leaves – than for any other late quartet; they even surpass those Beethoven required for his work on the Ninth Symphony and the *Missa Solemnis*. Notwithstanding, Johnson believes Beethoven must have worked on many others since parts of the Quartet are represented only in a fragmentary manner in the score sketches. These have since acquired trophy status and are now scattered in several libraries in Europe and America.[lxxxvi]

The score sketches vary in their musicological elaboration. Typically they consist of melodic, single-line fragments without clef or key signature. However, in his tireless pursuit for perfection, Beethoven wrote out no fewer than fifteen full-score versions of the last four bars of the variations in the C-sharp minor Quartet – all finished in detail.[lxxxvii] The English music scholar Basil Lam refers to twelve bars of the Quartet that Beethoven wrote out in full score as 'Beethoven's search for perfection'.[lxxxviii]

Of the last five quartets and the *Great Fugue*, only the autograph of the Quartet in A minor, Op. 132 has survived intact. The autographs of Opp. 127, 130, 131 and 135 were early in their history dismembered and sold off, movement by movement, to different collectors and institutions.[lxxxix]

The first movement of the C-sharp minor Quartet is unique among Beethoven's sixteen quartets insofar as it opens not with a sonata-form *allegro* but with an *adagio* that the performers' are requested to play *ma non troppo e molto espressivo*. Perhaps in this carefully measured opening fugal adagio, Beethoven was consciously looking back to, and enlarging upon, an older style of slow introduction?[xc] Matthews refers to the music's 'noble pathos' and with others detects the influence of Bach in the movement's later pages. For him, however, the counterpoint is far removed from the aggressive assertiveness of the *Grosse Fugue*. He draws attention to the heavily stressed A and D naturals, characterising them as being 'intensely personal' and the manner in which he considers they add 'strength and poignancy' to the movement's closing measures.[xci] Violinist Arnold Steinhardt perceives the Quartet's opening statement as a 'dramatic event' not only because it is announcing the fugue subject, that permeates the movement, but because of the manner in which the motif of the first two bars is used in later movements as well.[xcii]

Bekker's estimation of the opening *Adagio* is worthy of being quoted in full: 'In this movement the poetic idea of the whole movement is proclaimed. The return to life, to joyful thought and emotion, an *incarnates est* in the human rather than in the religious sense, is presented in each section of this twofold movement, the first representing the mystical rebirth, a return form the world of visions and dreams to the world of reality, the second, the homophonous D major section, confirming and giving actuality to the new-won hope in life.'[xciii] In much the same spirit, Scott similarly empathised with this 'noble and gravely beautiful music'. She suggests: '[We] shall not be far wrong, if we see in the fugal motto theme a symbol of Life, eternal and unchangeable behind the shifting phenomena of the temporal worlds, and manifesting itself through them, now here, now there.'[xciv] With more measured objectivity, Cooper remarks on the movement's suggestions of the Phrygian mode that he considers 'betrays the ecclesiastical influence of its conception'. Here he is reminding us, as previously noted, that Beethoven had thoughts regarding the composition of a Mass in the key of C-sharp minor.[xcv]

Wagner imagined a day in the life of Beethoven – 'the sacred genius' – and selected the C-sharp minor Quartet as a basis upon which to construct his imagery. He commences: 'The long opening *Adagio*, surely the saddest utterance ever made in notes, I should call the awakening of the dawn of a day which "in its whole long course shall not fulfil a single wish, not one" [Goethe's *Faust*] ... It is at the same time a penitential prayer, a communing with God out of a firm belief in the Eternal God.'[xcvi] Nearer our own time and, with the benefit of a performer's insights, cellist David Soyer proclaimed: 'For me the first movement has a pervading tragic quality, a sense of foreboding; it's a magnificent prelude to all that's to come.'[xcvii] In Joseph de Marliave's analysis of the movement he suggests the opening theme can be split into two elements, the first phrase seeming to him 'to express a profound sadness' and the second phrase to be a motif 'of still resignation' – each motif serving as the basis for a development of its own. Regarding the introduction as a whole, he likens it to 'a lamentation at once passionate and resigned, labouring under restraint, an endless melodic line'. In his opinion 'not one phrase could be taken away without marring the continuity of the idea'. He continues in his analytical manner: '[The] complete double theme breaks forth in the expression of defiant grief. Sombre and fierce instead of despairing, the theme rolls in the cello in augmentation [and] semibreves and crotchets take the place of the minims and crotchets of the opening statement.'[xcviii] Contrary to these views, Cooper finds no hint of sadness *per se* in the opening fugue. He writes of the music's 'life-enhancing beauty' of 'contemplative art' and if there is sadness it is the sadness 'occasioned by the transience of beauty or the mutability of everything human — such as we often find in Schubert'. He cites the latter's achingly moving *Adagio* from the C major Quintet. Cooper concedes, if there is an element of sadness it is 'no more than a streak of sombre colour that runs through much (though by no means all) of the movement without ever dominating it entirely'.[xcix]

Concerning Beethoven's interest in, and awareness of, the art of fugue it is known from his studies with Christian Gottlob Neefe that as a boy of twelve he was proficient in the performance of all of Bach's *The Well-Tempered Clavier* — a remarkable achievement. We recall Bach's stated intentions in composing 'the forty eight' were 'for the profit and use of musical youth desirous of learning, and especially for the pastime of those already skilled in this study'. Of significance here is that Beethoven possessed, in his relatively small collection of books, a copy of Johann Philipp Kirnberger's six-volume *The Art of Strict Composition in Music.* The extent to which Beethoven absorbed Bach's influence in the art of fugal composition is indirectly evident in the contrapuntal studies of his piano pupil Carl

Czerny. He based his 1838 edition of the *The Well-Tempered Clavier* in part on his recollections of hearing many of these preludes and fugues played by Beethoven. Authorities consider the composer's presence can be detected in this edition as reflected in many of Czerny's prescriptions concerning tempos and dynamics. This is relevant to our discussion as Michael Steinberg elucidates: 'Forty-two years later, Beethoven revisits [the art of fugue] and transports us into the world of the sublime C-sharp minor. But it is more the manner and the manners of this fugue that creates an air of Apollonian calm in contrast to the Dionysian abandon of Op. 133.' Steinberg concludes: 'The way the Op. 131 fugue looks on the page seems to confirm the accuracy of Czerny's representation of Beethoven's highly inflected manner in which he played Bach.'[c]

Beethoven became more preoccupied with fugal writing as he progressed from his so-called second period to his third. In our previous writing we have cited examples of this in both his string quartets and piano sonatas. As Harold Truscott states: 'His early works abound with beautifully written fugal passages, but significant content expressed in fugue rather than in fugal passages, within a different structural framework, this he left mainly for what would be his final period.'[d] In support of this contention we may cite the fugal passages in the D-major Cello Sonata, the *Hammerklavier* Sonata, the A-flat Sonata, Op. 110, the *Gloria* and *Credo* of the *Missa Solemnis*, the majestic *Diabelli* Variations, and the B-flat major Quartet.

With regard to the adoption of fugal writing in Beethoven's lifetime, Philip Radcliffe writes: 'Since the death of Bach and Handel fugues had usually been brisk and animated; sometimes full of suppressed excitement, as in the remarkable *sotto voce* fugal finales of some of Haydn's Op. 20 quartets, and sometimes fierce and argumentative, as in Mozart's' Fugue in C minor.' He continues: 'But it was left for Beethoven, in his Quartet in C-sharp minor, to recapture the brooding and meditative atmosphere of Bach's fugue in the same key, from the first book of the *Forty-Eight.*'[cii] Several authorities identify Beethoven's fugal writing in his Op. 131 with that of Bach. Among these is Martin Cooper who comments: 'The similarity with the first half of this [the fugue's] theme and that of the C-sharp minor fugue in the first book of J. S. Bach's *48* can hardly be fortuitous, particularly in view of the extreme rarity of the key of C-sharp minor in Beethoven's music.' He also makes reference to the composer's projected plans for a Requiem Mass that was to be set in the same key. He speculates: 'Whether the opening fugue was at any time or in any way associated with that scheme we do not know.'[ciii]

Cooper likens the opening fugal movement of the C-sharp minor Quartet to being 'as unmistakably the first scene of a drama as the *Grosse Fuge* is the last'.[civ] Kinderman makes the same evaluation: 'In the C-sharp minor Quartet ... Beethoven inverts the position of the fugue, treating it as the point of departure instead of the outcome of the work.'[cv] To quote Cooper once more, he remarks on Beethoven's departure from strict contrapuntal orthodoxy in the Quartet's fugal writing: '[Beethoven] is no longer reconciling, or even demonstrating, like the Creator himself, the principle of order or *kosmos* inherent in the theme that he has chosen, drawing it out and revealing it with a kind of awe, that sense of wonder that he shares with the great poets and mystics and never lost to the end of his life.'[cvi] Steinberg, no less respectful of the composer's achievement, allows himself a moment of levity: 'It is as though Beethoven, after the inspired and magisterial audacities of the *Grosse Fuge*, were rendering a peace offering to the fugue gods.'[cvii]

Reflecting on the pioneering studies of Gustav Nottebohm — one of the first musician-musicologists to carry out a close study of Beethoven's sketchbooks and sketch-leaves — Bekker calls attention to what he identifies as the 'organic connection' to be found between the string quartets Opp. 132, 130 and 131 that has characterised them, in Beethoven musicology, as being 'a triptych'. By this is meant the thematic bond that unites them. Nottebohm had shown that the fugue theme of Op. 130, and the opening of the A minor Quartet Op. 132, are contemporaneous and closely associated. Moreover, he showed that the fugue theme served a threefold purpose. To quote Bekker: 'This theme formed not only the main subject of the first movement of Op. 132 and the fugue subject of Op. 130 (now Op. 133), but, by a change from ascending sixths to descending thirds, it became the principal theme of the first, and, reversed, of the last movement of Op. 131.'[cviii]

Beethoven gives the melody initially to the first violin, unaccompanied over five bars, following which it is taken up by the second violin and cello in turn. Over the next fourteen bars the counterpoint is complete. Commenting on his workmanship, from the musician's viewpoint, cellist David Soyer enthuses: 'It's fascinating to observe how Beethoven develops the two part of the fugue subject independently as the movement evolves — in segments, in inversion, in diminution, in augmentation: the material sometimes appears in three different time values. The whole movement seems to unfold naturally, almost like a song; and the performance must above all preserve continuity, a sense of inevitability from beginning to end.' Violinist David Soyer endorses his colleague's remarks: 'In general the writing is a model of contrapuntal clarity. The performer should, however, be conscious of those places where one voice has only a segment of the fugue subject while another will at the same time be stating it in its entirety.'[cix] In his textual analysis, Radcliffe cites the movement's later transition to A major that he describes as 'a moment of the most ethereal beauty [that] seems to become a new character'.[cx]

The philosopher-musicologist Theodore Adorno remarks on Beethoven's 'extraordinary treatment of form' in the C-sharp minor Quartet and what he describes as its 'harmonic correlates'. He elaborates: 'In late Beethoven there is no longer any *fabric*. Instead of *durch-brochene Arbeit* [technique in which melody fragments alternate between different instruments] there is frequently a mere division of the melody.'[cxi] Kerman makes a related, but wider-ranging, generalisation embracing the Op. 127 and Op. 131 Quartets: 'These are the two quartets containing fugues. The dance movements shrink and become strikingly popular, even childlike in tone. The slow movements no longer feel so central — for there are now two slow movements in each quartet — and, in consequence, the finales are treated with new complexity and emphasis.'[cxii]

As late as the early 1900s, the episodic fugue that characterises the opening *Adagio* perplexed some. For example, the discerning English musician and educator Ernest Walker — a champion of such modernist composers as Hugo Wolf and Claude Debussy — could write in a monograph *Beethoven* (1905) that to him the C-sharp minor Quartet was 'a mystery' and the contemporaneous *Grosse Fuge* as being 'quite beyond the pale'.[cxiii] A few years later the French polymath Romain Rolland declared the opening fugue to be 'mystic' and 'organ-like' in character — the former description of which would have doubtless appealed to Walker who was himself a life-long mystic.[cxiv] The views of violist Michael Tree are consonant with the foregoing. Not only does he consider the fugal material of the first moment to be 'of the utmost seriousness and grandeur' but also to be 'a mystical meditation and yet deeply human'. He cites such passages as the duet between the viola and cello (bars 73—9) as being 'tender beyond words'.[cxv] Perhaps with such responses to the music in mind, Matthews describes the fugue as 'appearing from the shadows as though from a vast distance' but acknowledges how the fugue 'quickly generates surprising rhythmic energy'.[cxvi] In his study of Beethoven's string quartets (1935), the American composer and musicologist Arthur Shepherd so esteemed Beethoven's fugal writing, as expressed in the *Grosse Fuge, the Hammerklavier* Sonata, and the *Et vitam venture* from the *Missa Solemnis*, that he considered 'even Beethoven could climb no higher' and 'returns to the world of normal, glad emotion and concepts' by way of the C-sharp minor Quartet but bringing with him also 'the great illumination' to which he had attained in the finale of the B-flat major Quartet, Op. 130.[cxvii]

In his admiration for Beethoven's fugal writing, Radcliffe considers it to be highly characteristic of Beethoven to write within a short space of time two such dissimilar fugues as that in the *Grosse Fuge* — 'extended ... to enormous dimensions, so as to include a bewildering variety of mood and incident' — and the fugue in the C-sharp minor Quartet — 'achieving a different kind of spaciousness by maintaining on a very broad scale a mood of deep and unbroken thoughtfulness'. Radcliff's observations call to mind Beethoven's assertion: 'I never repeat myself.' He maintains that many hearings are required to reveal all that happens in the fugue, citing 'its features and incidents that merge in an atmosphere' that Radcliff considers to be quite unlike that of any other of the composer's fugues. He suggests: 'Perhaps the nearest approach can be found, on a much smaller scale, in the thirtieth of the *Diabelli* Variations, which has something of the same deeply brooding quality, expressed in a musical texture which is not strictly fugal, but contains a certain amount of counterpoint.'[cxviii]

Some words of William Kinderman take us to a consideration of the Quartet's second movement: 'The end of the *Adagio, ma non troppo e molto espressivo* in Op. 131 ... assumes a narrative significance ... This passage foreshadows the ensuing *Allegro molto vivace*, while simultaneously distilling essential relationships from the outset of the fugue that re-emerge with a vengeance in the finale.'[cxix]

Thus far in the music we have had 'intense contemplation' that is now followed by 'scintillating innocence'. Harold Truscott, whose words we have quoted, considers the second movement of the C-sharp minor Quartet to be 'thematically and emotionally all of a piece'. He perceives the movement to be a response to the dramatic tension of the opening fugue but in a way to be mutually interdependent — 'the two movements are really one movement, each requiring the other to complete the sense'.[cxx] Could the movement be 'a sort of intermezzo ... playful yet pregnant', as suggested by the anonymous contributor to the Preface of the Philharmonia Miniature score.[cxxi] Steinberg is in no doubt that the movement is a scherzo 'quick in tempo [and] gentle in mood' — here we have the first pianissimo in the Quartet in which 'the rhetoric is modest ... but the effect is of a delightful freshness'.[cxxii] Kerman is less sure how the movement should be described: 'One gropes ... for a way to characterise this movement — at once so straightforward and so strange, at once lucid and elusive, with its evaporating octaves everywhere and its pedals ... its shimmering rhythms and its dreamlike false security in the Neapolitan region.' He quotes Wagner's characterisation of the music: 'The inward eye then traces the consoling vision ... perceptible by it alone, in which that longing becomes a sweet but plaintive playing with itself: the image of the innermost dream takes waking form as a loveliest remembrance.'[cxxiii]

As the *Allegro molto vivace* brings before the imagination a new musical sense, de Marliave cites the delicately wrought writing for the first violin that, in his words, 'dissipates the sombre despair of the *Adagio*' and which, quoting Wagner once more, 'fades away into wistful memory'. He adds his own views: 'The movement assumes increasing ardour and fire ... A heroic inspiration gives life to this episode [and], like a cloud passing over the sun, gives it a contemplative cast.'[cxxiv] Radcliff draws attention to the compositional challenge Beethoven had to confront following the sombre closing of the first movement fugue: 'To follow the fugue with a movement in fully developed sonata form might run the risk of excessive solidity; on the other hand, a sequel of too frivolous a character would have produced a jarring anti-climax.' He suggests the *Allegro molto vivace* is a successful compromise: 'It is in a highly compressed sonata form with no development and an engagingly naïve main theme, which produces an odd and curiously touching contrast to what has gone before it.'[cxxv] To quote the performers once more whom we have previously cited, David Soyer: 'The new movement is immediately most lively; it's light, airy, elegant, and scherzolike. But I sense as well am element of sadness, a bittersweet quality.' Arnold Steinhardt: '[The] character is dancelike. I wouldn't be surprised if, consciously or not, Beethoven derived this material from some sort of folk music.'[cxxvi]

With regard to Beethoven's craftsmanship, de Marliave esteemed this section of the Quartet for its 'remarkable [and] ingenious harmonies' and the development that ensues for being 'a veritable mosaic of thematic design, fashioned out of the artist's fantasy, and yet moving with perfect balance and unerring logical sequence'.[cxxvii] Martin Cooper is more restrained. Although he too found the material of the second movement to be suggestive of a scherzo, or perhaps even a rondo-finale, he regarded it as being 'no more than a bridge passage, however important'. In fairness to him, he also proposes the movement's melody 'to be something hummed under the breath with a secret, interior delight'.[cxxviii] Wagner was not restrained when writing of the C-sharp minor Quartet on the occasion of Beethoven's Birth Centenary. In his characteristically florid style he enthused: 'And now 'tis as if the Master, grown conscious of his art, were settling to work at his magic ... The mind's eye ... perceives the consoling vision which it alone can descry, wherein the longing becomes a sweet and playful though plaintive daydream. The image of the dream takes waking form as the loveliest of memories.'[cxxix]

To quote our cited performers once more, David Soyer: 'One often hears this movement played too fast. The marking is *Allegro molto vivace*. "Alegro", yes — but *molto vivace* indicates the character; it's not a tempo marking.' And Michael Tree: 'The melodic line must be gently caressed ... The performance of this movement should convey effortlessness, fluency, and continuity. But, in fact, it takes a considerable effort within the Quartet to achieve that result.'[cxxx]

The ensuing *Allegro* in hardly more than a string-quartet flourish. With a performing time of under a minute it is almost a case of blink and you will miss it — or should that be allow the attention to wander and the fourth movement will have arrived. The music is a transitional passage that serves as a bridge 'from the emotional sphere of one main movement to the next'.[cxxxi] 'The soul, newly returned to human life, seems to ask the question, "What next?" — to seek and to find new tasks.'[cxxxii] Wagner resorts to similar word-imagery: 'Then, with a short transitional passage (*allegro moderato*), it is as if the Master, recalling his art, were settling down to practise its magic.'[cxxxiii]

The first violin is allowed a declaration 'ardent and passionate' in a run of thirty-second notes that are 'proudly elegant' and, to some ears, declamatory 'in the manner of Handel'.[cxxxiv][cxxxv] In the eleven measures Beethoven allows for the *Allegro*, six may be considered as 'conversational exchanges between the instruments', briefly recalling the genre of the classical quartet when such a dialogue between the four instruments was the norm.

A 'coloratura flourish' from the first violin has the effect of 'pushing memories of the *serious* [opening] fugue still further away'.[cxxxvi] The stage is now set for the sequence of variations found in the fourth movement

To borrow a phrase from Misha Donat, the fourth movement of the C-sharp minor Quartet is its 'expressive heart'.[cxxxvii] It consists of a serene and expansive set of variations; in performance they extend for almost a quarter of an hour. Perhaps it was natural, almost inevitable, that Beethoven, who had once lionised Vienna's salons with his improvisations as a virtuoso pianist, should make recourse to the variation form for one of the profoundest discourses in music. As Basil Lam remarks: 'When action gives place to contemplation a set of variations seems the natural resource for a composer who intends a "still centre" for a major work, where tension and contrast can be banished.'[cxxxviii] The heading to the fourth movement itself provides an indication of the richness and diversity of the music that is to unfold: *Andante, ma non troppo e molto cantabile — Andante moderato e lusinghiero — Adagio — Allegretto — Adagio, ma non troppo e semplice — Allegretto.*

The opening theme 'one of Beethoven's profound inspirations' is inspirational in the manner of its presentation as it is gently intertwines 'with infinite tenderness' between the various instruments.[cxxxix] The theme consists of two eight-bar phrases with repeats varied in a disarming manner 'simple and almost childlike both melodically and harmonically'.[cxl] That Beethoven is about to take us on an extended musical journey is evident from the outset. The two underlying eight-bar phrases duly expand to thirty-two measures. The atmosphere is 'full of shining clarity — the incarnation of innocence' (to quote Wagner once more) as the two violins interlace the opening melody in the upper and lower registers.[cxli] The theme is set in the key of A major — Beethoven's 'key of relaxation' — that he favoured for other of his late slow movements; consider, for example, the *Arietta* of the Piano Sonata, Op. 111.[cxlii] Cooper remarks on the 'smiling mood' of the A major tonality that pervades many of the Quartet's variations in what he describes as a 'combination of purely melodic metamorphosis'.[cxliii]

'In the variation tune, lyricism unfolds with perfect freedom, simplicity, and uncertainty ... we identity this tune ... as a sister of the variation melody of the Quartet in E flat, Op. 127 — younger, less soulful and serious-minded.'[cxliv]

Contemplating the effect of the fourth movement as a whole, Wagner enthused: 'Its power summons afresh in order to conjure up one graceful figure, the blessed embodiment of native innocence, and [Beethoven] finds unending rapture in that figure's ceaseless, unheard-of transformations under the prismatic lights which his immortal genius casts upon it.'[cxlv] Kerman likens the ensuing variations to 'an incandescent chain'[cxlvi] as does Kinderman, 'like the variations in Op. 109, these transformations of the theme take the form of a brilliant chain of revelations'.[cxlvii]

Commentators have remarked on the disarmingly (and deceptively) simple design of the variation-theme. Steinberg comments: 'This [opening] page is of such simplicity that the music seems hardly to have been consciously scored at all.' But he acknowledges how amazing it is citing 'the subtle difference between the way the second violin quietly supports the first violin's phrases, while the first violin stays silent when the second speaks'. He also draws attention to the contrast between the viola's long notes and the pizzicatos in the cello.[cxlviii] To quote Lam: '[In] these variations, both the harmonic scheme — itself of great simplicity — and the phrase structure are easily recognisable in every variation.'[cxlix] As so frequently, however, in Beethoven's compositional process arriving at simplicity cost him much effort. From Schindler we learn: 'The master's repeated attempts to work out the motif of the fourth movement of the C-sharp minor Quartet, as they appear in the sketchbooks ... demonstrate how fastidiously he elaborated his themes until he was satisfied that they were just right and could be correctly performed. Before his quartet themes could be employed, they had to pass as rigid requirements as the subject for a fugue. This motif in the C-sharp Quartet even had to be adaptable to different time signatures. In the sketchbook it is first noted in 6/8 time, then 4/4, then twice again in 6/8 (the second time marked *Meilleur*), then in 3/4, the sixth version in 4/4, and finally, the last time, in 4/4 with variations. The published version also had the theme in different rhythms.'[d]

In Kerman's view the effect of the *Andante* of Op. 131 does not depend so much upon its musical architecture as upon 'the series of brilliant, astonishing revelations in the individual variations'. He discerns Beethoven adopting the manner that he had explored in the *Diabelli* Variations. Following on from what we have quoted from Schindler, he draws attention to the variations' changes in time signature and tempo that he asserts is 'a sure sign that variety is of the essence'.[di]

Some observations of Barry Cooper are relevant here. He draws attention to the manner in which, in his later compositions, Beethoven was prone to insert additional qualifying terms into his scores than hitherto in order to convey to interpreters of his music the ever-increasing demands he was imposing upon them — bearing upon such considerations as the degree of flexibility he was demanding, more precise interpretation, and stricter, and more sophisticated, regulation of variations in tempo. Of the C-sharp minor Quartet he writes: 'New words are added in Beethoven's quest for precision in the fourth movement of the String Quartet, Op. 131 ... The effect of these painstaking directions adds to the intensity in performance. These qualifying marks for tempo and mood are closely related to the increased number of terms and signs used to express volume, attack, and phrasing.'[clii]

Bekker describes the fourth movement variations as being 'a song of joy' — all the more telling when we recall the adverse circumstances Beethoven was enduring at the period of their composition.[cliii] Igor Stravinsky was not so in awe of the composer's late quartets as to refrain from making critical remarks about them — the prerogative of one very great man contemplating the craftsmanship of another. But, with regard to the C-sharp minor Quartet, he considered 'the lustre of the instrumentation [to be] unique' and the manner in which in this music 'one's "soul" actually seems to migrate'. He was indeed so moved as to quote Shakespeare: 'Singing masons building roofs of gold.' [*Henry V*, Act 1, Scene 2][cliv] Others, likewise, have been moved to quote Shakespeare in support of their emotional response to the fourth movement. Lam found mystery here as deep as the feeling expressed in Shakespeare's allegorical poem *Phoenix and the Turtle*. Its subject, the death of ideal love, disposed him to cite the lines: 'Reason in itself confounded/Saw division grow together/To themselves yet either neither/Simple were so well compounded.'[clv]

Others find the variations, 'contemplative',[clvi]

'enigmatic',[clvii] 'possessed of wonderful variety',[clviii] and 'unique in their range of textures'.[clix] De Marliave regarded the variations of the *Andante* of Op. 131 to be 'much more than the medium by which a single idea finds more complete expression'. For him they demonstrate 'the continual changing of an idea' as it follows 'the changing fantasy of the artist' and as it is 'moulded afresh by the influence of inner vitality'. He summates: 'To this continual changing of imaginative idea is bound the change of musical idea, constantly charged with new thought (not merely technical variations of the same thought); and these new thoughts in their turn give rise to flexible thematic combinations that express their most delicate shades of meaning.'[clx]

With regard to interpretation, Radcliff urges performers to play the music at a pace that 'precludes the slightest suspicion of jauntiness' so as to allow 'suitable breadth for the beautifully timed rising crotchets'.[clxi] 'The sonority should be unforced, neither too loud not too soft, like the natural sound of your voice as if you were singing to yourself.' [Arnold Steinhardt] 'The movement as a whole evolves more organically when the tempo relationships aren't set in arbitrary moulds ... In marking *Andante ma non troppo* Beethoven implies a tempo flowing, but not too brusquely. A little too fast and it sounds trite; a little too slow and it becomes heavy.' [David Soyer] 'This is one of the most inspired melodies in all Beethoven. You won't find a lovelier tune. It has a Schubertian quality.' [Michael Tree][clxii]

The serenity of the variation theme, heard at the outset of the movement, takes on a 'dance-like character.[clxiii] The theme's 'tender, almost willowy gracefulness' are muted into 'a stiff double-dotted rhythm' that is maintained by the inner instruments while the violin and cello 'punctuate and comment'.[clxiv] When writing about this movement on the occasion of Beethoven's Death Centenary, violist Rebecca

Clarke enthused 'how expressive are the conversations held between the instruments'.[clxv] Beethoven's inventiveness with the theme, with which he struggled in his sketchbooks, soon becomes apparent: '[During] the first eight bars it moves from a dark to an ethereal colouring.' In the repeats the texture is 'more broken', the rhythm becomes 'increasingly vivacious' and the harmonic details 'increasingly plentiful'.[clxvi] As the variation proceeds 'the texture becomes ever more elaborated, subtilized, [and] unpredictable'.[clxvii] 'The polyphony thickens by added movement in the inner parts ... alternation in note values in the last bars of the variation imparts to the development a quality of bubbling life.'[clxviii]

An exchange between violin and cello follows during which the middle instruments are reserved to provide 'a simple tick-tick accompaniment'.[clxix] After the interlocked manner of quartet writing heard so far, the instruments are now more individually exposed. This poses a challenge to the performers' resourcefulness as they execute an unaccompanied dialogue. Some detect a Rossinian flavour in the music; Rossini we recall had been 'all the rage' in Vienna but a few years previously and had been warmly received by Beethoven. Notwithstanding: 'It is Beethoven who shines through in these moments of imitation of the Italian opera composer.'[clxx] Others detect a rustic, country-dance character in the music. But it is 'pastoral freshness' wearing 'hob-nailed boots' as the variation acquires an energetic character with even the suggestion of a 'persistent drum rhythm'.[clxxi] An innovation in this variation is the adoption of pizzicato in the base. This was so visionary for the period that it must have seemed frivolously capricious to the ears of the work's first audiences. Lam regards this, and other features of Beethoven's scoring, as 'a marvel of the deaf composer's aural imagination'.[clxxii] Stravinsky was deeply moved by Beethoven's writing declaring: 'The most affecting music of all, to me, is the beginning of the *Andante moderato* variation. The mood is like no other ... and the intensity, if it were to endure much longer, would be intolerable.'[clxxiii]

In accordance with Beethoven's instruction *attacca*, the music proceeds without a break. A reminder of the interconnectedness that unifies the late quartets is the composer's quotation here from the first movement of the A minor Quartet, Op. 132. The character of the music is that of a slow march. From Truscott we have a paean of praise: '[This] music is indescribable: for me it is one of the highest peaks of profoundly suggestive writing Beethoven ever attained. Its impact in sound could never be gathered from the printed notes, without the ability to translate these into sound.'[clxxiv] Being march-like the pace is slower. The markings for the players is *lusinghiero* — 'flattering, coaxing, caressing' but Steinberg suggests *seductive* is not too strong a translation.[clxxv] Recalling what we have said — quoting Barry Cooper's observations concerning Beethoven's propensity to carefully annotate his late scores — he fastidiously writes *dolce* over the cello's and viola's first phrases.

In his youth Beethoven wrote out many contrapuntal exercises, in part in response to the requirements of his teachers but in addition under the self-promptings of his desire to more fully come to terms with his art. Could Beethoven perhaps be recalling such exercises in the manner in which he sets out this variation? Martin Cooper characterises the piece as 'a kind of mock contrapuntal exercise' and, regarding the instruction *lusinghiero*, he asks: 'What effect did Beethoven wish to obtain?' He suggests: 'Perhaps a schoolroom precision and correctness seen after nearly half a century, in an affectionate, wistful light?[clxxvi] Alongside Cooper, Kerman describes Beethoven's later working as having 'the old schoolroom smell ... but perfumed with in a quite indescribable way.'[clxxvii] De Marliave praises the composer for his 'polished dialogue' as it unfolds in imitation in canon. Of Beethoven's writing more generally he states: 'This is pure "quartet form". But its apparent ease and grace make way for a broadening of the design, a glistening web of sound in which the voices and *motifs* are blended to attain a brilliant dramatic effect in the last bars.'[clxxviii]

Perhaps there is a trace of Beethoven's youthful contrapuntal studies in the manner in which the two violins engage in a canonic dialogue that is taken up by the viola and cello. The mood changes as trills 'take charge of the proceedings with sudden spurts of energy'.[clxxix] In his late works the trill assumes far greater importance than being a mere ornamental device. For example, in the *Hammerklavier* Piano Sonata they number some one hundred and twenty. In the fourth variation, Beethoven contents himself in a 'halo of trills', a memorable phrase attributed to Donald Tovey.[clxxx] De Marliave considered the music 'reveals an imaginative power and charm' that has a capacity to astonish us today as it did audiences of Beethoven's generation. Concerning the response of the composer's contemporaries, he adds: 'Listening to this expression of an ecstatic inner vitality, we can understand what the friends of the musician meant by the phrase: "The Master has a *raptus* [seized – inspired] again today".'[clxxxi]

Martin Cooper regarded the fifth variation to be 'possibly the subtlest piece of writing in the movement' through the manner in which he considers the harmonies of the original theme are gradually changed as they 'descend in the first strain' and '[are] built up in a similar manner in the second'.[clxxxii] Steinberg expresses similar thoughts: 'Here is one of Beethoven's strangest and most haunting pages. It begins with what sounds like tuning. Everything at first is off the beat, rhythmically "soft", virtually devoid of melody.'[clxxxiii] Radcliff perceives the 'reticent mood' of the fifth variation recalls that of the third but being different in character: 'The mysterious simplicity of this variation gives it a strangely individual character and its laconic understatement makes it a remarkably effective interlude between the grace of its predecessor and the extraordinary depth of what follows.' He suggests the music's 'enigmatic syncopated rhythm' anticipates similar procedures adopted some years later by Schumann.[clxxxiv] Martin Cooper believes this variation has affinities with the *Diabelli* Variations 'insofar as everything is here pared down to the bone' and considers how we are given 'a blueprint of the [original] theme with the perspective drastically foreshortened'.[clxxxv] Matthews is more succinct and refers to the music's 'harmonic concentration'.[clxxxvi] Rebecca Clarke draws attention to the 'mysterious way the chords melt into each other'.[clxxxvii] De Marliave gives vent once more to his spacious eloquence: 'It seems as if shadows fall over the scene. Through strange harmonies, the distorted theme, with only its bare outlines left, is re-clothed in the garb of a chorale sustained by long organ notes ... The contemplative character of this variation anticipates the prevailing atmosphere of earnest supplication that fills the sixth and last variation.'[clxxxviii]

Kerman refers to the closing variation as the 'heaviest link in the chain'. In response to the designation *Adagio ma non troppo e semplice*, he maintains the climax has weight (gravitas) that imparts 'a sublime, hymn-like mood' very characteristic of Beethoven's late slow movements. He speaks of the movement's 'earnest contemplation' that for him calls to mind 'the atmosphere of prayer ... One almost thinks of the *Heiliger Dankgesang* of Op. 132'.[clxxxix] 'Slowly pulsating chords now outline the familiar harmonies and shapes ... for the most part the music moves in the world of *piano, pianissimo*, and *sotto voce* ... All in all ... this is music of spellbinding stillness.'[cxc] '[How] divinely calm and beautiful is the simplicity of the sixth variation' responds Rebecca Clarke empathetically.[cxci] '[The] harmonies of the theme are given a new, simple but heart-searching shape.'[cxcii] For John Dalley: 'The atmosphere is extraordinary ... hymn like'. For Arnold Steinhardt: 'The mood is hushed and sustained. The bow strokes are silken and floating ... Beethoven indicates *semplice* and the music — so inward and reverential — should be expressed as simply as possible.'[cxciii]

Composition was never as spontaneous for Beethoven as it was for Mozart or Schubert and, as so frequently with him, music that suggests it fell effortlessly from his pen caused him a great deal of heart searching. He labored over this passage more than any other in the entire Quartet. Twelve versions are fully sketched out alongside of which Beethoven wrote *besser* (better/preferably) or *meilleur* (best/better). On the basis of his study of Beethoven's sketchbook, Radcliff comments: 'Some of the sketches are slightly simpler and others slightly more complicated than the final version [indicative of] not only Beethoven's great sensitiveness to detail, but also the difficulty with which he made his final choice.'[cxciv] In Martin Cooper's estimation, the variation's gently oscillating motion combined with Beethoven's *sotto voce* and *cantabile* markings, suggest more a nocturne than a hymn — 'despite the almost Mendelssohnian suavity of bars 7—8 and 15—16'. He adds words of caution: 'Is Beethoven's marking *semplice* a warning against any hint of exaggerated soulfulness in performance?'[cxcv]

'The variation comes to no settled end. It is caught up ... with a cadenza-like figure of triplets which is passed gradually to each instrument in turn and leads to a passage of shakes and changing harmonies [and] ends with broken phrases moving quietly at last to a pizzicato final tonic chord.'[cxcvi]

We have remarked that the fourth movement of the C-sharp minor String Quartet has six variations, but a fragmentary, putative seventh variation morphs into the closing coda. The passage in question has been described as 'a half variation'.[cxcvii] Florid triplets, shared by the four instruments, herald the would-be variation for the duration of eight bars. Their progress is halted by a series of trills whose effect is to convey 'a strange sense of vastness'.[cxcviii] To Cooper's ears the 'full-blown ornament conveys not the sound of the string quartet but that of a string orchestra, 'with percussion furnished by the cello'. Cooper's study of the sketch sources reminds us of Beethoven's diligence. He cites no fewer than fifteen separate versions in the sketchbooks of passages that bear testimony to his attention to detail in such matters as 'the repetition of a pizzicato note, the harmony provided by a quaver chord or two semi-quavers, the exact disposition of rests etc.'.[cxcix]

In drawing our discussion of the fourth movement to a close, we give the final words to Joseph de Marliave. 'If one reviews the musical course travelled over, from the exposition of the original theme to these final chords, it seems as if the artist has moved through countless changing phases of spiritual experience on his way, scattering abroad the wealth of his imaginative resource as he passed ... Few pages in musical literature reach the depths of poignant introspection realized here ... Of this luminous phrase Beethoven might have said with Goethe: "Ich habe da viel hinein geheimnist" — Here I have hidden many secret thoughts.'[cc]

The fifth movement of Op. 131 is a Beethoven scherzo that he designates *Presto — Molto poco adagio*. We open our account of this movement with the thoughts of two professional interpreters. Writing in 1927 on the occasion of Beethoven's Death Centenary, violist Rebecca Clarke was disposed to enthuse: '[The] variations lead into a *presto* which is perhaps the most amazing of all Beethoven's many amazing scherzo movements. No modern writer has ever obtained more astonishing effects from a quartet of strings than are here to be found; but Beethoven, unlike modern composers, never wrote effects for themselves alone, and here they are always an integral part of his idea ... This movement is brilliant, funny, and "unbuttoned" beyond words; and the joke is that it is built up on tunes so absurdly simple they might be those of a child!'[cci] Fellow violist Michael Tree, of the Guarneri Quartet, tells us: 'We regard the opening two bars as a curtain raiser — a sort of miniature overture.'[ccii] Echoing what Clarke says, regarding the music as having childlike simplicity, Adorno offers the generalisation: 'In late Beethoven [one finds] a kind of theme which might seem folkloristic and which I should like to most compare to verse-saying from fairy-tales ... An example [may be found] in the *scherzo* of the String Quartet in C-sharp minor, Op. 131.'[cciii]

Discerning ears find a connection with the opening melody of this fifth movement with another of the composer's late compositions, namely, the G major Bagatelle, Op. 126, No. 1 — in particular bars 1–6.[cciv] [ccv] De Marliave looks back to earlier times when Beethoven was making his first venture into writing for the string quartet: 'The theme ... is played in unison at the octave on the two violins and recalls the days of the artist's youth and happiness, being none other than the *motif* written about twenty-eight years earlier for the first movement of the Quartet in G, Op. 18, No.2.' He qualifies his observation by remarking on the deep-seated difference in inspiration between the two works. He reminds us that the G major Quartet had earned the sobriquet *The Compliment Quartet*, for its politely-reserved classical nature, whereas in the C-sharp minor Quartet he detects 'a certain air of pomp and flourish, like a popular song or tune of a village fair' — characteristic traits he also suggests may be found in Beethoven's lighter melodies that typify some of his later music.[ccvi]

Tovey considered the *Presto* to be 'the most childlike of all Beethoven's scherzos'. With respect to its working-out he draws attention to 'the joints of the form ... the humorous treatment of its first four notes' and the manner in which 'the humour ... is heightened at each recurrence'.[ccvii] De Marliave identifies 'a 'fierce gaiety [that] runs through the entire movement, filling it with riotous life from beginning to end'.[ccviii] For Kinderman the *Presto* is 'naively playful'.[ccix] For Bekker it is 'high spirited'.[ccx] For Kerman the E-major *Presto* 'is perhaps the most childlike of all Beethoven's scherzos'. He considers it to be close in spirit to the *Alla danza Tedesca* of the B flat Quartet, maintaining: 'There is really very little "refinement" about it; it is Beethoven's most childlike scherzo in his most mature and complex work of art.' He perceives the piece as 'serving a special role in the total drama of the C-sharp minor Quartet ... a genuine resting place in the total journey, a moment (but a timeless moment) of play before the *Adagio* in C-sharp minor will lead back to concerns broached by the opening Fugue'.[ccxi]

Radcliffe likens the repetitiveness of the theme to the manner in which such a characteristic is to be found in nursery rhymes. But he urges the listener to look beyond the music's apparent naiveté: 'Here the high spirits, which had a curiously tentative air in the second movement, find far fuller and more uninhibited expression.' Calling to mind Beethoven's teacher, he avers: 'If Haydn had lived to hear it, he might have thought it puerile and vulgar, but it contains some of his high spirit and, with all its wayward hilarity, it does nothing as strange as the odd harmonic digressions and feints that occur in the finale of Haydn's Piano Sonata in C major, No. 50.'[ccxii]

Rey Longyear makes reference to the challenges that string players of Beethoven's day found when performing his quartets — and still do! He suggests that here in the *Presto* he seems to be depicting the confusion that must have frequently happened in rehearsal and even in performance. In his words: 'In the *scherzo* of the String Quartet, Op. 131 (measures 444—69) Beethoven creates the effect of musicians who have gotten lost and are trying to get back together; when they do (measures 470—86), they scape away *sul ponticello*. Previous statements of the initial motive, at the opening and at measures 167 and 333, give the impression of an overeager cellist who starts before his colleagues are ready.'[ccxiii]

In his commentary on Beethoven's workmanship, Truscott suggest that here we have a case of 'complexity that lies at the heart of simplicity' — which calls to mind Picasso's assertion that it had taken him a lifetime to learn how to draw like a child. Regarding the scherzo, Truscott describes it as being 'all harmonic simplicity [that] revolves round its own tonic, dominant, subdominant ... It is all completely through-composed'.[ccxiv] Describing the working-out of the movement, Kerman states: 'Like a child repeating a joke, Beethoven makes us go through the process five times identically — for the full alternation scheme is: Scherzo (with repeat) — Trio — Scherzo — Trio — Scherzo (with repeat) — (Trio) — (Scherzo).'[ccxv] Matthews describes this structure as 'a continuum' with 'folk-like themes in regular four-bar phrasing'.[ccxvi] Likewise de Marliave: 'Following on without break [from the variations movement] it forms an unbroken stream of sound, a single melodic sequence, built upon a little *motif* that anybody could hum over as they left the concert, a *motif* ... transformed into the loveliest music imaginable.'[ccxvii]

In his estimation of the fifth movement, Wagner

heightens the discourse in his characteristically elevated manner: 'Here again the world appears before [Beethoven] ... and his inward joy illuminates everything around him. It is as if he were listening for strains of unearthly music, as visions pass before his gaze in perfect harmony, once ethereal, now embodied in material form.'[ccxviii] 'Then we see him, profoundly happy by virtue of his own effort, direct his glowing vision upon the outer world. Once more nature stands afresh before him as in the *Pastoral* Symphony, radiant with his inner joy ... It is as if he heard the native accents of the apparitions that dance before him in a rhythm now gay, now gross.'[ccxix]

Stravinsky makes reference to the *Pastoral* Symphony: 'The *Presto* recalls the *Pastoral* Symphony, incidentally, in the character of the second theme and its accompaniment ... the echoed hallooings, the silences like the pauses before the storm in the Symphony.'[ccx]

Beethoven gives the cello a prominent role, allowing its plucked strings to halt the music with sonorous pizzicatos. He also makes unusual — and innovatory — demands on the other instruments by requiring them to play in their highest register with the bow virtually on the bridge. The resulting ghostly effect has been likened to 'rats' feet on broken glass'.[ccxxi] Basil Lam describes the effect as 'the weird toneless rustling that strikes a chill note'.[ccxxii] Perhaps a modern-day parallel can be found. We recall the occasion during a rehearsal when the conductor Sir Thomas Beecham thought that his female soloist was playing less than adequately on her fine Italian cello. He stopped the orchestra and declared: 'Madam, you have between your legs an instrument capable of giving pleasure to thousands, and all you can do is scratch it!'

'For all its plain speech the *Presto* shows the hand of the master-magician everywhere, whether in the rhythmic subtleties that combine epigrammatic wit with the continuous development of phrase-structure, or in the highly original way in which the themes are connected.'[ccxxiii] 'The effect of the whole movement, with its brilliance and high spirits, is electrifying in its deeply thoughtful surroundings and seems to laugh good-naturedly at those who regard the posthumous quartets as an unfathomable mystery.'[ccxxiv]

The penultimate movement is a short *Adagio* with the qualification *quasi un poco andante*. 'We suddenly find ourselves drawn into the world of the *Adagio* ... What a dolorous and mournful piece it is!' [Arnold Steinhardt] 'This is without doubt, one of the most moving passages in all music. What a moment for the viola!' [Michael Tree][ccxxv] According to the Belgian musicologist-composer François-Joseph Fétis, Beethoven may have derived the movement's melody from an old French folksong.[ccxxvi] In Steinberg's opinion, the Op. 131 Quartet has no real slow movement that he considers comparable to the variations in the E-flat major Quartet, Op. 127 or the *Cavatina* in the B-flat major Quartet, Op. 130. He acknowledges, however, that the *Adagio quasi un poco andante* passage of Op. 131 functions primarily as 'a major structural and expressive marker' in the Quartet that he also considers serves as a bridge between the scherzo and finale.[ccxxvii]

A more plausible origin than Fétis', for the source of Beethoven's inspiration for the opening theme of the *Adagio*, may be traceable to the following circumstance. In 1825 the Viennese Jewish community approached Beethoven with a view to him composing a cantata for the dedication of a new synagogue. Beethoven contemplated the proposal, as he had many times similarly considered suggestions for opera projects, but the cantata suggestion, like the opera projects, was not fulfilled. However, it is believed that in his consideration of the cantata, Beethoven may have become familiar with the Kol Nidre, the prayer sung in Jewish synagogues at the beginning of the service on the eve of Yom Kippur — the Day of Atonement.[ccxxviii] The point to be made is that some commentators detect, in the *Adagio's* profound depth of feeling, something of the sense of lamentation that permeates the Kol Nidre.[ccxxix]

In the *Adagio*, Wagner describes Beethoven as giving expression to 'a contemplation [that is] short-lived but profound — as if he were buried for the moment in the depths of his own soul'.[ccxxx] The *Cavatina* of the B-flat major Quartet has been mentioned. The music's 'pensive and hesitating' manner has affinities, in its intensity, for Radcliff, with this work. He accepts though it is confined to a much smaller format than the *Cavatina* and is possessed of simpler textures and a more melancholy mood.[ccxxxi] 'Reproachfully the viola begins a beautiful mourning song in G-sharp minor, *Adagio quasi un poco andante* ... For a moment the simplicity of the tune and its unabashed emotionality suggest a new *cavatina*.' So writes Joseph Kerman but qualifies his remarks: 'However, the present tune is probably too slight to make a real *cavatina* or full movement of any sort.'[ccxxxii] Cooper cautions against making too close a comparison with the *Cavatina* of Op. 130 arguing 'the scope, character and function of the two movements are entirely different'. His take on the *Adagio* is that of 'a transitional piece, an introduction to the tragic finale but still restrained, almost hymn-like and concise in form'.[ccxxxiii]

Beethoven compresses his feelings in the *Adagio* within the compass of a mere twenty-eight bars that have a performing time of just two minutes. For Clarke these say 'more than many a longer movement, the force and fire of which almost make one forget the frequent awkwardness which its key brings'.[ccxxxiv] (As a professional violist she is making reference to the challenges of hand position the lower instruments have to negotiate.) Whilst the overall structure is that of sonata form, there is a hint of the fugal theme that 'stirs, as it were in its chrysalis, striving to emerge as aria'.[ccxxxv]

Encomia have been showered on the *Adagio*. '[Beethoven] looks on life and seems to ponder (brief *Adagio*) how to fashion the tune for life itself to dance to — a short but gloomy spell of brooding, as if the master were sunk to the lowest depths of his dream.'[ccxxxvi] 'Nowhere in all the quartets is there expressed a resignation so deeply felt, an introspection so profound ...'.[ccxxxvii] '[Beethoven's] magnificent sanity and his mundane common sense never left him, and the penultimate movement of Op. 131 hints at tragedy with a Mozartian quietness even more moving than the utterly genuine eloquence of the heart-broken speech of the *Cavatina* in Op. 130 ... Unlike the *Cavatina* which, as its name implies, has something of a deliberately pathetic monologue, this brief *Adagio* is "true as truth's simplicity".' [*Troilus and Cressida*][ccxxxviii]

Beethoven draws the C-sharp minor String Quartet, Op. 131 to a close with 'a savage tonic-dominant theme in quavers and crochets' to be followed by 'a wild yet square-cut tune in dotted rhythm and tragically sardonic mood'.[ccxxxix] The melody is declaimed by all four players in fortissimo octaves that centre about the initial notes of the theme heard in the first movement. The members of the Guarneri String Quartet endorse the spirit of the words of Donald Tovey whom we have just quoted. 'It's savage — utterly savage — the culmination of the entire work.' [David Soyer] 'Grotesque and wild! It has invincible energy.' [John Dalley] 'A relentless dance, a demonic dance — and yet, what wonderfully tender moments, what an enormous range!' [Michael Tree] '[Beethoven's] shaking his fist at destiny. It's terrifying — but suddenly everything is released and it overflows with joy, with ecstasy.' [Arnold Steinhardt][ccxl] To quote David

Soyer once more: 'Having already played for half an hour with the intense concentration demanded throughout this work, to come to this wood-tearing, flesh-tearing movement has quite a vitalizing effect. I feel exhilarated, much as I do when playing the *Grosse Fuge*.'[ccxli] Steinberg regards the lyric theme that Beethoven adopts to be perhaps the Quartet's 'greatest marvel ... richly scored ... whose phrases end in leaps that most extraordinarily convey both serenity and ecstasy'.[ccxlii] De Marliave considers the first violin 'lifts a melody of sublime purity, like a glimpse of blue sky among storm-clouds, imposing a sense of mysticism and spiritual vitality upon the essentially material texture of the movement'.[ccxliii] Wagner's word-imagery is equal to the drama of the music: 'In a flash the world is again illuminated before him; [Beethoven] awakes, and invokes from the violin music the like of which the world has never imagined. This is the fury of the world's dance of fierce pleasure, agony, ecstasy of love, joy, anger, passion, and pain; lightnings flash and thunder rolls; and above the tumult the indomitable fiddler whirls us on to the abyss. Amid the clamour he smiles, for to him it is nothing but a mocking fantasy aa the end the darkness beckons him away, and his task is done.'[ccxliv]

Kerman considers the 'violence' of the main theme and its 'pent up emotion' look back some twenty years 'to the days of defiance after the *Heiligenstadt Testament*'. He also identifies the mood and even specific details with the final theme of the E-minor *Razumovsky* Quartet Op. 59, No. 2.[ccxlv] Lam finds resemblances in the persistent dotted rhythms in the finale of Op. 131 with those in that in the first *Razumovsky* String Quartet, Op. 59, No.1. He also casts his gaze back further and ventures to suggest Beethoven may have drawn inspiration from *Bach's Musical Offering*.[ccxlvi] Other commentators are content to identify the spirit of the closing *Allegro* in the C-sharp minor Quartet with the Op.

59 set of quartets. Cooper remarks on the transformations the theme underwent in the sketchbooks, appearing first in a 'mild form' before acquiring its final 'rhythmic, stamping shape' that to him recalls the finale of Op. 59, No. 2. He refers to the *espressivo* passage 'that carries a note of exultation' and concludes: 'This, like the *Grosse Fuge*, is the Dionysian obverse of such great moments of Apollonian contemplation as the finale of Op. 111, the *Heiliger Dankgesang* of Op. 132, or the opening fugue of the present work.'[ccxlvii] Simpson, alongside Kerman, identifies the dominating dotted rhythm of the Allegro with the last movement of the E minor *Razumovsky* Quartet, but affirms 'there is a vast sweep and scope completely beyond the terms of the earlier work'. He asks: 'Is there a more marvellous piece of quartet writing than in this passage?'[ccxlviii] Griffiths also finds affinities with the E minor *Razumovsky* in the *Allegro's* 'galloping rhythm' of the kind that is found in the urgency of the writing to which Schubert gave expression in his D minor Quartet, *Death and the Maiden*.[ccxlix]

For Kerman the finale 'crowns' the C-sharp minor Quartet in practically every way 'in force of expression, intellectual intensity, breadth of action, and integrative power over the composition as a whole'. For him the C-sharp finale 'heightens and purifies the famous C-minor mood of Beethoven's early years'. His great accomplishment he suggests lies in the manner in which Beethoven preserves 'all the force and innocence and heroic thrust while discounting any suspicion of overextension of feeling'.[ccl] Beethoven's recourse to fugal writing invites some commentators to adopt the metaphor of a circle being completed. 'Intensely rhythmic but with a wondrous lyricism and opening up of texture; and its manifest links with the opening fugue complete the circle of the quartet that Beethoven thought his best.'[ccli] 'As the music progresses, Beethoven forges more and more links to establish the sense that a great circle is closing'.[cclii]

In the *Allegro*, Scott sees Beethoven attaining the heights at which he aimed in the Ninth Symphony. For her: 'I know of few things in music which seem so to transcend temporal existence as the passage beginning at bar 56 and its counterpart later on.'[ccliii] De Marliave considers the first violin 'lifts a melody of sublime purity, like a glimpse of blue sky among storm-clouds, imposing a sense of mysticism and spiritual vitality upon the essentially material texture of the movement'.[ccliv]

Kinderman likens the opening fugue and the finale to 'stern outer columns framing a fantastic range of diverse inner episodes'. In considering how Beethoven brings about 'a synthesis of contemplation and action' he invokes Schiller's terms of 'an unblinkered awareness of suffering [that is] merged with a capacity to resist these feelings and therefore not accept them as permanent and irremediable'. He also draws attention to Beethoven's dramatic use of silences 'hardly less important than the notes themselves'.[cclv] In his analysis of Beethoven's construction, Bekker perceives the *Allegro* as plunging the music once more 'into the maelstrom of active life' as it follows the relative 'calm' of the sixth-movement 'interlude'. He cites the introductory fugue as being 'symbolic of action', of the effect of its key transformations — 'C sharp — B sharp — A — G sharp', of it 'amazing expressiveness and versatility', and how it appears 'in ever-varying forms' until the *coda* when, at the moment of greatest tension, 'it becomes a choral-like hymn of victory ... The spirit of man, illuminated through the anguish of moral conflict and assured of Will and Fate, of Freedom and Necessity, returns once more to earth.'[cclvi]

As the movement proceeds, Beethoven has further invention to release: 'Whole notes ring out in octaves — the only passage of sustained octaves anywhere in the Beethoven quartets.'[cclvii] Lam regarded the development as being 'as terse and concentrated as, say, that in Mozart's *Prague* Symphony'.[cclviii] Of the closing pages, de Marliave first remarks: 'From this point to the last bar of the finale is a veritable orgy of wild joy, a passage unparalleled in the literature of chamber music.' Consistent with the views of others we have noted, he considers the only works of Beethoven that even anticipate the last movement of Op. 131 are the finales of the Quartets in E minor, Op. 59, No. 2, and in C, Op. 59, No. 3, to which he adds the *scherzi* of the Quartet in E flat, Op. 74, and that in the Quartet in F minor, Op. 95.'[cclix] In the movement's recapitulation, Kerman finds Beethoven reviving a procedure that he describes as 'an expanded triumphant return' and, with others we have cited, he quotes Wagner — in a somewhat modified translation: 'The dance of the whole world itself, wild joy, the wail of pain, love's transport, utmost bliss, grief, frenzy, riot, suffering; the lightning flickers, thunders growl; and above it the stupendous fiddler who bans and bends it all, who leads it haughtily from whirlwind into whirlpool, to the brink of the abyss.'[cclx] Tovey is succinct: '[The] ensuing coda is unsurpassed anywhere in Beethoven for tragic irony.'[cclxi]

So closes 'the last of Beethoven's great tragedies in music'.[cclxii] '[The] spirit of the artist is wholly emancipated from all doubt and suffering'. In a 'Bacchic frenzy' all four instruments draw the movement and the Quartet to a close upon two gigantic chords of C-sharp minor, 'setting a massive seal to Beethoven's most powerful chamber work'.[cclxiii] At the close of String Quartet in C-sharp minor, Op. 131, Marion Scott asks as to Beethoven's meaning of the three quartets Opp. 132, 130 and 131. She responds: 'How far was he the conscious channel for these great works ... and how far was he the arbiter? ... Whatever the relation, he was a willing co-operator, not a trance medium. As to Beethoven's meaning, each person must take or make their own share of it from the music.'[cclxiv]

We have related that Schubert, on hearing a performance of the C-sharp minor Quartet — when prostrate on his deathbed — remarked admiringly: 'After this what is there left to write?' It was a proposition that was to confront fellow musicians through the nineteenth century — and beyond. The youthful Mendelsohn sought to emulate Beethoven in his earliest quartet writing but, notwithstanding his remarkable precocity, his efforts go little beyond Beethovenian imitation. Brahms, ever beneath the shadow of Beethoven, was prone to lament: 'You do not know what it is like to be followed by Him.' Many would agree that it was not until Béla Bartók wrote his six string quartets that the sound world, so wonderfully explored by Beethoven in his Quartet Op. 131, would be re-examined with similar powers of penetration and invention. As for Beethoven, his response to 'What is there left to write?' was the composition of the String Quartet in F major, Op. 135 — his last complete work. It is to this that we next direct our narrative. As for Schubert, we can but conjecture how he may have enlarged the genre of the string quartet had he been granted even a few more years to his tragically short life.

---

[i] Adapted from Elliot Forbes, editor, 1967, p. 982. Misha Donat expresses similar views to Holz: 'Beethoven completed this most unconventionally-shaped of all his string quartets [Op. 131] in the summer of 1826. His preceding three quartets (Opp.127, 132 and 130) had been commissioned by Prince Nikolas Galitzin of St Petersburg, but the abundance of Beethoven's inspiration seems to have impelled him to continue the series without the need for an external stimulus.' Misha Donat, *String Quartet in C sharp Minor, Op. 131: Notes to the BBC Radio Three Beethoven Experience*, Sunday 5 June 2005, www.bbc.co.uk/radio3/Beethoven

[ii] William Kinderman, 1997, pp. 282–3. Reflecting on the creation origins of the late quartets — perceived as an entity — Kinderman comments: 'Yet we know from studies of the autograph manuscripts and sketchbooks that each of these pieces was originally conceived on a still lager scale. In different ways, Beethoven ultimately limited the size of each of these huge works by

rearranging or abridging his material.'

[iii] Michael Steinberg, *String Quartet in C-sharp minor, Op. 131* in: Robert Winter and Robert Martin editors, *The Beethoven quartet companion*, 1994, p. 246.

[iv] Paul Bekker, 1925, p. 32 quoted by Joseph de Marliave, 1925 (reprint 1961), pp. 296—7.

[v] Marion M. Scott, 1940, p. 266.

[vi] Denis Matthews, 1985, p. 145.

[vii] Barry Cooper, 1991, p. 208.

[viii] *Ibid*, p. 73.

[ix] Reginald Barrett-Ayres, 1974, pp. 29—30.

[x] Arthur Shepherd, 1935, p. 59.

[xi] See, for example Barry Cooper 1991, p. 159 and 2000, p. 339.

[xii] Tully Potter writing in Robin Stowell editor, *The Cambridge companion to the string quartet*, 2003, pp. 43—4.

[xiii] Emily Anderson, editor and translator, 1961, Vol. 3, Letter No. 1481, pp. 1283—4. Schlesinger so admired Beethoven string quartets that he assured him he considered they were 'as much masterpieces as an oratorio and would live a long', cited by Barry Cooper, 2000, pp. 334—5.

[xiv] With acknowledgment to Barry Cooper, 1995, p. 35.

[xv] See, for example, Barry Cooper, 1990, p. 68 and 2000, p. 337. Additionally, sketches for the B-flat major Quartet, Op. 130 suggest Beethoven had already contemplated the key of C-sharp minor for this work.

[xvi] Theodor Adorno, 1989, p. 56.

[xvii] Paul Griffiths, 1983, p. 107.

[xviii] Arthur Shepherd, 1935, pp. 56—7.

[xix] Joseph Kerman, 1967, p. 326.

[xx] Marion M. Scott, 1940, p. 273.

[xxi] Maynard Solomon, 1977, p. 325

[xxii] See, for example, Robert Winter and Robert Martin editors, *The Beethoven quartet companion*, 1994, p. 4 and Joseph Kerman, 1994, p. 235.

[xxiii] See, for example, Wilhelm Altman's commentary to the C-sharp minor Quartet, Eulenberg Miniature Score, 1911.

[xxiv] As propounded by such commentators as Arthur Shepherd, 1935, p. 59.

[xxv] David Wyn Jones, *Beethoven and the Viennese Legacy* in: Robin Stowell, editor, *The Cambridge companion to the string quartet*, 2003, p. 225.

[xxvi] Joseph Kerman, 1967, p. 334.

[xxvii] Arthur Shepherd, 1935, p. 57.

[xxviii] Derived from Oscar George Theodore Sonneck, *Beethoven: impressions of contemporaries*, 1927, pp. 149—54. See also, Peter Clive, 2000, pp. 127—8.

[xxix] *Ibid*, pp. 159—61.

[xxx] For contextual remarks see Theodore Albrecht, translator and editor, 1996, Vol. 2, Letter No. 315, pp. 255—6. The Härtel portrait was destroyed during World War II and is now known only from reproductions. See, for example, the frontispiece to Emily Anderson's *The Letters of Beethoven* Vol. 3 and Beethoven House, Digital Archives Library Document B. 362.

[xxxi] Theodore Albrecht, editor and translator, 1996, Vol. 2, Letter No. 286, pp. 204—6.

[xxxii] Emily Anderson, editor and translator, 1961, Vol. 3, Letter No. 1420, pp. 1240—1.

xxiii Elliot Forbes editor, *Thayer's life of Beethoven*, 1967, p. 973.
xxiv *Ibid*.
xxv Anton Felix Schindler, Beethoven as I knew him, edited by Donald W. MacArdle and translated by Constance S. Jolly from the German edition of 1860, 1966, pp. 314—5.
xxvi Emily Anderson, editor and translator, 1961, Vol. 3, Letter No. 1472, pp. 1278—79.
xxvii *Ibid*, Letter No. 1485, pp. 1286-7.
xxviii *Ibid*, Letter No, 1488, pp. 1288—9.
xxix For a discussion of Beethoven's relationship with Probst, see Peter Clive, 2000, pp. 271—2.
xl Emily Anderson, editor and translator, 1961, Vol. 3, Letter No. 1491, pp. 1290—1.
xli *Ibid*, Letter No. 1493, p. 1292.
xlii See: Barry Cooper, 2000, p. 341; Rebecca Clarke *The Beethoven quartets as a player sees* them in: *Musical Times*, Special Issue, Vol. VIII, No. 2, 1927, pp. 184—90; and Joseph de Marliave, 1925 (reprint 1961), p. 296.
xliii Emily Anderson, editor and translator, 1961, Vol. 3, Letter No. 1498, p. 1295.
xliv *Ibid*, Letter No. 1531, p. 1312.
xlv Theodore Albrecht, translator and editor, 1996, Vol. 3, Letter No. 447, pp. 156—9
xlvi Emily Anderson, editor and translator, 1961, Vol. 3, Letter No. 1535, pp. 1314—15.
xlvii *Ibid*, Letter No. 1545, p. 1325.
xlviii Gerhard von Breuning, *Memories of Beethoven: from the house of the black-robed Spaniards*, 1992 (reprint) p. 92 and endnote 156.
xlix Theodore Albrecht, translator and editor, 1996, Vol. 3, Letter No. 450, pp. 164—5.
l Peter Clive, 2000, p. 401.
li Emily Anderson, editor and translator, 1961, Vol. 3, Letter No. 1553, pp. 1334—35.
lii Emily Anderson, editor and translator, 1961, Vol. 3, Letter No. 1558, pp. 1338—39.
liii Theodore Albrecht, editor and translator, 1996, Vol. 3 Letter No. 461, pp. 183—5. By way of evidence of Beethoven's receptivity to antiquarian influences, Albrecht cites the researches of Alan Tyson 1982, pp. 161—191 (especially p. 163) and Johnson-Tyson-Winter, pp. 315—7.
liv Elliot Forbes, editor, *Thayer's life of Beethoven*, 1967, pp. 1044.
lv Theodore Albrecht, editor and translator, 1996, Vol. 3, Letter No. 466, pp. 191—5.
lvi Emily Anderson, editor and translator, 1961, Vol. 3, Letter No. 9, Appendix 1, pp. 1425—3.
lvii *Ibid*, Letter No. 1561, pp. 1340—41.
lviii It is probable that Stephan von Breuning played a part in assisting Karl to be admitted to von Stutterheim's regiment; Breuning was a colleague of Stutterheim's in the War Department. See: Peter Clive, 2000, p. 361.
lix Elliot Forbes, editor, *Thayer's life of Beethoven*, 1967, pp. 1038—9.
lx Theodore Albrecht, editor and translator, 1996, Vol. 2, Letter No. 475, pp. 231—2.
lxi *Ibid*, Letter No. 479, pp. 222—4.

lxii Wilhelm Altman, Eulenberg Miniature Score, 1911.

lxiii For facsimile reproductions of various early editions of the C-sharp minor Quartet, see: Beethoven House, Digital Archives, Library Documents: H. C. Bodmer, HCB C Md 79, 10; C 131/1; C 131/2; c 131 /10; Schorn 80b; and J. van der Spek C Op. 131

lxiv Theodore Albrecht, editor and translator, 1996, Vol. 3, Letter No. 487, pp. 244–7.

lxv *Ibid*, Letter No. 487, pp. 244–7.

lxvi Robin Wallace, *Beethoven's critics: aesthetic dilemmas and resolutions during the composer's lifetime*, 1986, p. 43. See also Robert Winter *Performing the Beethoven quartets in their first century* in: Robert Winter and Robert Martin, editors, *The Beethoven quartet companion*, 1994, p. 41.

lxvii As quoted by John Daverio, *Manner, tone, and tendency in Beethoven's chamber music for strings* in: Glenn Stanley editor, *The Cambridge companion to Beethoven*, 2000, pp. 147–64.

lxviii Quoted by Joseph de Marliave, 1925 (1961 reprint), p. 229.

lxix Michael Steinberg, *String Quartet in C-sharp minor, Op. 131* in: Robert Winter and Robert Martin editors *The Beethoven quartet companion*, 1994, p. 245.

lxx Quoted by Anne-Louise Coldicot in: Barry Cooper, 1991, p. 297.

lxxi Originally published In *La Correspondent* in 1837 and reproduced from a translation by Jacques Barzun in: John L. Holmes, *Composers on composers*, 1990, p. 378. Philip Radcliffe also gives a brief account of the concert in question, 1978, p. 177.

lxxii Stephen Johnson, 1998, p. 74.

lxxiii William Kinderman, 1997, p. 9.

lxxiv As quoted by Robert Winter, *Performing the Beethoven quartets in their first century* in: Robert Winter and Robert Martin editors, The Beethoven quartet companion, 1994, pp. 41–3 and p. 52.

lxxv Natali Bauer-Lechner, *Recollections of Gustav Mahler*, 1980, pp. 118–9 and pp. 136–7.

lxxvi Helena Matheopoulos, 1982, p. 16.

lxxvii Quoted by Leon Botstein, *The patrons and publics of the quartets* in: Robert Winter and Robert Martin editors, *The Beethoven quartet companion*, 1994, pp. 108–9.

lxxviii *Ibid*.

lxxix Derived, in part, from Otto Erich Deutsch, *Schubert: a documentary biography*, 1946, pp. 820–21 and Alfred Einstein, *A short history of music*, 1948, p. 87.

lxxx Holtz's remarks are so well intended that it seems churlish to reproach him in any way whatsoever. The point to be made here, however, is that in speaking as he did he unwittingly characterised Schubert as being a *mere* composer of songs – as indeed he was considered by so many of his contemporaries. Holtz was not to know that by the time of his death, Schubert had written sonatas and string quartets the equal of Beethoven's but which would languish, largely unperformed, for almost a century.

lxxxi Beethoven House, Digital Archives, Library Documents BSK22 and MH 96.

lxxxii Beethoven House, Digital Archives, Library Document, H. C. Bodmer, HCB Mh. See also Anton Felix Schindler, Beethoven as I knew him, edited by Donald W. MacArdle and translated by Constance S. Jolly from the German edition of 1860, 1966, pp. 438–41.

lxxxiii Richard Kramer in: Christoph Wolff and Robert Riggs, *The string quartets of Haydn, Mozart and Beethoven: studies of the autograph manuscripts: a conference at Isham Memorial Library*, March 15–17, 1979, pp. 234–5.

lxxxiv Barry Cooper, 2000, pp. 322–3.

lxxxv Douglas Porter Johnson, editor, 1985, pp. 471–4.

lxxxvi The number of sketch pages that Beethoven used in the creation of the C-sharp minor Quartet may in fact extend to some 650, more than four times as many as he needed to write out the finished score in its entirety. See: Robert Winter and Robert Martin, 1994, p. 4.

lxxxvii Ernest Walker, 1946.

lxxxviii Basil Lam, 1975, p. 125.

lxxxix Richard Kramer in: Christoph Wolff and Robert Riggs, *The string quartets of Haydn, Mozart and Beethoven: studies of the autograph manuscripts*: a conference at Isham Memorial Library, March 15–17, 1979, pp. 234–5.

xc As suggested by Paul Griffiths, 1983, p. 106.

xci Denis Matthews, 1985, pp. 145–6.

xcii Arnold Steinhardt, first violin of the Guarneri Quartet, in conversation with David Blum, 1986, p. 172.

xciii Paul Bekker, 1925, p. 334.

xciv Marion M. Scott, 1940, p. 273 and p. 274.

xcv Barry Cooper, 1990, p. 68.

xcvi Richard Wagner, writing in celebration of Beethoven on the occasion of the Centenary of his birthday, quoted by Jacques Barzun, *Pleasures of music: an anthology of writing about music and musicians*, 1977, p. 96. The original source is *Beethoven*, by Richard Wagner, translated by A. Lasvignes, 1902, p. 68.

xcvii David Soyer, cellist of the Guarneri Quartet, in conversation with David Blum, 1986, p. 171.

xcviii Joseph de Marliave, 1925 (reprint 1961), pp. 296–7.

xcix Barry Cooper. The precise location of this quotation has not been preserved. It may be Cooper, 1990, p. 68 *passim*.

c Michael Steinberg, *String Quartet in C-sharp minor, Op. 131* in: Robert Winter and Robert Martin editors, *The Beethoven quartet companion*, 1994, p. 247.

ci Harold Truscott, 1968, p. 101.

cii Philip Radcliffe, 1978, p. 148.

ciii Martin Cooper, 1970, p. 391.

civ *Ibid*.

cv William Kinderman, 1997, p. 309.

cvi Martin Cooper, 1970, p. 392.

cvii Michael Steinberg, *String Quartet in C-sharp minor, Op. 131* in: Robert Winter and Robert Martin editors, *The Beethoven quartet companion*, 1994, p. 247.

cviii Paul Bekker, 1925, p. 328.

cix John Dalley cellist and David Soyer second violin, in conversation with David Blum, *The art of quartet playing: the Guerneri Quartet*, 1986, pp. 171–2.

cx Philip Radcliffe, 1978, p. 149.

cxi Theodor W. Adorno, 1998, p. 132.

cxii Joseph Kerman, 1967, p. 302.

cxiii As quoted by Phillip Radcliffe, 1978, p. 186.

[xxiv] Romain Rolland, 1917, p. 189.
[xxv] Michael Tree, viola member of the Guarneri Quartet, in conversation with David Blum, 1986, p. 171.
[xxvi] Denis Matthews, 1895, p. 146.
[xxvii] Arthur Shepherd, 1935, p. 58.
[xxviii] Philip Radcliffe, 1978, p. 149—50.
[xxix] William Kinderman, 1997, p. 315.
[xxx] Harold Truscott, 1968, p. 106.
[xxxi] Preface to Wiener Philharmonischer Verlag, Wien, undated.
[xxxii] Michael Steinberg, *String Quartet in C-sharp minor, Op. 131* in: Robert Winter and Robert Martin editors, *The Beethoven quartet companion*, 1994, pp. 249—50.
[xxxiii] Joseph Kerman, 1967, p. 334.
[xxxiv] Joseph de Marliave, 1925 (reprint 1961), pp. 301—2.
[xxxv] Philip Radcliffe, 1978, p. 150.
[xxxvi] Derived from David Blum when in conversation with members of the Guarneri Quartet, 1986, p. 183.
[xxxvii] Joseph de Marliave, 1925 (reprint 1961), pp. 301—2.
[xxxviii] Martin Cooper, 1970, p. 394.
[xxxix] Jacques Barzun, 1977, p. 96 and Jack Sullivan, 1990, p. 130.
[xxxx] Derived from David Blum when in conversation with members of the Guarneri Quartet, 1986, p. 183 and p. 189.
[xxxxi] Arthur Shepherd, 1935, p. 59.
[xxxxii] Paul Bekker, 1925, p. 334.
[xxxxiii] Quoted by Jacques Barzun, *Pleasures of music: an anthology of writing about music and musicians,* 1977, p. 96.
[xxxxiv] Michael Steinberg, *String Quartet in C-sharp minor, Op. 131* in: Robert Winter and Robert Martin editors, *The Beethoven quartet companion*, 1994, p. 251.
[xxxxv] Joseph de Marliave, 1925 (reprint 1961), p. 303.
[xxxxvi] Denis Matthews, 1985, p. 146.
[xxxxvii] Misha Donat, *String Quartet in C sharp Minor, Op. 131:* **Notes to the BBC Radio Three Beethoven Experience**, Sunday 5 June 2005, www.bbc.co.uk/radio3/Beethoven
[xxxxviii] Basil Lam, 1975, p. 120.
[xxxxix] Misha Donat, *String Quartet in C sharp Minor, Op. 131:* **Notes to the BBC Radio Three Beethoven Experience**, Sunday 5 June 2005, www.bbc.co.uk/radio3/Beethoven
[cd] Phillip Radcliff, 1978, p. 152.
[cdi] The words quoted derive from Joseph de Marliave, 1925 (reprint 1961), p. 305.
[cdii] With acknowledgement to Alec Harman, Anthony Milner and Wilfrid Mellers, 1988, p. 654.
[cdiii] Martin Cooper, 1970, p. 396.
[cdiv] Joseph Kerman, 1967, pp. 334—5.
[cdv] Quoted by Jacques Barzun, 1977, p. 96.
[cdvi] Joseph Kerman, 1967, p. 214.
[cdvii] William Kinderman, 1997, p. 316.
[cdviii] Michael Steinberg, *String Quartet in C-sharp minor, Op. 131* in: Robert

cxlix Winter and Robert Martin editors, *The Beethoven quartet companion*, 1994, pp. 251–2.
cl Basil Lam, 1975, p. 121.
cli Anton Felix Schindler, *Beethoven as I knew him*, edited by Donald W. MacArdle and translated by Constance S. Jolly from the German edition of 1860, 1966, p. 309.
clii Joseph Kerman, 1967, pp. 213–4.
cliii Barry Cooper, 1991, p. 283.
cliv Paul Bekker, 1925, p. 334.
clv Igor Stravinsky, 1972, p. 262.
clvi Basil Lam, 1975, p. 120.
clvii Harold Truscott, 1968, p. 108.
clviii Theodor W. Adorno, 1998, p. 132.
clix Simpson Robert, 1973, p. 274.
clx Denis Matthews, 1985, p. 146.
clxi Joseph de Marliave, 1925 (reprint 1961), pp. 303–4.
clxii Philip Radcliffe, 1978, p. 153.
clxiii The views of members of the Guarneri Quartet in conversation with David Blum, 1986, pp. 191–2.
clxiv *Ibid*, Arnold Steinhardt's response to the first variation, the effect of which he describes as 'quite startling'. Its texture and its simplicity he founds reminiscent of the middle section of the second movement of Op 132.
clxv Martin Cooper, 1970, p. 396.
clxvi Rebecca Clarke, *The Beethoven quartets as a player sees them* in: *Musical Times*, Special Issue, 1927, Vol., VIII, No. 2, pp. 184–90.
clxvii Philip Radcliffe, 1978, p. 153.
clxviii Michael Steinberg, *String Quartet in C-sharp minor, Op. 131* in: Robert Winter and Robert Martin editors, *The Beethoven quartet companion*, 1994, p. 252.
clxix Joseph de Marliave, 1925 (reprint 1961), p. 306.
clxx Michael Steinberg, *String Quartet in C-sharp minor, Op. 131* in: Robert Winter and Robert Martin editors, *The Beethoven quartet companion*, 1994, p. 253.
clxxi Harold Truscott, 1968, p. 109.
clxxii Martin Cooper, 1970, p. 397 and Joseph de Marliave, 1925 (reprint 1961), p. 307.
clxxiii Basil Lam, 1975, p. 121.
clxxiv Igor Stravinsky, 1972, p. 262.
clxxv Harold Truscott, 1968, p. 109.
clxxvi Michael Steinberg, *String Quartet in C-sharp minor, Op. 131* in: Robert Winter and Robert Martin editors, *The Beethoven quartet companion*, 1994, p. 253–4.
clxxvii Martin Cooper, 1970, p. 397.
clxxviii Joseph Kerman, 1967, p. 335.
clxxix Joseph de Marliave, 1925 (reprint 1961), p. 307.
clxxx Michael Steinberg, *String Quartet in C-sharp minor, Op. 131* in: Robert Winter and Robert Martin editors, *The Beethoven quartet companion*, 1994, p. 253–4.
clxxxi Basil Lam, 1975, p. 121.

[cxxxi] Joseph de Marliave, 1925 (reprint 1961), p. 307.
[cxxxii] Harold Truscott, 1968, p. 110.
[cxxxiii] Michael Steinberg, *String Quartet in C-sharp minor, Op. 131* in: Robert Winter and Robert Martin editors, *The Beethoven quartet companion*, 1994, pp. 255–6.
[cxxxiv] Philip Radcliffe, 1978, p. 155.
[cxxxv] Martin Cooper, 1970, p. 398.
[cxxxvi] Denis Mathews, 1985, p. 146.
[cxxxvii] Rebecca Clarke, *The Beethoven quartets as a player sees them* in: *Musical Times*, Special Issue, 1927, Vol., VIII, No. 2, pp. 184–90.
[cxxxviii] Joseph de Marliave, 1925 (reprint 1961), p. 310.
[cxxxix] Joseph Kerman, 1967, pp. 334–5.
[cxc] Michael Steinberg, *String Quartet in C-sharp minor, Op. 131* in: Robert Winter and Robert Martin editors, *The Beethoven quartet companion*, 1994, p. 256.
[cxci] Rebecca Clarke, *The Beethoven quartets as a player sees them* in: *Musical Times*, Special Issue, 1927, Vol., VIII, No. 2, pp. 184–90.
[cxcii] Harold Truscott, 1968, p. 111.
[cxciii] The views of members of the Guarneri Quartet in conversation with David Blum, 1986, pp. 204–5.
[cxciv] Philip Radcliffe, 1978, p. 157.
[cxcv] Martin Cooper, 1970, p. 398.
[cxcvi] Harold Truscott, 1968, p. 110.
[cxcvii] Joseph Kerman, 1967, p. 337.
[cxcviii] Philip Radcliffe, 1978, p. 157.
[cxcix] Martin Cooper, 1970, pp. 399–400.
[cc] Joseph de Marliave, 1925 (reprint 1961), pp. 310–11.
[cci] Rebecca Clarke, *The Beethoven quartets as a player sees them* in: *Musical Times*, Special Issue, 1927, Vol. VIII, No. 2, pp. 184–90.
[ccii] Michael Tree in conversation with David Blum, *The art of quartet playing: the Guarneri Quartet in conversation with David Blum*, 1986, p. 212.
[cciii] Theodor W. Adorno, 1998, p. 135.
[cciv] As suggested by Harold Truscott, 1968, p. 116.
[ccv] Basil Lam also finds a similar connection with the Bagatelle in B minor, Op. 126, No. 4.
[ccvi] Joseph de Marliave, 1925 (reprint 1961), pp. 316–17.
[ccvii] Donald Francis Tovey, 1949, p. 292.
[ccviii] Joseph de Marliave, 1925 (reprint 1961), p. 314.
[ccix] William Kinderman, 1997, p. 317.
[ccx] Paul Bekker, 1925, p. 334.
[ccxi] Joseph Kerman, 1967, p. 338.
[ccxii] Philip Radcliffe, 1978, pp. 158–9.
[ccxiii] Rey M. Longyear, *Beethoven and romantic irony* in: Paul Henry Lang, *The creative world of Beethoven*, 1971, p. 156.
[ccxiv] Harold Truscott, 1968, pp. 111–12.
[ccxv] Joseph Kerman, 1967, p. 339.
[ccxvi] Denis Matthews, 1985, p. 146.
[ccxvii] Derived from Joseph de Marliave, 1925 (reprint 1961), p. 314.

ccxviii   *Ibid*.

ccxix   Derived from Jacques Barzun, 1977, pp. 96–7. Barzun himself quotes Wagner from *Beethoven's Day*, in: *A Pilgrimage to Beethoven*, Leipzig, 1883, pp. 96–7.

ccxx   Igor Stravinsky, 1972, p. 262.

ccxxi   Michael Steinberg, *String Quartet in C-sharp minor, Op. 131* in: Robert Winter and Robert Martin editors, *The Beethoven quartet companion*, 1994, p. 258.

ccxxii   Basil Lam, 1975, p. 126.

ccxxiii   *Ibid*.

ccxxiv   Philip Radcliffe, 1978, pp. 159.

ccxxv   The views of members of the Guarneri Quartet in conversation with David Blum, 1986, pp. 220.

ccxxvi   As reported by Phillip Radcliff, 1978, pp. 159–60.

ccxxvii   Michael Steinberg, *String Quartet in C-sharp minor, Op. 131* in: Robert Winter and Robert Martin editors, *The Beethoven quartet companion*, 1994, p. 260.

ccxxviii   As mentioned by Paul Nettle, 1975 and David Blum, 1986 p. 220.

ccxxix   One of Beethoven's 'gruff shrugs'. Romain Rolland, 1917, p. 190.

ccxxx   As quoted by Joseph de Marliave, 1925 (reprint 1961), p. 319.

ccxxxi   Philip Radcliffe, 1978, pp. 159.

ccxxxii   Joseph Kerman, 1967, p. 400.

ccxxxiii   Martin Cooper, 1970, p. 400.

ccxxxiv   Rebecca Clarke, *The Beethoven quartets as a player sees them in: Musical Times*, Special Issue, 1927, Vol. VIII, No. 2, pp. 184–90.

ccxxxv   Alec Harman with Anthony Milner and Wilfrid Mellers, 1988, p. 655.

ccxxxvi   Richard Wagner, quoted by Jacques Barzun, 1977, p. 97.

ccxxxvii   Joseph de Marliave, 1925 (reprint 1961), pp. 316–17.

ccxxxviii   Basil Lam, 1975, p. 126.

ccxxxix   Donald Tovey, 1949, p. 293.

ccxl   The views of members of the Guarneri Quartet in conversation with David Blum, 1986, pp. 220.

ccxli   *Ibid*.

ccxlii   Michael Steinberg, *String Quartet in C-sharp minor, Op. 131* in: Robert Winter and Robert Martin editors, *The Beethoven quartet companion*, 1994, p. 261.

ccxliii   Joseph de Marliave, 1925 (reprint 1961), p. 322.

ccxliv   Quoted by Joseph de Marliave, 1925 (reprint 1961), p. 319.

ccxlv   Joseph Kerman, 1967, pp. 341–42.

ccxlvi   Basil Lam, 1975, p. 128. *The Musical Offering* BWV 1079 is a collection of keyboard canons and fugues and other pieces of music by Johann Sebastian Bach, all based on a single musical theme given to him by Frederick the Great (Frederick II of Prussia), to whom they are dedicated.

ccxlvii   Martin Cooper, 1970, pp. 402.

ccxlviii   Robert Simpson, *The Chamber Music for Strings* in: Denis Arnold and Nigel Fortune editors, *The Beethoven companion*, 1973, p. 274.

ccxlix   Paul Griffiths, 1983, pp. 106–7.

ccl   Joseph Kerman, 1967, pp. 340–41.

ccli   Denis Matthews, 1985, p. 146.

- ccliiMichael Steinberg, *String Quartet in C-sharp minor, Op. 131* in: Robert Winter and Robert Martin editors, *The Beethoven quartet companion*, 1994, p. 261.
- ccliiiMarion M Scott, 1940, p. 273.
- ccliv Joseph de Marliave, 1925 (reprint 1961), p. 322.
- cclv William Kinderman, 1997, p. 319 and p. 323.
- cclvi Paul Bekker, 1925, p. 335.
- cclviiMichael Steinberg, *String Quartet in C-sharp minor, Op. 131* in: Robert Winter and Robert Martin editors, *The Beethoven quartet companion*, 1994, p. 261.
- cclviii Basil Lam, 1975, p. 128.
- cclix Joseph de Marliave, 1925 (reprint 1961), p. 325.
- cclx Joseph Kerman, *The Uncanny* in: William Kinderman editor, *The string quartets of Beethoven*, 2005, p. 276.
- cclxi Donald Francis Tovey, 1949, pp. 295–6.
- cclxiiMichael Steinberg, *String Quartet in C-sharp minor, Op. 131* in: Robert Winter and Robert Martin editors, *The Beethoven quartet companion*, 1994, p. 261.
- cclxiii Joseph de Marliave, 1925 (reprint 1961), p. 327–8.
- cclxiv Marion M. Scott, 1940, p. 274.

STRING QUARTET IN F MAJOR, OP. 135

'It is amazing where the newest composers are heading, with technical and mechanical dimensions raised to the very highest levels; their works end up no longer music, for they go beyond the scope of human emotional responses and one cannot add anything more to such works from one's own spirit and heart.'

Johann Wolfgang von Goethe in recorded conversation with his secretary Johann Peter Eckermann. As quoted in: Robert Winter and Robert Martin, editors, *The Beethoven quartet companion*, 1994, p. 77.

'Those diligent folk who pride themselves on their ability to distinguish Beethoven's various

> styles would surely come to grief over this movement [of the F major String Quartet] if the time and conditions of its composition were known, for is not this finale similar in style and clarity to many of the quartet movements of an earlier period? The same is true of the fourth and sixth movements of the C-sharp minor Quartet, and no less true of the second, fourth, and fifth movements of the A minor Quartet. Who can deny that one meets in these last works the deepest depths of obscurity right next to the brightest light of clarity? A sustained style can be found only in the four movements of the Quartet in F major, Op. 135.'

Anton Felix Schindler, *Beethoven as I knew him*, edited by Donald W. MacArdle and translated by Constance S. Jolly from the German edition of 1860, 1966, p. 308.

In March 1877 George Bernard Shaw, acting in his role of music critic, gave an account of a performance of the Op. 127 and Op. 135 String Quartets. He writes:

> 'The selection was an admirable one, for the two works in question illustrate some phases of feeling which belong peculiarly to the great master's individuality. The Quartet in F major, Op. 135 contains one of those majestic slow movements which occur in Beethoven's earliest and latest works, and in which he has conveyed intense melancholy without sacrifice of dignity or suggestion of morbid sentimentality.'

George Bernhard Shaw, originally published in *The Hornet*

and reproduced in: *Bernhard Shaw, How to become a musical critic*, 1960, pp. 18—19.

> 'Like the F major Symphony, Op. 93, the F major Quartet, Op. 135 stands at the close of a phase of development and possess the peace of a goal attained. It lacks moments of great spiritual tension, of wild excitement over deep questions and problems. These, having been exhausted in preceding works, are merely subjects of imaginative reminiscence ... The F major is in the nature of an epilogue, a retrospective ... There is a return to the four-movement quartet type, and the individual movements are not so great a scale as those of the preceding works.'

Paul Bekker, *Beethoven*, 1925, p. 335.

> 'In actual dimensions this work is much more concise than the Quartets Opp. 127, 130, 131, and 132. It is not their inferior from the point of technique, but its imaginative significance is infinitely less; here can be traced no psychological meaning, as in the earlier works of Beethoven's later manner. The first, second, and third movements are, rather, a fluent play of brilliant but irresponsible wit. By way of contrast, the *Adagio*, in spite of its circumscribed form, is one of the most profound expressions of Beethoven's genius that his work can offer, and the quality of its inspiration shows that he wrote it with an instinctive foreboding of the end.'

Joseph de Marliave, *Beethoven's quartets*, 1925 (reprint

1961), p. 355.

> 'The last of the quartets, that in F major, Op. 135, is shorter and slighter than any other of the period. It is strange, and perhaps characteristic, that as Beethoven's life drew near to its end his music became happier and more light-hearted, as we have already seen in the case of the finale of the B flat Quartet, written about the same time.'

Rebecca Clarke, *The Beethoven quartets as a player sees them in: Musical Times*, Special Issue, 1927, Vol. VIII, No. 2, pp. 184—90.

> 'The Quartet in F major, Op. 135 is the cheeriest and most directly accessible of Beethoven's late quartets. It impresses us as serene and cheerful — "above the fray", as it were. Critics have occasionally compared it to *Falstaff* that quicksilver, comedic affirmation of life and living Giuseppe Verdi chose as his valedictory after a long career of depicting storm and stress. Others have described this final quartet as "Beethoven sunning himself on the heights".' Tim Page, quoting from J.W.N. Sullivan's, *Beethoven: His Spiritual Development,* 1927. Page adds: 'It is the work of a man who is fundamentally at peace. It is the peace of a man who has known conflict, but whose conflicts are now reminiscent ... If we may judge from this quartet — and also from Beethoven's actual last composition, the present finale of the B-flat Quartet — it would appear that at the end of his life the inner Beethoven who expressed himself in music was content.'

Tim Page, *Liner notes to the F major String Quartet, Op. 135*, Juilliard String Quartet, undated.

> 'Let us not fall too readily into a bland acceptation of prevalent critical estimates of this work. In certain respects, it is the most advanced of all, in a *modernistic* sense. Size, length, and weightiness have nothing to do with the question. Consider, instead, its wit, its mellowness, its intriguing instrumental badinage, all made the more telling in relation to the deeply subjective and heartfelt *Adagio*.'

Arthur Shepherd, *The string quartets of Ludwig van Beethoven*, 1935, pp. 75–6.

> 'Closing the pages of this F major Quartet to gaze in retrospect upon Beethoven's whole career, his words take on a new meaning. "Muss es sein?" Destiny seems to brood over the composer as over his compositions. Beethoven the man had to be; his music had to come into being. Everything is as it should be. "Es muss sein!" we say quietly and that answer is true for it is not of Death but of Life.'

Marion M. Scott, *Beethoven: The master musicians*, 1940, p. 277.

> 'This Quartet does not stand out as either a very significantly integrative work or as a dissociated one; Op. 135 is not pre-eminently an exploratory work at all, any more than Op. 18, No. 5, or Op.

74 (though each of these has its exploratory aspects). There is no reason to doubt Beethoven's integrity, or to doubt that he was producing a work of integrity, besides accomplishing exactly what the course of his artistic development required at the particular juncture ... That the piece is very different from the Quartets in B flat and C-sharp minor is of course true, and it should not be necessary to have to insist on the individuality of these three last quartets. There individuality, or authenticity, is the measure of their greatness.'

Joseph Kerman, *The Beethoven quartets*, 1967, pp. 377–6.

'This Quartet, Beethoven's last completed full-scale work, has often been described as a return to the early simpler style of the classical composers. Haydn has been mentioned as a comparison. I can think of no assessment more wide of the mark. It is true that, in the main, Beethoven's thematic material here is simpler than in many of the other of these late quartets; this is a simplicity which reaches its apex in two themes: the main theme of the second group in the first movement and the corresponding theme in the finale. But the work which uses these themes has a complexity which is different in kind from that of Haydn, and far more intense, although Haydn could be complex enough.'

Harold Truscott, *Beethoven's late string quartets*, 1968, p. 120.

'There is ... considerable resemblance between the eighteenth-century good humour and good manners, and even the slightly self-conscious touch of Biedermeir-domesticity ... found in the new finale of Op. 130 and the neo-Haydn exterior of the first movement and the final *Allegro* of Op. 135. It is not a matter merely of appearances. In both these works Beethoven seems to have exorcised the angels and the demons, pity and terror, to have momentarily have finished with supra-mundane contemplations and the Dionysian assertion of the significance of life's struggles and contradictions.'

Martin Cooper, *Beethoven: the last decade, 1817–1827*, 1970, pp. 403–4.

'The weaknesses are obvious: the shortness of breath, the failure to push the argument, the stylistic jolt of the final movement with its musical snuff-box tune; but the strengths outweigh and outnumber them. The Quartet is said to be short on innovations, too, but the repeated figure in the *Vivace* is the newest and most astonishing idea Beethoven had.'

Igor Stravinsky, *Themes and conclusions*, 1972, p. 263.

'Beethoven's final quartet, the F major, Op. 135, is his last completed composition, except for the second finale to Op. 130. It has the light touch of infinite wisdom and clarity; smaller than the others in scope as well as dimensions, it is nevertheless something only the vastly experienced Beethoven could have written.'

Robert Simpson, *The Chamber Music for Strings* in, Denis Arnold and Nigel Fortune editors, *The Beethoven companion*, 1973, p. 276.

> 'If, in the event, Op. 135 becomes a strangely individual work, this was only to be expected from a composer for whom self-conscious revivals of past styles (neo classicism) were as unthinkable as rigid *a priori* systems.'

Basil Lam, *Beethoven string quartets*, 1975, p. 130.

> 'With the Quartet in F major, Op. 135, Beethoven came "home" at last. This is not to say that it is a conservative or anachronistic work — the hallmarks of the late style are too deeply imprinted in it for such a judgement to be viable.'

Maynard Solomon, *Beethoven*, 1977, p. 325.

> 'The Quartet in F major, Op, 135, has none of this "all-embracing" quality; it is concise in form, spare in texture and intimate in mood ... It is appropriate to the part played by Beethoven's string quartets in his whole output that they should end, not with a monumental structure on the scale of the Ninth Symphony, but with a short and intimate work like the Op. 135. In its extreme terseness it recalls the Piano Sonata in F-sharp major, Op. 78, for which Beethoven himself had a particular affection, and in all probability his last quartet meant at least as much to him as its slightly

earlier predecessor.'

Philip Radcliffe, *Beethoven's string quartets*, 1978, p. 165 and pp. 171–2.

'Like Schubert's G major Quartet, Beethoven's Op. 135 is once more in the four usual movements, with a sonata-form *allegretto* followed by a *scherzo*, a slow movement in D flat and a finale. But for Beethoven, of course, this was a conscious return, and not without point. On one level there is a parallel with the Seventh Symphony, and even more so the Eighth, coming after a group of more insistently revolutionary works in the same form, for similarly the Op. 135 Quartet is a work of reflection and control not denying the eccentricities and the battles of its predecessors, but seeing them with a certain detachment.'

Paul Griffiths, *The string quartet*, 1983, pp. 110–11.

'To regard Op. 135's reversion to a Mozartian time-scale as somehow retrograde is a serious misapprehension. After the grandeur of its predecessor it may seem closer to the world of comedy than tragedy but it radiates a spiritual serenity and philosophy of acceptance that transcends both ... Beethoven in his last completed work summed up his life's struggles, his resignation and his ultimate philosophy and faith, in music of disarming lightness and simplicity.'

Denis Matthews, *Beethoven: The master musicians*, 1985, pp. 146–7.

> 'By virtue of its brevity and its *normality* of design, Op. 135 stands apart from the other late quartets. What if Beethoven could have recovered from the dropsy and cirrhosis that laid him low at the end of 1826? What if he had lived? Such speculations are in an obvious sense useless, but they need not be uninteresting. In the case of Beethoven, one question that immediately presents itself is whether the Tenth Symphony and whatever quartets and other works that followed would have continued on the path of new simplicity suggested by Op. 135 and the *Allegro* of Op. 130 ... Do we, in the works of the second part of 1826, have the beginning of a fourth period, vastly different from the awesome third, or would Op. 135 have come to seem like an intermezzo?'

Robert Winter and Robert Martin editors, *The Beethoven quartet companion*, 1994, p. 273.

> 'Having recently drawn inspiration from the old modes and a-cappella style in the *Heiliger Dankgesang* of Op. 132 and the fugue of Op. 131, Beethoven now looked to the late eighteenth century and the world of Haydn. Nevertheless [in Op. 135] there are still some unmistakable Beethoven hallmarks ...'.

Barry Cooper, *Beethoven: The master musicians*, 2000, p. 342.

> 'Beethoven's last quartet opens the era of Roman-

tic music. Beethoven's near contemporaries condemned the quartet for its looseness in construction, and judged it a work of decline. Others acclaimed it as a prophetic vision of the romantic future. Perhaps it is neither. The quartet is typical Beethoven, and there are elements of his great style, as exemplified in the *Lento*, and also the lesser art of brilliant humour. Although Beethoven noted "the last quartet" at the end of the manuscript, he could not foresee it was to be his last work. This quartet was Beethoven's *intermezzo*, which death converted into a finale.'

Electra Slonimsky Yourke editor, *Nicolas Slonimsky: writings on music*, 2003–2005, p. 171.

Reflecting on the gestation of the new finale for the B-flat major Quartet and the stylistic manner of the F major Quartet, Op. 135, Maynard Solomon remarks 'they reflect a tranquil and confident return to a happier, Haydnesque play world'.[i] Discussing Beethoven's preparedness to turn to traditional models, Nicholas Marston describes Beethoven's very last quartet as being 'the composer's most successful evocation of the style of Haydn and Mozart'.[ii] Paul Bekker, amongst others (see later), offers words of caution: 'High-spirited laughter is no longer accepted as the final wisdom. Wherefore the humour of this Quartet, it has not the elfishness, levitation or vibrating tempo of the Eighth Symphony ... An earnest mood prevails and the work is inspired more by reflection than gaiety.'[iii] Arthur Shepherd expressed similar thoughts. He believed the poetic idea of Beethoven's last quartet, or the first half of it at least, arose from the same impulse that had brought into being various other works to which he refers as being 'imbued with a rustic spirit'. In support of this contention he cites the *Pastoral* Piano Sonata, Op. 28, of 1801 and the *Pastoral* Symphony of 1808.[iv] In his consideration of the reflective nature of the F major Quartet, Martin Cooper states metaphorically: '[Beethoven] is now content to cultivate his garden, to smile and to remember, to mock a little perhaps at his own dramatization of cosmic problems and to exercise his incomparable gift for sheer musical invention.'[v] Robert Winter and Robert Martin assert that in his Op. 135, Beethoven did not have to be 'simple' but they perceive him voluntarily turning away from 'the crescendo of complexity' that can be traced from Op. 127 to Op. 131. They qualify their observation: 'Op. 135 no more expresses nostalgia for the good old days of Op. 18 than the Eighth Symphony expresses longing for a quest for the ideal *multum in parvo* ['much in little'].' They pose the challenge confronting Beethoven, as he set to work on the String Quartet in F major, Op, 135, in the form of a rhetorical question: 'How would it be to provide an aesthetically and emotionally rich experience, divorced from the staggering complexities and expansive scale of the preceding quartets, particularly Opp. 130 and 131?'[vi] We shall consider Beethoven's response to this self-imposed challenge as our narrative unfolds.

Basil Lam perceives the more diminutive structure of the F major Quartet as being, in part, Beethoven's reaction against 'the superhuman concentration' expended upon the composition of its predecessors – Opp. 127, 132, 130, 131, and 133. Not surprising, then, that he should return 'unaffected by romantic nostalgia, to the less exacting world of his youth'. He qualifies his remark with the caution: 'We must not make rash generalisations on the basis of his last compositions, for their status as such is purely accidental.' He elaborates. 'All that can be said is that [Beethoven] was pleased, in 1826, to occupy himself with music less exploratory than re-creative.'[vii]

We have seen in the E-flat major Quartet, Op. 127, that Beethoven settled upon a four-movement design (having initially contemplated a six-movement format). In the A minor Quartet, Op. 132 he expanded the genre to five movements — although Beethoven regarded the work as having six. The B-flat major Quartet, Op. 130 has six movements; and the C-sharp minor no fewer than seven movements. In the F major Quartet, Op. 135, Beethoven made life easier for himself by reverting to the four-movement structure that he had adopted in the Op. 127 Quartet. Moreover, in the F major Quartet there is a return to conciseness; the four movements are shorter and less discursive than its predecessors. Harold Truscott considers the scale of Op. 135 is more implicit than explicit. He explains: 'The *scale-of-size* [our italics] of this quartet is as large as that of any of the others [late quartets], whereas Haydn's scale-of-size, even at his most profound, remains small with quick reactions.' Truscott regards this as being quite unique to the F major Quartet: 'There are no themes in Haydn's work as I know it, or in that of any other classical composer, which could produce anything like the scale-of-size of this Quartet [Op. 135].'[viii]

Beethoven gives the opening movement the designation *Allegro*. It has been suggested that since this movement has a moderate tempo, the usual order of the following movements is changed. The second movement is *Vivace* — a pulsating Beethoven scherzo with syncopation. A variation movement follows — *Lento assai e cantante tranquillo*. The work concludes with the most famous movement of all — arising as a consequence of the anecdotes connected with it: *Der schwer gefasste Entschuluss. Grave (Muss es sein?) — Allegro (Es muss sein!) — Grave, ma non troppo tratto — Allegro.*

Although the F major String Quartet was Beethoven's last major composition, authorities are in agreement that it does not represent an end but a new beginning. In their estimation of Beethoven's originality in his Op. 135, Winter and Martin ask the question: Do we, in the works of the second part of 1826, have the beginning of a fourth period, vastly different from the awesome third, or would Op. 135 have come to seem like an intermezzo?' They respond: '[This] quartet sounds like the utterance of a heart and mind miraculously refreshed ... And, we may add, ready for new endeavours.'[ix] Truscott asserts: 'The [Op. 135] Quartet is not a third period work at all, or a first or second period either, but the beginning of new fourth, phase.' He elaborates: 'Beethoven is true to his nature in that, as always with a new start, he goes even more than usual to the root of things, to the origins of classical speech.' He refers to Beethoven's 'boldness' in the manner of his handling something new, prompting him to suggest that Op. 135 has one thing the late quartets have not given us — 'comedy'. In his estimation, Op. 135 is 'a comedy of the spirit'. Philosophically he concludes: '[Like] all comedy, it is basically serious, because one cannot laugh at, or with, something which has no standard of truth.'[x] Shepherd reminds us: 'Up to the very end Beethoven was true to his own dictum that "Art demands of us that we shall never stand still".'[xi] For Marion Scott, however, the F major Quartet sounds a valedictory note: '[Op. 135] was to Beethoven much what the *Requiem* was to Mozart, and the *Four Serious Songs* to Brahms.'[xii]

Before progressing to a discussion of the creation origins of the F major Quartet, we pause for a moment to reflect on some of the more personal aspects of the composer's life at the period when he was working on the late string quartets.

In 1824 Beethoven received a rare honour from the French Emperor. In 1823, Louis XVIII had been a subscriber to the composer's *Missa Solemnis*. On receipt of the manuscript he instructed his First Chancellor the Duc d'Achâts that 'it had pleased his Majesty to honour the artist with a gold medal showing the King's head'. This honorary gift had the weight of twenty-one louis d'or and inscribed on the reverse were the words: 'Donné par le Roi à Monsieur Beethoven.'[xiii] Beethoven was clearly touched by this as is evident from a letter he wrote some time later (early March) to the journalist and editor Joseph Karl Bernard. He requested news of his honour should be made more widely known by being announced in the *Wiener Zeitung*, of which Bernard was then editor. Beethoven refers to Louis XVIII as being 'a generous King and a man of refined feeling'.[xiv]

We derive an impression of Beethoven's appearance from an account of him left by the poet and music critic Ludwig Rellstab; it is Rellstab who remarked that the first movement of the Piano Sonata Op. 27, No. 2 suggested moonlight on Lake Lucerne, giving rise to its nickname *Mondscheinsonate — Moonlight Sonata*. The writer visited Beethoven a number of times in 1825 and was cordially received. He had hopes the composer would set a number of his poems to music but Beethoven was too unwell to fulfil the commission; it fell to Schubert to confer immortality on Rellstab by his own setting of the texts. When Rellstab met the composer he found him unwell. Looking about his room he observed a table 'completely covered with treasures, with notes in Beethoven's hand, and with the work with which he was busy at the moment'. Of his features, Rellstab writes: 'His hair, almost totally grey, rose bushily and in disorder from his head; not soft and curly, not stiff, a mixture of all three.' Comparing Beethoven's appearance, with that portrayed in later romanticized portraits, Rellstab remarks:

'There was nothing which expressed that brusqueness, that tempestuous, unshackled quality which has been lent his physiognomy in order to bring it into conformity with his works.'[xv]

In our previous discussions we have made passing reference to Beethoven's possessive relationship with his nephew Karl. In Cooper's eloquent words: 'Karl's tragedy was that, when still a child, he was asked to be a vessel into which an aging and ill genius discharged all the pent-up tenderness and possessiveness that had never found its normal outlet in the relationship first of husband and then father.'[xvi] As we have seen (C sharp-minor String Quartet) the pressures on Karl resulted in him attempting to take his life. The traumatic effect on the composer can only be imagined. Karl spent a period of convalescence together with Beethoven on his brother's estate at Gneixendorf — where much of the work on the F major Quartet was completed. On Karl's full recovery — he had only slightly wounded himself — Beethoven's long-time friend Stephan von Breuning arranged for Karl to enter the regiment of Baron von Stutterheim, as a cadet, and also agreed to act as his co-guardian. We take leave of Karl by saying, when allowed to follow his chosen vocation — and free of the stifling influence of his demanding uncle — he had a successful military career, eventually rising to the rank of officer.

Beethoven's failing health at this period should be noted. From April 1825 the composer received treatment from Dr. Anton Braunhofer. According to Anton Schindler, Braunhofer maintained a firm attitude to his stubborn patient and held his own against him. He prescribed a strict diet, to assist his inflamed digestion, and insisted the composer should abstain from alcohol and coffee — Beethoven liked to start his working day by grinding his own blend of coffee. Beethoven's adherence to Braunhofer's strict regimen appears to have been successful — at least for a period — and enabled him to resume work on his composition.[vii] In his final illness Beethoven received regular treatment from Professor Dr. Andreas Wawruch, one of the directors of the Medical Clinic at the University of Vienna. He was a specialist in the therapy of internal diseases, relevant to Beethoven's dropsy and inflamed digestion. Doubtless congenial to Beethoven was that Wawruch was interested in music and was an accomplished cellist. In recognition of the care and solicitude that Waruch bestowed upon him, Beethoven gave his physician a copy of the score of Handel's *Messiah* — Handel then being the composer whom he placed above all others. On 20 May 1827, following Beethoven's death, Wawruch wrote a detailed account of the composer's many illnesses that was eventually published in April 1842.[xviii]

Beethoven's association with the violinist Ignaz Schuppanzigh will redirect us to the genre of the string quartet. As we have seen in our previous discussions, Schuppanzigh and his Quartet had premiered the first performance of the String Quartet, Op. 95 and later his ensemble gave first performances of the Quartets Op. 127, Op. 132, and Op. 130, with the *Great Fugue* on 21 March 1826, and, following Beethoven's death, with the new finale on 22 April 1827. Beethoven thought highly of Schuppanzigh and as Tully Potter writes: 'The knowledge that this faithful servant was once again available was undoubtedly a stimulus to Beethoven, who always had performance in mind for even his most advanced music.'[xix]

The F major String Quartet was composed during the later months of 1826 when Beethoven was residing on his bother Johann's estate at Gneixendorf. A contemporary account paints a somewhat idealised picture of the composer amidst these surroundings: 'Just as Beethoven's works carry the stamp of the highest and, no doubt, often bizarre originality, we also see the master moving about within, or rather outside, the bustle of the world with the greatest peculiarity.' This can be taken as a reference to his demeanour as perceived by others when he was outdoors. The author of the piece in question attributes the nature of Beethoven's works to his isolation: 'His works receive all the more value precisely because of the fact that they are pure, unadulterated products of his innermost spiritual life, weakened and modified as little as possible by external impressions.'[ix] Beethoven certainly found relief in the countryside as is apparent in a letter he sent at this time to Bernhard Schotts: 'I am using what remains of the fine weather to take a holiday here in the country.' He concludes: 'The district where I am now staying reminds me to a certain extent of the Rhine country which I so ardently desire to revisit. For I left it long ago when I was young.'[xxi]

An unfortunate incident occurred during Beethoven's sojourn at Gneixendorf that bears testimony to Rellstab's description of his negligent appearance. Beethoven, his brother Johann and others paid a social visit to a Dr. Keller — a surgeon friend of Johann. Frau Keller, anxious to be an attentive hostess, offered her guests a glass of wine. Seeing a rather shabbily dressed figure sitting alone on a bench — and assuming it was the coachman — she obligingly poured some wine into an earthenware pot, saying kindly: 'Here is a draught for you too!' Dr, Keller, who had been away when the party arrived, immediately realised his wife's unintended slight and exclaimed: 'What have you done!' He gently reproached her for not having recognised 'the greatest composer of the age'.[xxii]

The composition and completion of the F major Quartet can be traced through his negotiations with his publishers to which we now make reference.

Central to this part of our narrative is the music publisher Schlesinger — more correctly the Schlesingers. The main branch of the business was conducted from Berlin, by its founder Adolf, with support from the Paris office whose affairs were looked after by Adolf's son Maurice (Moritz). Maurice was in Vienna from late August until late September 1825. We have seen elsewhere that his subsequent meeting with Beethoven was fruitful insofar as it resulted in the Schlesingers' publishing the String Quartet, Op. 132. The Schlesingers' had previously collaborated with Beethoven in the publication of his last great keyboard trilogy, Piano Sonata Op. 109 (Berlin 1821 and Paris 1822), Piano Sonata Op. 110 (Berlin/Paris 1822), and Piano Sonata Op. 111 (Paris 1823).

On 15 April 1826, Adolf Schlesinger wrote to Beethoven in the hope that he would compose an opera on the subject of the mythological spirit *Melusine* (*Melusina*) to a word setting by the dramatist Franz Grillparzer. At the close of his letter Adolf added: 'If you perhaps have something on hand that you could send me, I request your obliging news about it.'[xxiii] Of related interest is that Maurice, as remarked representing the publishing firm in Paris, also wrote to Beethoven at this time in the same vein. Before his move to Gneixendorf, Beethoven wrote from Vienna to Maurice on 22 September: 'I inform you that another new quartet will be finished in two or three weeks at latest.' This is taken to be a reference to the String Quartet in F major, Op. 135. Anticipating Maurice's acceptance of the work he added: 'Please arrange, therefore, that the sum of 80 Imperial and Royal gold ducats be paid to me immediately.' Beethoven urged Maurice to act promptly: 'And let there be no delay, for quartets are now in demand everywhere; and it really seems that our age is taking a step forward.'[xxiv]

From the foregoing we can infer that the String Quartet Op. 135 was not composed directly in response to a commission. It appears to have been conceived more in answer to the inner promptings of Beethoven's personal desire to write yet another string quartet — of which he had now become supreme master. In the words of William Kinderman: 'Thus, in writing each of these [late] works, Beethoven conceived material that spilled over beyond the composition immediately at hand. His fertility of invention refused to be contained within the boundaries of the singular work.'[xxv]

At this time the violinist Karl Holz was assisting Beethoven with his daily business affairs. Sometime in July 1826, Holz was in contact with Maurice Schlesinger who asked about the progress Beethoven's was making with the Quartet. By then Holz appears to have learned from the composer that he was not contemplating a work on such a gigantic scale as its predecessors. Mindful of this, Holz is recorded as saying to Schlesinger: 'You will not punish him [Beethoven] if it is short. Even if it should have only three movements it will still be a quartet by Beethoven, and it would cost less to print it.' Holz made known this conversational exchange to Beethoven. It later transpired Schlesinger agreed to purchase the Quartet for 80 ducats but subsequently sent 360 florins instead — that was not an equivalent monetary conversion. The circumstance drew from Beethoven a characteristic response: 'If a Jew [a reference to Schlesinger's religion] sends circumcised ducats he shall have a circumcised quartet.'[xxvi]

Beethoven wrote to Adolf Schlesinger on 13 October from Gneixendorf. He informed him that having returned to the country he was feeling 'in a good mood once again'. He reassured his publisher: 'The Quartet [Op. 135] is finished, but not entirely copied out, but will be ready for delivery in a few days.' The parts for Op. 135, in Beethoven's hand, are today preserved in the Archives of the Beethoven Haus, Bonn. Beethoven took the opportunity to raise a subject very dear to him, namely, the publication of a complete edition of his works. To facilitate this he was prepared to revisit certain of his earlier compositions, to write additional works in order to fill missing gaps, and to add metronome indications. Having consulted with friends, he suggested a price of 4000 ducats 'does not seem to be too sizable'. Nothing, however, came of this suggestion. Beethoven then apologized for his delay in not making progress with Grillparzer's libretto for *Die Schöne Melusine* stating, 'I am only now beginning to regain my composure, since this summer flew by in a very disturbing manner.' Beethoven's death, a few months, later put an end to his long cherished hope of creating a new work for the lyric theatre following the eventual success of his only work in that genre — *Fidelio*.[xxvii]

Later in the month, Beethoven arranged for payment of the F major Quartet to be made to Schlesinger by courtesy of his agent in Vienna Tendler & Manstein — a firm of booksellers well known to the composer: 'I am sending you by my brother [Johann] my latest violin quartet [Op. 135] composed for Herr Schlesinger; and I request you to hand to the former the fee of 80 ducats deposited with you for this purpose.'[xxviii]

At the close of October 1826, Beethoven corresponded with Maurice Schlesinger in Paris. He opens: 'Just see what an unfortunate fellow I am.' He explains how challenging it has been for him to work adding: 'I composed it [Op. 135] solely because I had promised it to you and needed the money'. His next sentence has considerable extra-musicological significance: 'That it was difficult for me to do so you can infer from the *Ess muss sein*?' Beethoven is making reference here to the fourth movement of the F major Quartet to which he gave the title *Der schwer gefasste Entschluss*. The precise meaning of Beethoven's enigmatic words *Ess muss sein* have been the subject of much speculation that we consider later in our discussion of the Quartet's individual movements. Beethoven closed his letter by reflecting on the effort he had had to expend writing out the parts himself because, residing as he was in the countryside, there was no copyist available to him. He closes: 'Well, that was a gruelling piece of work, in truth! Ugh, it is finished. Amen!'[xxix]

A few days later Beethoven wrote once more to Maurice in similar terms: 'Here my dear fellow is my last quartet. It will be the last; indeed it has given me much trouble. For I could not bring myself to compose the last movement.' We recall that Holz had wondered if the F major Quartet might have only three movements. Beethoven reaffirmed that he had resolved to compose a fourth movement so as not to disappoint his publisher: 'And that is the reason why I have written the motto: *The decision with difficulty — Must it be? — It must be, it must be!* [Beethoven's italics] Explaining once more that he had written out the parts in his own hand, he expressed the hope that Schlesinger's engraver 'will be able to read my scrawl'.[xxx]

On 11 November, Adolf Schlesinger replied to Beethoven: 'I very much enjoyed your honoured letter of 13 October in which you expressed your satisfaction now, having returned to the country, again to be able to live for the Muse. How eager I am to see your new masterwork [Op. 135] brought to light soon.' It will be recalled Beethoven wanted it to be made public that Louis XVIII had honoured him with a gold medal. Eager to oblige, Adolf requested an impression of the medal to be sent with a copy of the Emperor's citation; the publisher's intention was to make the requested announcement in the *Berliner Allgemeine Musikalische Zeitung* that had, in part, been founded by Adolf Schlesinger. His esteem for the composer can be judged from the style of his closing remarks: 'Gladden me soon with a letter about you and your works, my very worthy Herr von [sic] Beethoven and accept the assurance of my greatest respect.'[xxxi]

We have seen that Karl Holz was taking a close interest in the progress of the F major Quartet and raised the question with Beethoven why he had chosen the key of F major; Op. 135 was in fact Beethoven's third string quartet in this key.[xxxii] The composer's response is not on record. Barry Cooper offers the following explanation: 'Presumably Beethoven felt that the other two (Op. 18, No. 1 and Op. 59, No. 1) were so much earlier that they were no longer relevant; he would have been more concerned with the immediate neighbours of the quartet, and certainly each of the late quartets is in a different key from the others.' As Cooper further remarks, it was Beethoven's habit — more properly a feature of his creative process — when composing sets of works (typically three) in close proximity to choose different keys to maximise the contrast between them.[xxxiii]

Meanwhile, Beethoven's health was worsening. On 17 February 1827, he wrote to his childhood friend and physician Gerhard Wegeler. He informed him of his deteriorating condition and his anticipation of the need for a fourth abdominal operation to relieve dropsy: 'I must expect a fourth operation ... I cultivate patience and think — Well, sometimes some good comes from all this evil'.[xxxiv]

Turning to the progress of the F major Quartet, in our discussion of the creation origins of the C-sharp minor Quartet, we have seen that its dedicatee was to have been Beethoven's ardent admirer Johann Nepomuk Wolfmayer. The composer had a late change of mind in favour of the

Lieutenant Field-Marshall Baron von Stutterheim to whom he had become indebted when, as we have seen, he assisted in Karl's rehabilitation. Wolfmayer received the dedication of the F major Quartet instead. Anton Schindler explains how this came about. In March 1827, with Beethoven on his deathbed, he placed ever more reliance on those near to him to assist him with his business transactions. According to Schindler: 'It was ... on 18 March that Beethoven asked me to take care of the dedication of his last Quartet in F major, and he wanted to choose one of his worthy friends ... Since I knew how highly he regarded Johann Wolfmayer, and how much this man had done for him (he was one of the quietist and most helpful of the Master's patrons), I recommended this name to the publisher.'[xxxv]

The String Quartet in F major, Op. 135 was published posthumously in September 1827 — Beethoven having died on 26 March. Wolfmayer duly received his recognition as the work's dedicatee: 'Dix-septième / QUATOR / POUR / deux Violins, Alto et Violin-celle, / Composé, / et Dédié à son Ami / JEAN WOLFFMEYER / PAR / L. Van Beethoven. / Œuv. 134. Prix: 9f / Œuvre Posthume. / À PARIS, chez Maurice SCHLESINGER, Md. De Musique du ROI, Éditeur des Œuv. De Mozart, Hummel, Rossini, etc. /Rue de Richelieu, No. 97 / BERLIN, chez A. M. SCHLESINGER — LONDRES, chez CLEMENTI, COLLARD et COLLARD. / Propriété des Éditeurs.'[xxxvi] The Paris edition, bearing the incorrect opus number (see above) was announced on 22 August by Maurice Schlesinger in the *Bibliographie de la France*. This edition was created from the set of parts that, as we have seen, was sent to Maurice at the close of October 1825.[xxxvii] The Berlin edition of the Quartet appeared almost contemporaneously with its Paris counterpart.[xxxviii]

On 23 March 1828, Ignaz Schuppanzigh led the first

performance of the F major Quartet at what was described as 'A Beethoven Memorial Concert'. According to Schindler: 'The performance was a success, since the work offered no stylistic, harmonic, or technical peculiarities.'[xxxix] As we shall shortly see, others of his contemporaries were not so readily disposed to concur with this somewhat sanguine assessment.

One of the earliest evaluations of the F major Quartet came from the pen of the musicologist Adolf Bernhard Marx. He is recognised for his intellectually and musically informed reviews of Beethoven's most recent works and his wider appreciation of the composer as propounded in his *Ludwig van Beethoven: Leben und Schaffen*, Berlin, 1859. Marx published a review of the two Quartets Op. 132 and Op. 135 in the fifth volume [1828?] of the *Berliner Allgemeine Musikalische Zeitung* that he had co-founded in 1824. For Marx, these quartets represented a significant step in the progress of musical art. He confidently predicted that in the future they would present no more difficulties to the performer, just as Haydn's quartets had ceased to be difficult for Marx's contemporaries. Marx compared Beethoven's quartets to a painting by Rubens, 'in which one must first become acquainted with a mass of detail before proceeding to understand the sense of the whole'. In short, he urged patience on his readers in their own coming-to-terms with the composer's latest creations.[xl]

Sometime in 1829, Germany's distinguished musically minded, polymath man-of-letters Wolfgang Goethe had occasion to write to his friend the German composer and conductor Carl Friedrich Zelter. Goethe, although no modernist in his musical preferences, eagerly attended quartet evenings directed by the violinist Karl Möser at which Beethoven's quartets were performed, alongside those of Haydn and Mozart. In his letter to Zelter he remarked: 'Möser's quartet evenings ... are when it comes to instrumental music, the most comprehensible to me: one hears four rational people talk among themselves, one believes that one gains something from their discourse and becomes acquainted with the idiosyncrasies of their instruments ... [Möser] so electrifies his fellow players that the hearer also does not know what is happening to him. One believes that one is playing along; one understands the unfathomable, one is possessed — one does not know by what.'[xli] Years before, on meeting Beethoven at the spa town Teplitz, Goethe had written to Zelter expressing his impressions of the composer: 'His talent astounded me; but unfortunately he is a quite intractable person ... he does not make things enjoyable either for himself or for others.'[xlii]

In France, Beethoven's late string-quartet music struggled to gain acceptance. This can be inferred from a piece written in the *Revue musicale* of 27 June 1834 by the Belgian musicologist François-Joseph Fétis. He speaks of 'the caprice which mars the admirable qualities of Beethoven's last works ... In the two last quartets by this celebrated musician ... there is much to occasion surprise; it is difficult to imagine how so powerful an inspiration could be linked with so much sheer extravagance'.[xliii]

In England an edition of the F major Quartet was entered in the records at Stationers Hall in London on 11 October 1827 by Clementi and his Partners as their property. Muzio Clementi may be described as the polymath of music — composer, pianist, pedagogue, conductor, music publisher, editor, and piano manufacturer! He enjoyed a long association with Beethoven having made his acquaintance in 1807; at this time he secured the publishing rights to Beethoven's music in England. The Law of Copyright then required eleven copies of newly printed works to be deposited at Stationers' Hall, the London home of the

Worshipful Company of Stationers and Newspaper Makers – a Livery Company that regulated the affairs of the printing and publishing industry. On receipt of new works, the Company then passed these to the eleven libraries that were privileged to exercise their right of demand to receive new works – the equivalent of today's system of Legal Deposit. As Pamela Willets explains in her study of *Beethoven and England*: 'This is the principal source of the collections of the English Beethoven [first] editions preserved in the British Museum, the Bodlian Library at Oxford, [and] the University Library at Cambridge.[xliv] Clementi's edition is a direct copy of the French edition; his publishing house did not publish separate editions of Beethoven's works – as was common practice amongst English publishers of the period who had similar arrangements to Clementi with a Parisian firm. The principal concession made for English musicians was to replace the foreign title page with an English translation.[xlv]

It required some years for the late quartets to be performed in England. The principal proselytiser of new music was the journal *Music Weekly* that concerned itself with 'the present state of music' and was dedicated to publishing contemporary revues of music and musical activities. In its issue for 17 March 1837 it included an assessment of the F major Quartet. At this period it made reference in its writings to Beethoven's late quartets as 'oeuvre posthume'. The reviewer approached Beethoven's late compositions with caution. Of a performance of the Op. 135 Quartet he wrote: 'The principal feature in the bill was Beethoven's much-talked-of posthumous Quartet [Op. 135]. With all its many phrases and passages of distinguished beauty, we must honestly confess, that hitherto we have not been able to perceive any distinctness or continuity of design in this singular composition. The fault probably lies with ourselves, and most willingly we prefer it should be so, than that a great man should underwrite himself ... As a whole it is ultra-Beethoven, and assuredly we presume not to decide upon it after so slight an acquaintance.'[xlvi]

Richard Wagner's Beethoven Centennial essay of 1870 did much to influence the positive reception of the composer's late style. Commenting on this, Kinderman remarks: 'Beethoven's deafness, which was previously regarded as the handicap that explained the eccentricities of these works, was seen by Wagner as an enabling factor that had shielded Beethoven from the turmoil of the outer world and enhanced his ability to dwell in the inner-world of the imagination. For Wagner, Beethoven was a deaf "seer" who led the way to new artistic perspectives.'[xlvii]

We direct our attention now to the compositional origins of the F major String Quartet as they are revealed in Beethoven's surviving sketch sources. In our previous discussions of the companion late string quartets, we have made reference in some detail to the sketch sources Beethoven used at this period. We confine the following remarks, therefore, to a summary outline of these sources insofar as they bear on Op. 135

As in the case of the String Quartets Opp. 127, 132, 130, and 131, Beethoven set out his musical thoughts in the form of miscellaneous sketch leaves, desk sketchbooks and score sketches. We have seen that Beethoven worked on the F major Quartet through the latter part of 1826. Despite his many illnesses and other tribulations he appears to have worked quickly. This may be explained, in part, as a consequence of the small scale of the composition — relative to its predecessors — but also, and not least, because of Beethoven's, by now, supreme command of the genre.

From the autumn of 1825 until November 1826, Beethoven used a compilation of sketch leaves — today numbering 62 — that were purchased by Domenico Artaria at the *Nachlass* auction of the composer's effects in November 1827. Later they came into the possession of the composer Franz Kullak who subsequently gave them, in sketchbook form, to the Berlin Royal Library — Berlin Staatsbibliothek Preussischer Kulturbesitz. The first part this sketchbook contains ideas for Op. 130, Op. 131 and the *Grosse Fuge*. In the latter part, all movements of the F major Quartet are represented at folios 47v—48r, 49r—51r, and 52r—58r. From late June-July of 1826, Beethoven used a compilation of sketch leaves known as Artaria 205 Bundle 3. Today, 18 leaves are known that are believed to have formed part of a once larger gathering. The fist part of the sketchbook is devoted to Op. 131 but the second part reveals Beethoven turning his mind to ideas for Op. 135: first movement (p. 19, pp. 29—30), second movement (p. 16, p. 28, pp. 30—40), third movement (p. 29, p. 32, p. 350). A collection of 29 and two further leaves comprise a set of pocket bifolia (double format sheets) known as MS 62 and MS 66 in the nomenclature of the Bibliothèque National, Paris where that are now preserved. Sketches for movements two, three and four of Op. 135 are distributed through these pages.[xlviii]

Worthy of reiteration is that in his work on the Quartets Opp. 127, 132, 130, 131 and 135, Beethoven introduced an innovation into his sketching procedures. He made use of manuscript paper ruled in the form of quartet-score sheets. These enabled him to set down more extended compositional drafts encompassing all four instruments — doubtless prompted, in part, by the challenges posed by the growing contrapuntal complexity of the music evolving in his mind. As Cooper remarks, the composer's 'limitless aspirations' required a new method of composing: '[He] began making frequent use of sketching in open score on four staves, instead of merely on one or two as before.' This was to assist with what Beethoven himself described as 'a new kind of part writing'. Cooper adds: 'The score sketches did not supplant other types of sketching, but ran in parallel with them.' Since Op. 135 is laid out on a much smaller scale than its immediate predecessor Op. 131, there are fewer score sketches. Some 69 leaves are preserved today in the Staatsbibliothek Preussischer Kulturbesitz, Berlin.[xlix]

The first of the four movements of the F major Quartet is an *Allegretto*; this was an innovation for Beethoven who had more typically opened his string quartets with an *Allegro*. Nicolas Slonimsky considers: 'This departure from rule indicates the lighter nature of the Quartet as a whole.'[l] 'This is the most modestly proportioned among Beethoven's late string quartets, and one whose opening movement, in particular, seems imbued with the spirit of Haydn.'[li] In musicologist David Jones estimation: 'The thematic material of the first movement is quite eccentric: the merest suggestion of a motif for the first subject and a second subject that could be taken from a *quatuor concertante* by any number of composers from the 1780s and 1790s.'[lii] 'What astounds us is not only the extreme simplicity of tone but how soon it is over.'[liii] The *Allegro* has a typical performing time of a little over six minutes. Paul Griffiths asks: 'Is Beethoven trying to be earnest but not quite serious?[liv] The uncertainty lies in the nature of the opening statements.

As just intimated, the opening sounds suggestive of Haydn are heard in the manner of the music's 'off-balance, harmonically ambiguous gesture'.[lv] Joseph de Marliave describes this as 'the little sprightly *motif* which underlays the movement that Beethoven develops 'with extraordinary fullness of inventive power' and in the course of which 'the various thematic elements are combined with striking ingenuity'. Whilst the initial design might have come from the pen of Haydn, he acknowledges, 'the voice of Beethoven is distinctly heard'.[lvi] Perhaps de Marliave had in mind the manner in which, after the opening light-hearted statement, the four instruments 'switch to a solemn, even austere passage of unharmonised octaves'.[lvii]

Robert Simpson calls to mind the sense of ambiguity, to which we have made reference, in his telling observation: 'There is much quiet humour in [the first movement] as well as the mystery of all perfect things.' (Shades of Edgar Allen Poe's line: 'There is no beauty without some strangeness.'). Lam finds Beethoven drawing on what he had learnt from his previous quartet writing. He cites such passages as Variation II in the second movement of Op. 127, the *Andante* of Op. 130, and the *Neue Kraft fühlend* section of the *Heiliger Dankgesang* of Op. 132. Simpson looks back further still: 'Even so far back as the coda of the *Andante cantabile* of Op. 18, No. 5, we can find the beginnings of this particular genius, a delicately ambling style, light and airy, never mincing, the parts very free and strong and fine, with a great variety of detail, and deep subtlety of harmony.' He is in no doubt: 'It is the most sensitively coloured quartet-writing in existence.'[lviii]

In our discussion of Beethoven's Op. 18 set of string quartets, we remarked how the interplay between the four instruments have the manner of informed conversation; we recall Goethe's words to this effect in which he considered the string quartet sounded to him 'like four rational people talking among themselves'. To some ears the *Allegretto* is imbued with this spirit: 'The opening at once suggests an atmosphere of quiet and sophisticated conversation.'[lix] 'This gently conversational first movement — *Allegretto* — is an enchanting mixture of the plain and the curious.'[lx] The movement has a 'light interplay' between the parts.[lxi] There is evidence of 'urbane wit'.[lxii] There is 'a light teasing intimacy which makes it very responsive to players'.[lxiii] There is a 'questioning character'.[lxiv] These are musical characteristics that Haydn would have recognised and, indeed, frequently employed in his own writing for the string quartet. In this respect, Kerman describes Op. 135 as being imbued with a 'self-conscious classicism' that centres around 'a quite explicit *homage* to Haydn' with perhaps a 'symmetrical-architectural' shape that adheres to a Mozartian ideal. Notwithstanding, Kerman has cause to reflect. He asks: 'Why does the movement seem, in its way, to be tranquil? ... All sense of conflict seems to have been eliminated.' He proposes not too close a parallel should be made with Haydn: 'Here the technique is quintessentially classical, and in so many places reminiscent of Haydn ... But the spirit of Haydn is so different; lacking is Haydn's ceaseless enthusiasm, that down-to-earthness ... For Beethoven, wit is an urbane stylistic reflex, not really a sense of fun, as for Haydn ... The whole vision is too abstracted — or abstract — to count as humorous.' He concludes: 'Certainly the first movement of the Quartet in F is not straining at the frontiers opened up by the *Great Fugue* and the Quartet in C-sharp minor.'[lxv] Martin Cooper detects traces of Haydn's influence in the *Allegretto's* 'humour and deliberate unexpectedness' and, alongside Kerman, finds characteristics of Mozart 'in its formal symmetry and freedom from all those mercurial changes of mood and direction that have marked the quartets since Op. 127'. Cooper suggests Beethoven's return to the spirit of his own past and to his own former models 'is so clear that we feel it must have been conscious and deliberate'. In so doing, however, he maintains '[Beethoven] no more ceases to be Beethoven than Stravinsky ceased to be Stravinsky when he wrote *Pulcinella*'.[lxvi]

Despite the compressed format of the *Allegretto* it is rich in Beethovenian invention; a sequence of motifs appear in rapid succession. We have 'a terse example of Beethoven's technique of thematic generation ... the basic material of the Quartet germinates as we listen'.[lxvii] 'This first movement is an example of pure *quartet* technique, in the fluent polyphonic style proper to the genre, and obviously written at one effortless stroke.'[lxviii] Perhaps Joseph de Marliave, whom we have just quoted, was being a little too generous here since the sketches for the movement suggest, as almost always with Beethoven, that he arrived at apparent simplicity only after much compositional striving.

In his formal analysis of the music, Harold Truscott accepts the *Allegretto* may be 'very simple' but behind this is 'innate complexity'. He suggests the multiplicity of themes, and their relation to each other, reveal more thematic material than is to be found in any other sonata movement in the late quartets — 'and it is still the shortest'. He elaborates: '[So] far in 27 bars we have had no less than eight significant themes, varied in size but all equally important.' Concerning the construction of the movement as it evolves he adds, with characteristic eloquence and insight: 'The development proper, beginning at bar 62, is the kernel into which nearly all of these themes fit like an embryo in its mother's womb. Thrown out so casually — the casualness of great artistic care — they fit and combine together in combinations which, although we know nothing like all the possibilities are actually used, suggest the infinity that is really alive in them.'[lxix] Philip Radcliffe also maintains supressed thematic material is inherent in the *Allegretto*. He suggests the 'reticent quality' of the movement arises from the manner in which Beethoven 'rigorously controls the material and never allows it to expand'.[lxx]

To quote Truscott once more: 'This movement is light, with no pretentions, bare and yet full in its sound. It exposes the quartet medium in its stark skeletal and fully clothes it at the same time; and yet it is compact with meaning in which no single note is superfluous or too few, and in its comic grasp it sounds the depths as not even the greatest tragedy could.'[lxxi]

The second movement accelerates the tempo. Beethoven designates it *Vivace* and as such it functions as the Quartet's scherzo, although Beethoven does not describe it as such. In his suggestion of the hidden depths that Lam considers lay at the heart of the second movement, he invokes word-imagery to suit: 'If [the] wonderful *Allegretto* reconciles stylistic opposites with the equanimity attributed to Chinese philosophers, the *Vivace* feigns a confusing of hawks and hacksaws and is perhaps the most disquieting movement in the quartets, not because its humour is *black*, but rather on account of a suspicion that we who hear it are the object of its mockery.'[lxxii] Others are content to discuss the *Vivace* in similar but les less metaphorical terms. Cooper suggests: 'Whereas the first movement is an extension of the witty chamber music addressed to an audience of connoisseurs, the second belongs to Beethoven's stylized out-of-door scenes, like the corresponding movement in the Sixth Symphony.'[lxxiii]

The reader will recall Beethoven prefaces his Sixth Symphony, *The Pastoral,* with the words, 'Awakening of cheerful feelings upon arrival in the country' and later in the music suggests an encounter 'with country-folk merrymaking'. Kerman describes the manner in which the violin in the second movement of the F major Quartet, playing in the low cello register, creates 'well-calculated grinding clashes'. He describes these as 'Beethoven's last rustic parody' and 'his last broad joke at the expense of the counterpoint books'. Perhaps, as he further intimates, the *Vivace* is 'heir to the raucous trios' of the E-minor *Razumovsky* Quartet and of the String Quartet Op. 74. He adds: 'The piece is as swift and quirky as a bagatelle, a fact [though] that should not obscure its very ominous undertones.' With regard to Beethoven's construction, he considers the working-out of the second movement 'stands in the main stream of technical, stylistic, and expressive exploration' as exemplified by the late quartet as group.[lxxiv]

Cooper, with further allusions to country-folk merry-making, likens the sounds of the two lower instruments to the execution of 'a hobbledehoy dance' to rhythms provided by the upper two instruments in their 'different cross accents'. In the spirit of art concealing art he maintains: 'All the elements are simple to the point of banality, their amalgamation subtle to the point of sophistication.'[lxxv] In more musicological terms: 'The movement opens in canon so that the two violins and the viola enter on different beats, while the cello plays an independent melody staccato.'[lxxvi] For some the second movement *Vivace-scherzo* is 'Beethoven's middle-period rhetoric restated in epigrams' in which 'its tonal shocks are rarefied in the tenuous texture'.[lxxvii]

'The melody in the first violin is simplicity itself, just a shuttling back of forth along the first three notes of the F-major scale — F, G and A ... [whilst] the second violin's syncopations add breathless excitement.'[lxxviii] As Radcliffe remarks, the key sequence F, G, and A was unusual for the period and for him it imparts 'an atmosphere of nightmarish obsession'. Of related interest is that he finds a parallel expression of feeling here similar to that produced by Elgar in the third movement of his second symphony and passages in Vaughn Williams' 'Triumph of Satan' in *Job*.[lxxix] De Marliave makes reference to the manner in which 'the original *piano* becomes a *pianissimo*, increasing the ethereal remoteness of effect'.[lxxx]

Radcliffe considers the *Vivace* has all the energy of the *Presto* of the C-sharp minor Quartet 'but with a decidedly sardonic undercurrent'. After the 'innocent main theme' has run its course he equates the persistently reiterated E flat to 'an extraneous intrusion'.[lxxxi] In what Rebecca Clarke describes as Beethoven's 'typical love of horseplay', in the middle section of the movement the three lower instruments are required to play the same bar approaching some fifty times while the first violin improvises a dance-like theme above. Notwithstanding the humour, she considers this sustained passage 'gives a richness and sonority almost like that of an organ'.[lxxxii] In her take on the passage in question, Marion Scott delights in saying how the passage is 'unplayable for the first violin, but immensely playable'. It disposed her to quote from Houseman's *A Shropshire Lad*: 'The tree of man was never quiet', words she considered 'fit this strange scherzo'.[lxxxiii] The music critic Adolf Bernhard Marx was initially confused by Beethoven's musical eccentricity. Writing of the composition in the *Berliner Allgemeine Musikalische Zeitung,* he remarked how easy it was to regard the repeated bars as being 'sheer nonsense' but maintained: 'Beethoven is based on a fundamental idea, which when understood can clarify the meaning of the most obscure passages.'[lxxxiv]

Although many of Beethoven's early critics perceived his wayward humour as deriving from his deafness, or being attributable even to mental decline, as Nicolas Slonimsky asserts 'it is quite in keeping with the spirit of the whole scherzo'.[lxxxv] Cooper, though, expresses words of caution insofar as he considers the music's many repetitions of a single phrase reveal what he describes as 'Beethoven's natural tendency to excess'. He explains: 'He had, as we know, in life as in his art, moments of regardlessness when he felt an inferior prompting to break every barrier, to let himself run completely wild. This trio is one of these moments.'[lxxxvi]

Marx, whom we have already quoted, gave further expression to his uncertainty asking: 'Is the musical picture here obscured within the spirit by the throbbing auditory nerves of a sick man (this would be an extraordinary case of the influence of the physical state upon the imaginative in Beethoven's work), or is it merely meant to impress upon the mind some persistent idea?' De Marliave comes to the composer's defence: 'It seems that the second suggestion may be the true explanation of the passage, if one is to understand here the subjective working-out of a stubborn persistence, with a veritable force.' He elaborates with invocations of a celebrated contemporary poet: 'The musical scene presented in this trio [is] rather after the manner of Heine — the marching of thousands of troops, with lances and shields, and colours flying in the wind.'[lxxxvii] The musicologist Walter Riezler found passages of the *Vivace* to be even more extreme in their fury than episodes in the *Grosse Fuge*. Notwithstanding he avers: 'Even when Beethoven seems to have lost all self-control, and to have worked himself up into a wild frenzy, he sees the world with eyes that are as clear as ever. But he is not afraid to draw aside the curtain that veils the abyss. He knows no fear of chaos, out of which matter is made form, because he is aware of his power to give form to all that his eyes have seen.'[lxxxviii]

Beethoven heads the third movement *Lento assai e cantante tranquillo* — to be played very slowly and in a calm, singing manner. This is the Quartet's slow movement and consists of a prefatory opening theme followed by a set of variations. It would be the last time Beethoven turned to the variation form that inhabits so much of his late music.

It is thought Beethoven may have originally conceived the theme to from the basis for an additional movement to the C-sharp minor Quartet, leaving the F major with only three movements. The reader will recall that Karl Holz had remarked to Maurice Schlesinger: 'You will not punish him [Beethoven] if it is short. Even if it should have only three movements.' However, as Bekker remarks, as Beethoven worked on the F major Quartet, with its alternate moods of pensiveness and gaiety, he realised 'a supplement or contrast of deeper emotion' was required. From this the D-flat major *lento* had its origins so as to create a movement, once more in Bekker's words, 'organically sound'.[lxxxix] Barry Cooper provides the following summation: 'The third movement, in D flat, was probably written particularly fast. Not only is it quite short — a mere fifty bars with relatively simple figuration — but its theme had been composed earlier, since it was originally planned as the extra eighth movement of Op. 131. Its middle section is in C-sharp minor, providing dark hints of the preceding quartet but otherwise the movement fulfils its previous designation as 'a sweet song of rest'.'[xc]

Having begun by building the tonic chord of the *Lento* from the closing notes of the *Vivace*, the various instruments establish the chord of D-flat major, sounding 'rich, soft and mellow'.[xci] 'A sublime melody moves like a spoken prayer above the harmonic base ... Mournful phrases, long drawn out, and harsh harmonic leaps give the theme an air of angularity; it settles down into a phase of calm repose and culminates in an episode of C-sharp minor ... The episodic theme has a tentative air, punctuated as it were by intermittent patches of light ... The prevailing mood of distress seems to linger ... chromatic harmonies maintain the melancholy tinge of C-sharp minor.' De Marliave, whose words we have quoted, further describes the music as having a 'mezzo tint' with effects that are 'a miracle of delicate subtlety'. He also suggests 'a sense of mysterious suspense' is felt in the manner in which the long opening notes are held in the tonic key.[xcii]

Others join with de Marliave in their admiration for this movement and express their feelings in no less a fulsome manner. Shepherd perceives the slow movement of the F major Quartet as 'directing us for the last time to that phase of the master's art which bears witness of his inner emotions'. For him: 'It is the final personal confession and prayer-like utterance in his long and unparalleled list of slow instrumental movements.' He concludes: 'Simplicity, directness and fervent emotion speak in every measure.'[xciii] Stravinsky concurred, but with more restraint: '[The] *Lento* is a meditation that crowns Beethoven's great series of flat-key movements.'[xciv] For Bekker: 'This movement is devout and religious in tone and reflects the mythic faith of the composer, a vision from which he can scarce turn his eyes to the things of earth.'[xcv] Others discern the *Lento* as 'a cross between aria and variation ... Melody dissolves into figuration'.[xcvi] Perhaps it is not surprising that the composer's admirers should express their thoughts in this way. Beethoven's sketchbook bears the following words in relation to the *Lento*, 'song of repose of peace'.[xcvii] The source in question was the Kullak sketchbook to which we have made reference. In this, Beethoven headed the *Lento* sketches with the words 'Süsser. Ruhegesang oder Friedensgesang'. As the instruments enter one by one, for Marian Scott the effect is 'among the loveliest ever composed ... as if out of the void a presence wavers together and stands there'. For her: 'Here is the supreme rest such as Brünnhilde invokes in her farewell to the dead hero in *Götterdämmmerung*. "Ruhe, ruhe, du Gott".'[xcviii]

Denis Mathews finds in the 'profound calm' of the slow movement, the 'subjective emotions' that many listeners detect in the *Cavatina* of the String Quartet, Op. 130. Recalling Beethoven's words, these feelings are here 'sublimated into the "song of rest and peace". Concerning the movement as a whole, relating to its theme and variations structure, he makes a comparison with the sets of variations in the Op. 127 and Op. 131 Quartets. Here, however, in the Op. 135 he finds 'the textures are sparer and simpler' consistent with Beethoven's *semplice* direction to performers.[xcix] Regarding Beethoven's workmanship, Radcliffe finds Beethoven being both economical and drawing, perhaps, upon the experience gained when composing one of his most dramatic piano sonatas. 'The theme is only ten bars long and is magnificently planned. The opening phrases move entirely by step, after which the compass is gradually extended by arpeggio-like phrases and culminates in a widely sweeping curve. The dark, rich colouring looks back to the central movement of the *Appassionata* Sonata and is often associated with the key of D minor.'[c] Lam describes the *Lento* as 'a concentrated meditation on and around the admirably plain melody' and, as with others we have just cited, regards it as 'a perfect example of the type to which the *Cavatina* of Op. 130 belongs' and, perhaps, 'the *Adagio* of the Violin Sonata, Op. 96'.[ci] Radcliffe, similarly, finds parallels in the *Lento's* 'solemn richness' with other of Beethoven's works. He finds in it the same 'serenity and profundity' as in the *Arietta* of the Piano Sonata in C minor, Op. 111. It may not necessarily be greater, he acknowledges, but 'it is certainly terser and more economical'.[cii] Could the second subject of the slow movement of Brahms's Fourth Symphony, perhaps, have an affinity with the theme of Beethoven's *Lento*?[ciii]

Cooper, alongside those we have mentioned, regards the *Lento* as the last of Beethoven's great variation movements and 'the simplest'. In formal musicological terms he describes the movement as 'a combination of song (A B A) and variations' that are as unified in their 'rapt lyricism' as any slow movement Beethoven ever wrote.[civ] Concerning

Beethoven's scoring, the writing for the first violin, designated *sotto voce* in its enunciation of the opening melody, has been described as 'Beethoven's most hymnal voice'. The author's of these words also remark: 'The scoring with the cello's double stops and the low-register musings of the second violin and viola are glorious.' They remind us that the acclaimed conductor Arturo Toscanini was a cellist at the outset of his career and – contrary to musical ethics – was occasionally tempted to perform the *Lento* with full orchestra. The effect of this, in the estimation of our sources, was 'effective in that form'.[cv] Joseph Kerman supports this contention. He writes: 'For a certain generation of musicians and listeners, this movement will stir memories of Arturo Toscanini, who used to perform and broadcast it at the beginning of orchestral concerts along with the second movement of Op. 135.' For Kerman the impression was 'unforgettable'. He acknowledges that from the purists' point of view Toscanini's action 'may have falsified Beethoven's texture' but for him 'the idea of magnifying the song in such a way ... corresponds to something very deep in Beethoven's conception.'[cvi]

The *Lento* has been described as 'a piece almost too simple to be misunderstood and too deep ever to be exhausted'.[cvii] Notwithstanding, its admirers find it as original in its way as the preceding *scherzo*: 'One really must not treat the Quartet in F as though in its way it shirked the stylistic and expressive adventure of the last quartets.' Joseph Kerman, whom we are quoting, expatiates: 'In the *Lento assai* of the Quartet in F, Beethoven seems to touch a true note of sublimity missing from the other hymn-like slow movements of the last years.' Even the hymn-like variations of Op. 127 and Op. 131 he suggests emanate 'a slightly sententious tone'. For him they recall the earnest religious maxims that Beethoven was disposed to jot down beside his manuscript sketches. In the slow movement of Op. 135, however, he asserts 'there is no suspicion of straining for solemnity, as in the *Cavatina* of Op. 130, or straining for asceticism, as in the *Heiliger Dankgesang* of Op. 132.' He concludes: 'The piece is neither operatic nor churchy, nor excessively humble either; it may look plain, but sonority is so calculated that the term *sobriety* hardly seems to do justice to the fullness of the effect.'[cviii]

In his summation of the music, Kerman invokes the views of the Austrian music critic and writer Theodor Helm: 'Never in his wanderings through the gulfs and labyrinths of the human soul had Beethoven sung anything more noble and so inward than this [*Lento assai e cantante Tranquillo*] of his last quartet — outwardly so small ... but inwardly so deeply significant.'[cix]

In his estimation of the variations that feature in Beethoven's late quartets, Radcliffe finds the dissimilarities between them to be nothing less than remarkable. In his words: The *Heiliger Dankgesang* from Op. 132, with its alternating Lydian and major tonalities, is perhaps the most original ... The *Andante* of Op. 131 the most complex and the most varied in mood and texture ... The *Adagio* of Op. 127 achieves the most perfect balance between the claims of variety and unity.' As for the slow movement of Op. 135, 'with its short and sublimely simple theme, [it] is concerned above all with concentration and continuity'.[cx] Radcliffe's latter remark is worthy of amplification. Although the third movement is musicologically a theme and variations, Beethoven intended it to have the effect upon the listener as a continuous, unbroken texture — like an unfolding length of fine fabric. As Lam remarks: 'It is now customary to describe this *song of repose of peace*, as Beethoven called it, in terms of a normal theme-and-variations structure, but such is not the effect on the hearer who listens to what the music tells him. It would be more useful to observe that Beethoven uses a *hidden* [italics added] variations element to give unity to a continually expanding *Gesang* [song].'[cxi]

Variation 1 emanates from the initial thematic statement at the thirteenth measure. '[It] is hardly more than a continuation of the melody, given a note of greater animation by the close-lying harmony in the higher register of the instruments and by the chromatic alterations ... It is as though the dream had shifted from darkness into light.'[cxii] Its higher register heightens the emotional intensity with 'chromatic touches of great beauty'.[cxiii] Variation 2 is marked *più lento* — to be played more slowly and slightly freer. Vincent d'Indy, in his *Beethoven: A critical biography*, was reluctant to consider this passage as a separate variation and saw it as being more like an 'episode'. Beethoven's additional designation *beklemmt* — oppressed — may account for the profoundly sombre mood that is expressed in broken phrases: 'Now the music moves in jerks ... all extraneous material has been removed from the frame's skeleton.'[cxiv] Stravinsky likened the music here to a dirge.[cxv] In variation 3, Beethoven returns to *tempo primo* and imparts to the music a canonic treatment that Kerman describes as 'trance-like'.[cxvi] The cello is given a prominent role whilst the other instruments provide an accompaniment. The atmosphere grows in intensity until the second violin and the viola prepare the way for the final variation. Variation 4 'does not seek extraordinary frontiers for its theme; it looks steadily in on the theme and seeks its pure essence'. In Kerman's imagery: 'Instead of unity in variety, the effect is simply of unity — the unity of a circle, not that of a crystal, a leaf, or a cathedral.' We recall Beethoven's instructions *cantante Tranquillo* as the violin sings 'exquisite arabesques'.[cxvii] The cello provides its peaceful accompaniment. The music is charged with pathos that disposed Stravinsky to sense 'the prescience of death'.[cxviii] The movement comes to an end: '[It] would be hard to imagine a more perfect conclusion, or truer realisation of the phrase *Süsser Ruhegesang oder Friedensgesang* — a sweet song of calm or peace.'[cxix]

The fourth and final movement of the F major Quartet is headed with the enigmatic words *Der schwer gefasste Entschluss. Grave (Muss es sein?) — Allegro (Es muss sein!) — Grave, ma non troppo tratto — Allegro*. Beethoven's adoption of his native language is of interest here. This may be seen, in part, in response to his frequently expressed desire to supplant Italian in favour of German. As long ago as 1817, he had written to his publisher Sigmund Anton Steiner: '[We] are resolved and hereby resolve that from henceforth on all our works, on which the title is German, instead of pianoforte *Hammerklavier* shall be used.'[cxx] His resolve was never fully realised though and only the majestic Piano Sonata, Op. 106 has retained his desired close identity with the German language. That said, in the Piano Sonata Op. 111 Beethoven used the expression *Langsam und sehnsuchtsvoll* — 'Slow and full of yearning'.[cxxi] Additionally, we have seen in the C-sharp minor Quartet, Beethoven headed the third movement *Heiliger Dankgesang eines Genesenden an die Gottheit, in der lydischen Tonart. Molto adagio* — 'Hymn of thanks in the Lydian mode offered to the Deity by a convalescent'. Thereby, Beethoven sought to provide performers with an emotional framework in order to encourage them to give the music its fullest expression. John Crabbe draws attention to this aspect of the composer's adoption of German in his intellectually inclined *Beethoven's empire of the mind*. He makes the following observation: 'Although the literary and emotional influences which helped to mould his instrumental art always found expression in purely musical terms, it is clear from the many elaborations of traditional instructions and titles in his scores that Beethoven wished to convey degrees of meaning which transcend the mechanics of performance ... [When] he could no longer trust his Italian he broke with tradition and employed German.'[cxxii]

Beethoven's words may be translated, 'The hard-won decision — Must it be? — It must be!' We consider how they came about and their musicological significance.

Beethoven's correspondence provides a suitable starting point. On 10 October 1824, he had occasion to write from Baden to the composer and publisher Tobias Haslinger. He urgently required a copy of the score of his Vocal Trio Op. 116 for chorus and orchestra, *Tremate empi tremate* — his own copy was in Vienna. The Trio was to be performed for a Court Festival in Vienna's Redoutensaal. He urged Haslinger to make haste with the expression *Es muss sein* — 'It must be done'. This was one of the composer's favourite exhortations on such occasions and, as we have seen, he adopted it in the heading to the fourth movement of the F major Quartet.[cxxiii] We have also seen that in late October 1826, Beethoven had written to his publisher Maurice Schlesinger remarking on the challenges he was confronting in bringing the composition to completion. 'Here my dear friend is my last quartet. It will be the last; and indeed it has given me much trouble. For I could not bring myself to compose the last movement. But as your letters were reminding me of it, in the end I decided to compose it. And that is the reason why I have written the motto: *The decision taken with difficulty — Must it be? — It must be, It must be!* [Beethoven's italics].[cxxiv] Slonimsky's offers an interpretation of Beethoven's adoption of these words. He suggests that whilst he was thinking about the possibilities of the themes he was going to use in the final movement, he fitted 'the question and answer' to them. This was, he further suggests, in essence 'a ponderous joke' of the kind to which Beethoven was prone.[cxxv] Shepherd expresses similar thoughts: 'It will profit [the Beethovenian] most to view the matter in the light of analogous manifestations in numerous other works showing the capricious and sometimes ironical oscillation between the grave and the gay or humorous.' With the final movement in mind, he elaborates: 'The introduction *Grave, ma non troppo*, is concerned wholly with repeated emphasis of the questioning motif, the answer to which *Es muss sein* forms the principal thematic element for the exposition in sonata-rondo design.'[cxxvi]

In his Biography of the composer, Anton Schindler offers an intriguing explanation for the origin of Beethoven's wordplay. He recalls how, at the period of composition the Op. 135 Quartet, his housekeeper 'Old Frau Schnapps' would wait patiently on Saturdays with her basket prompting Beethoven for the weekly payment. Schindler alleges, Beethoven's typical response was to sing in tones — 'Must if Be?'[cxxvii]

A variation on the foregoing anecdote derives from Beethoven's association at this time with the violinist Karl Holz; Holz was then assisting Beethoven as his secretarial assistant — having displaced Anton Schindler in that capacity who was temporarily out of favour. Beethoven wrote to Holz in the summer of 1826 when, as we have seen, he was at work on the F major Quartet. He requested of Holz: 'Wood — bring me some wood!' — a characteristic Beethovenian play on words — Holz, in German, meaning wood. More significantly, for our narrative, he exhorted Holz: 'Must it be? It must be!'[cxxviii]

A further anecdote that bears upon Beethoven's heading to the fourth movement concerns the music lover Ignaz Anton Aloys Dembscher. He was a Government official and ardent music lover. Having inherited a fortune he had the means to support music-making usually under the direction of the violinist Joseph Mayseder, with Dembscher himself playing the cello. From Thayer we learn 'there was a good deal of talk' at the start of 1826 concerning the performance of Beethoven's new string quartets. Ignaz Schuppanzigh's Quartet was then participating in the evening *Concerts spirituels* and in the string-quartet concerts then taking place in Dembscher's home. When Dembscher heard of the completion of the Quartet in E-flat major, Op. 127, he asked Beethoven for the honour of having it played for the first time in his house. Beethoven consented but on condition. He requested Dembscher should pay Schuppanzigh fifty florins for any loss that he (Schuppanzigh) might sustain at his forthcoming benefit concert — where the E-flat major Quartet was to be the main attraction. Allegedly, Dembscher sighed and said, 'Must it be?' On Holz relaying this to Beethoven, he responded: 'It must be!'[cxxix]

Beethoven's exchange with Dembscher had musical consequences. It stirred him to compose the Cannon WoO 196, 'Es muss sein — ja ja ja ja! Heraus mit dem Beutel!' — 'It must be! — yes yes yes yes! Out with your purse! The theme of this Canon, completed in July 1826, served Beethoven in the composition of the final movement of Op. 135. As Cooper remarks: 'Half-humorous, half-philosophical, it provided an ideal conclusion for a witty but profound quartet.[cxxx] In de Marliave's words: 'After relieving his boredom by musical caprice [WoO 196], he at once saw the use to which these themes could be put, and built upon them a movement of striking vigour and rhythmic force.'[cxxxi] The theme in the Quartet differs from that in the Canon, with general agreement that it improves upon it.[cxxxii]

Reflecting on the anecdotes relating to the words 'Muss es sein? — Es muss sein!' Bekker concludes, true of false, 'they do not affect the spiritual verities here revealed'. In his estimation the contrast between the two moods, as expressed in the music, are inherently psychological — 'the conflict between visionary quietism and disciplined activity'. He maintains: 'In the finale Beethoven asks a question of life and, as answer, proclaims the gospel of the Dead.'[cxxxiii] Scott's consideration of the words, and the music they presage, are consistent with Stravinsky's 'prescience of death'. She suggests Beethoven's prefatory words may be read as having 'an inner and darker meaning'. She asserts for Beethoven, by now a very sick man, 'the words came to have an ominous ring ... The finale is haunted again by the questioning, the recoil of that human heart from death ... In two passages of intense drama the phrase "Muss es sein?" approaches threateningly, and the answer is given like a pass-word "Es muss sein!" ... Yet at the end Beethoven deliberately brushes aside the manner and dissolves the answer into shadows. He goes to face the Unseen with gaiety.'[cxxxiv] Are there affinities, perhaps, in what she says with Keats' 'When I have fears that I may cease to be'? The distinguished physician-musicologist Anton Neumayr cautions though against relating the events in an artist's life to his psychological condition or creative activities.[cxxxv] Harold Truscott's words have particular resonance here: 'The only thing that concerns us is the music ... The music tells us all ... It tells us that in the introduction we have the only tragic note sounded in the entire work ... as the finale wings its way to a Paradise not unlike that of the children's Heaven in Mahler's Fourth Symphony.'[cxxxvi]

'The *Allegro* finale ... is halfway between sonata and fugue; and the texture grows increasingly rarefied until the theme has shed both sonata and operatic drama and becomes as simple as a folksong.' The authors of these words insist, however, that this is not 'a study of innocence', of the kind found in the *Pastoral* Symphony, but rather 'the innocence born of experience'. Beethoven, they assert, 'has gone back beyond sonata to opera; beyond opera to religious polyphony; beyond polyphony to song-melody ... beyond song to the source of melody in the undivided human consciousness'.[xxxvii] Scott finds the 'bare, spare lines' of the *Allegro* movement convey 'more the impression of a charcoal drawing than of colour'.[xxxviii]

Having described the character of the third movement as 'devout and religious', Bekker remarks on the transition of feeling to the fourth movement: 'From the world of quiet ecstasy [Beethoven] is called back to reality by the noise of battle.' For him, the words *Der schwer gefasste Entschluss* imply nothing less than 'determination made and held in the face of difficulty'.[xxxix] The introduction to the finale is a 12 bar passage that performers are requested to play *Grave, ma non troppo* – 'Seriously and slow, but not too drawn out'. *Muss es sein?* is presented by the cello and viola to which the violins offer their rejoinder – an 'impassioned commentary'. In more cheerful mood, the *Es muss sein!* figuration is heard. The melody here disposed Truscott to generalise: 'It is seldom that one finds Beethoven sounding definitely German; but this tune is like the essence of the lightest German fairy-tale.'[xl] Kerman discerns other and deeper procedures at work than the evocation of folk melody. He suggests the form of the opening may be regarded as an illustration of Beethoven's 'wordless recitative'. By way of illustration, he calls to mind the passage at the beginning of the finale to the Ninth Symphony where the cellos and bases recall themes heard in the previous movements. The implied meaning is then made evident when the baritone member of the vocal quartet proclaims: 'O friends, not these sounds; let us rather strike up something more seemly, more joyful'. In Kerman's estimation the finale to the F major Quartet exhibits all the rhetoric of a comparable 'solemn *recitativo accompagnato*'.[cxli]

Kerman's take on the music is not unrelentingly serious. He joins with Truscott in describing later passages of the music as 'a charming fairy march' that is scored and harmonized seductively: 'It really belongs in *A Midsummer Night's Dream*'.[cxlii] Stravinsky is more serious but no less discerning: 'The modulations are new and fresh ... but also abrupt some of them, as if the composer's restlessness had been translated to a dislike of being confined in any tonality for long.'[cxliii] With regard to the overall structure of his movements, in the piano sonatas and string quartets, Beethoven is usually categorical in his instructions to performers concerning which passages of the music are to be repeated. Here, however, in the closing *Allegro* he leaves this to the performers themselves: 'The second part to be repeated *if desired.*' [Italics added] David Wyn Jones offers an explanation. He suggests the more carefree, or apparently carefree, side of Beethoven's musical nature can be detected in the course of the movement – 'an inheritance from Haydn'. He elaborates: 'So certain is the composer of his craft that he allows the players to decide whether they want to repeat the development and recapitulation (*Se repete la seconda parte al suo piacere*)'. He further suggests 'the flippant pizzicato' has affinities with the finale of Haydn's String Quartet, Op. 76, No. 1.[cxliv] The playful pizzicato stays in *pianissimo* until a four-measure *fortissimo* 'brings this miracle of a quartet to its witty end'.[cxlv] 'Laughter, spontaneity, verve – these are the characteristics of this marvellous little *Allegro.*'[cxlvi] Alfred Einstein asks: 'Is Beethoven jesting or is he being earnest?' If the former, he posits: 'Cannot gaiety be sublime?'[cxlvii] Kinderman is in no doubt: 'Thus closes the F major Quartet, a fitting end to Beethoven's career and one of the finest examples of his humour in music.'[cxlviii] 'Finally ... all the instruments burst into a *fortissimo* unison for the four concluding bars of the Quartet. An almost humorous effect is created by the contrast between these last bars and the twenty-seven bars of *pianissimo* immediately before; it is as though Beethoven is laughing at himself and at his audience for taking this little motif seriously, and making such a mystery out of his whimsical *Muss es sein?* which was no enigma at all!'[cxlix]

'It seems to me that, in spite of the *accidental* nature of this "last opus" by the greatest suffering among composers, it forms a logical conclusion.'[d] 'If the first and last movements of Op. 135 do indeed represent a contraction of scope and a reduction of visionary power compared with the preceding quartets, they still retain potency of a different kind.'[cli] '[The] final movement could be regarded as providing a summing up not just of the quartet but of Beethoven's entire career, which had been replete with difficult decisions, both within his compositions and in everyday life.'[clii] 'To regard Op. 135's reversion to a Mozartian time-scale as somehow retrograde is a serious misapprehension. After the grandeur of its predecessor it may seem closer to the world of comedy than tragedy but it radiates a spiritual serenity and philosophy of acceptance that transcends both ... Beethoven in his last completed work summed up his life's struggles, his resignation and his ultimate philosophy and faith, in music of disarming lightness and simplicity.'[cliii]

As we take leave of the F major String Quartet, Op. 135, we do well to consider that although it was Beethoven's last major composition his mind was creatively and optimistically inclined to further compositions; the F major Quartet was by no means intended to be his last musical utterance. He had in hand in sketch form, and in some cases putative negotiations with publishers, ideas for the following compositions: A piano sonata for four hands — promised to the publisher Anton Diabelli and later published by him as a fragment titled *Beethoven's letzter musicalischer Gedanke* ('Beethoven's Last Musical Thought'). This was written in November 1826 at Gneixendorf when, as we have seen, Beethoven was staying at the house of his brother Johann. He had in mind a Tenth Symphony for the London Philharmonic Society for which substantial sketches survive; this was reconstructed, in part, by Barry Cooper in 1988. Beethoven had promised the Gesellschaft der Musikfreunde an Oratorio, *Bernard's Sieg des Kreuzes* ('Victory of the Cross'). He was seriously considering an Oratorio *Saul* to a text by Christoph Kuffner with choruses set in the old Hebrew modes; some authorities believe it was Kuffner who had provided the text to the composer's Choral Fantasy, Op. 80 from 1808. As already noted, Beethoven was contemplating setting Franz Grillparzer's *Melusine* libretto — an operatic project upon which he had meditated for a number of years. It was to have been in the romantic manner of Weber's *Der Freischütz* and *Euryanthe*. Plans were also in sketch form for an overture on the notes B-A-C-H. It is clear from the foregoing, to adapt Keats' words, that Beethoven's pen had much yet, beyond the F major Quartet, to 'glean his teaming brain'.

We draw our survey of the F major String Quartet, Op. 135 to a close by making reference to a selection of views that place Beethoven's achievement within the quartet genre itself.

> '[Beethoven'] quartets are my highest article of musical belief (which is a longer word for love, whatever else) as indispensable to the ways and meaning of art, as a musician of my era thinks of art, as temperature is to life. They are a triumph over temporality.'[cliv]

'The seventeen Beethoven string quartets are to chamber music what the plays of Shakespeare are to drama and what the self-portraits of Rembrandt are to portraiture.'[clv]

'Beethoven's quartets may not be summed up ... There is nothing else like them in the whole of music except in Beethoven's own work, and they reveal, like the sonatas and the symphonies, that of all composers he possessed the widest, deepest, most active and most realistically hopeful genius. It is a platitude to say that his range of expression is Shakespearean; so it is, but he has a commitment to humanity that Shakespeare does not reveal. There has been no greater artist; and it is to be doubted whether any can match him.'[clvi]

---

[i] Maynard Solomon, 1977, p. 283.

[ii] Nicholas Marston in: Barry Cooper, *The Beethoven compendium: a guide to Beethoven's life and music*, 1991, p. 235.

[iii] Paul Bekker, 1925, p. 336.

[iv] Arthur Shepherd, 1935, p. 79. Regarding the light-hearted mood of the F major Quartet, Shepherd adds: '[This is] all the more noteworthy in view of the distressing circumstances incident to its creation.'

[v] Martin Cooper, 1970, p. 404.

[vi] Winter Robert and Robert Martin editors, 1994, p. 273.

[vii] Basil Lam, 1975, p. 130.

[viii] Harold Truscott, 1968, p. 120.

[ix] Robert winter and Robert Martin editors, 1994, p. 273.

[x] Harold Truscott, 1968, pp. 120–21.

[xi] Arthur Shepherd, 1935, p. 76.

[xii] Marion Scott, 1940, p. 275.

[xiii] Anton Felix Schindler edited by Donald W. MacArdle and translated by Constance S. Jolly from the German edition of 1860, 1966, p. 242. See also Thayer-Forbes, 1967, pp. 923–6 and Emily Anderson, editor and translator, 1961, Vol. 3, Letter No. 1292, pp. 1127–29. The medal is now a prized possession of the Gesellschaft der Musikfreunde.

[xiv] The circumstance is recalled at length in: Elliot Forbes editor, *Thayer's life of Beethoven*, 1967, p. 828 and Gerhard von Breuning, *Memories of Beethoven: from the house of the black-robed Spaniards, 1874*, reprinted and edited by Maynard Solomon, 1992, p. 79 and endnotes 132 and 133.

xv Derived from, Oscar George Theodore Sonneck, *Beethoven: impressions of contemporaries*, 1927, pp. 176—91.

xvi Martin Cooper, 1970, p. 80.

xvii See Peter Clive, 2000 pp. 45—6 and Beethoven House, Digital Archives, Library Document, Sammlung H. C. Bodmer, HCB BBr 105.

xviii Peter Clive, 2000 pp. 187—8.

xix Tully Potter in: Robin Stowell editor, T*he Cambridge companion to the string quartet*, 2003, pp. 43—4.

xx Originally published as *Beethoven's Portrait* in *Allgemeine musikalische Anzeiger*, Frankfurt as quoted in: Wayne M. Senner, Robin Wallace and William Meredith editors, *The critical reception of Beethoven's compositions by his German contemporaries*, Lincoln: University of Nebraska Press, in association with the American Beethoven Society and the Ira F. Brilliant Center for Beethoven Studies, San José State University, 1999, Vol. 1, p. 90.

xxi Emily Anderson, 1961, Vol. 3, Letter No. 1535, pp. 1314—5.

xxii Quoted form Ludwig Nohl, *Beethoven depicted by his contemporaries*, 1880, pp. 313—22.

xxiii Theodore Albrecht, translator and editor, 1996, Vol. 3, Letter No. 430, pp. 135—6. As so typical of other putative opera projects, nothing came of the venture.

xxiv Emily Anderson, editor and translator, 1961, Vol. 3, Letter No. 1481, pp. 1283—4. Moritz's letter, thought to be of 13 September 1826, is now lost.

xxv William Kinderman, 1997, pp. 282—3.

xxvi Elliot Forbes editor, *Thayer's life of Beethoven*, 1967, p. 1009 and footnote 44.

xxvii Theodore Albrecht, translator and editor, 1996, Vol. 3, Letter No. 439, pp. 144—5 and note 4.

xxviii Emily Anderson, 1961, Vol. 3, Letter No. 1537, pp. 1317—8.

xxix *Ibid*, Letter No. 1538, p. 1318. For a facsimile reproduction of this letter see: Beethoven House, Digital Archives, Library Document, H. C. Bodmer, HCB BMh 6/46.

xxx Emily Anderson, 1961, Vol. 3, Letter No. 1538a, pp. 1318—9.

xxxi Theodore Albrecht, translator and editor, 1996, Vol. 3, Letter No. 443, pp. 151—2.

xxxii Elliot Forbes editor, *Thayer's life of Beethoven*, 1967, p. 1009.

xxxiii Barry Cooper, 1990, p. 121.

xxxiv Emily Anderson, 1961, Vol. 3, Letter No. 1551, p. 1333. Beethoven was too weak to write this letter; it was written for him by Schindler and signed by Beethoven.

xxxv Anton Felix Schindler, *Beethoven as I knew him*, edited by Donald W. MacArdle and translated by Constance S. Jolly from the German edition of 1860, 1966, pp. 324—5. It should be noted that MacArdle urges caution in taking Schindler's account too literally; it is known that he was given to elaborating — if not even falsifying — some of his accounts of his dealings with the composer. See MacArdle's endnote 264.

xxxvi Beethoven House, Digital Archives, Library Documents C 135/1 and H. C. Bodmer HCB C Md 79, 13.

xxxvii Emily Anderson, 1961, Vol. 3, Letters Nos. 1537—1539, pp. 1317—20.

xxxviii Alan Tyson, *The authentic English editions of Beethoven*, 1963, pp. 128—9.

xxxix Anton Felix Schindler, *Beethoven as I knew him*, edited by Donald W. MacArdle and translated by Constance S. Jolly from the German edition of 1860, 1966, p. 308. 'The weight of evidence seems to favour Schuppanzigh for this distinction.'

xl Adapted from Robin Wallace, *Beethoven's critics: aesthetic dilemmas and resolutions during the composer's lifetime*, 1986, pp. 58–8. See also Maynard Solomon, *Beethoven: Beyond Classicism* in Robert Winter and Robert Martin editors, *The Beethoven quartet companion*, 1994, p. 70.

xli *Ibid*, p. 77.

xlii Elliot Forbes, editor, *Thayer's life of Beethoven*, 1967, p. 521. See also H. C. Robbins Landon, 1970, pp. 143–4.

xliii As remarked by Joseph de Marliave, 1925 (reprint 1961), p. 229.

xliv Pamela J. Willetts, 1970, pp. 27–31.

xlv Alan Tyson, *The authentic English editions of Beethoven*, 1963, p. 130.

xlvi Victoria L. Cooper, *The house of Novello: the practice and policy of a Victorian music publisher, 1829–1866*, 2003, p. 140.

xlvii William Kinderman, *Beethoven*, 1997, p. 7.

xlviii Douglas Porter Johnson, editor, 1985, p. 313, p. 317, pp. 450–2, pp. 453–7; and Barry Cooper, 1990, p. 35.

xlix Douglas Porter Johnson, editor, 1985, pp. 471–4, Barry Cooper, 2000, pp. 322–3; and Richard Kramer in: Christoph Wolff and Robert Riggs, *The string quartets of Haydn, Mozart and Beethoven: studies of the autograph manuscripts: a conference at Isham Memorial Library*, March 15–17, 1979, pp. 234–5.

l Electra Slonimsky Yourke editor, *Nicolas Slonimsky: writings on music*, 4 Vols. 2003–2005, p. 169.

li Misha Donat, *String Quartet in F major, Op. 135: Notes to the BBC Radio Three Beethoven Experience*, Sunday 8 June 2005, www.bbc.co.uk/radio3/Beethoven

lii David Wyn Jones, *Beethoven and the Viennese Legacy* in: Robin Stowell editor, *The Cambridge companion to the string quartet*, 2003, p. 226.

liii Robert Winter and Robert Martin editors, *The Beethoven quartet companion*, 1994, p. 276.

liv Paul Griffiths, 1983, p. 111.

lv William Kinderman, 1997, pp. 329–30.

lvi Joseph de Marliave, 1925 (reprint 1961), p. 356.

lvii David Wyn Jones, *Beethoven and the Viennese Legacy* in: Robin Stowell editor, *The Cambridge companion to the string quartet*, 2003, p. 226. Robert Winter and Robert Martin editors, *The Beethoven quartet companion*, 1994, p. 276.

lviii Robert Simpson, *The Chamber Music for Strings* in Denis Arnold and Nigel Fortune, editors, *The Beethoven companion*, 1973, p. 276.

lix Philip Radcliffe, 1978, p. 165.

lx Robert Winter and Robert Martin editors, *The Beethoven quartet companion*, 1994, p. 276.

lxi Denis Matthews, 1985, p. 147.

lxii William Kinderman, 1997, pp. 329–30.

lxiii Rebecca Clarke, *The Beethoven quartets as a player sees them* in: *Musical Times* Special Issue, 1927, Vol. VIII, No. 2, pp. 184–90.

lxiv Electra Slonimsky Yourke editor, *Nicolas Slonimsky: writings on music*, 4

  Vols. 2003–2005, p. 169.
[lxv] Joseph Kerman, 1967, pp. 354–8.
[lxvi] Martin Cooper, 1970, p. 404.
[lxvii] Alec Harman with Anthony Milner and Wilfrid Mellers, 1988, p. 656.
[lxviii] Joseph de Marliave, 1925 (reprint 1961), p. 356.
[lxix] Harold Truscott, 1968, p. 124.
[lxx] Philip Radcliffe, 1978, p. 165.
[lxxi] Harold Truscott, 1968, pp. 126–7.
[lxxii] Basil Lam, 1975, p. 131.
[lxxiii] Martin Cooper, 1970, p. 406.
[lxxiv] Joseph Kerman, 1967, pp. 358–360.
[lxxv] Martin Cooper, 1970, p. 406.
[lxxvi] With acknowledgment to Electra Slonimsky Yourke editor, *Nicolas Slonimsky: writings on music*, 4 Vols. 2003-2005, p. 169.
[lxxvii] Alec Harman with Anthony Milner and Wilfrid Mellers, 1988, p. 656.
[lxxviii] Robert Winter and Robert Martin editors, 1994, p. 278.
[lxxix] Philip Radcliffe, 1978, p. 168.
[lxxx] Joseph de Marliave, 1925 (reprint 1961), p. 364.
[lxxxi] Philip Radcliffe, 1978, p. 167.
[lxxxii] Rebecca Clarke, *The Beethoven quartets as a player sees them* in: *Musical Times*, Special Issue, 1927, Vol. VIII, No. 2, pp. 184–90.
[lxxxiii] Marion M. Scott, 1940, p. 277.
[lxxxiv] Quoted by Robin Wallace, *Beethoven's critics: aesthetic dilemmas and resolutions during the composer's lifetime*, 1986, pp. 58–9.
[lxxxv] Electra Slonimsky Yourke editor, *Nicolas Slonimsky: writings on music*, 4 Vols. 2003–2005, p. 170.
[lxxxvi] Martin Cooper, 1970, pp. 407–8.
[lxxxvii] Joseph de Marliave, 1925 (reprint 1961), pp. 366–7.
[lxxxviii] Quoted by Joseph Kerman, 1967, p. 360.
[lxxxix] Paul Bekker, 1925, p. 336.
[xc] Barry Cooper, 2000, p. 242.
[xci] Robert Winter and Robert Martin editors, *The Beethoven quartet companion*, 1994, p. 280.
[xcii] Joseph de Marliave, 1925 (reprint 1961), pp. 368–70.
[xciii] Arthur Shepherd, 1935, p. 79.
[xciv] Quoted by Paul Griffiths, 1983, p. 111.
[xcv] Paul Bekker, 1925, p. 336.
[xcvi] Alec Harman with Anthony Milner and Wilfrid Mellers, 1988, p. 656.
[xcvii] Beethoven's words may alternatively be translated as 'song of rest and peace' or 'sweet song of rest or peace'
[xcviii] Marion Scott, 1940, p. 277.
[xcix] Denis Matthews, 1985, p. 147.
[c] Philip Radcliffe, 1978, p. 169.
[ci] Basil Lam, 1975, p. 132.
[cii] Philip Radcliffe, 1978, p. 173 and p. 174.
[ciii] *Ibid*, 1978, p. 184.
[civ] Martin Cooper, 1970, p. 408.

[v] Robert Winter and Robert Martin editors *The Beethoven quartet companion*, 1994, p. 280.
[vi] Joseph Kerman, 1967, pp. 221–2.
[vii] Robert Winter and Robert Martin editors, *The Beethoven quartet companion*, 1994, p. 279.
[viii] Joseph Kerman, 1967, p. 362.
[ix] *Ibid*, p. 221.
[x] Philip Radcliffe, 1978, p. 170.
[xi] Basil Lam, 1975, p. 132.
[xii] Martin Cooper, 1970, p. 409.
[xiii] Philip Radcliffe, 1978, p. 160.
[xiv] Martin Cooper, 1970, p. 409.
[xv] Igor Stravinsky, 1972, p. 263.
[xvi] Joseph Kerman, 1967, p. 219.
[xvii] *Ibid*.
[xviii] Igor Stravinsky, 1972, p. 263.
[xix] Philip Radcliffe, 1978, p. 160.
[xx] Emily Anderson, 1961, Vol. 2, Letter No. 737, p. 654.
[xxi] Beethoven may have been induced to promote his native language, at least in part, in response to national promptings to do so. We learn from his biographer Anton Schindler that the suggestion had gone out, sometime in 1817, that German composer's should substitute German terms in their music in place of Italian. Anton Felix Schindler, edited by Donald W. MacArdle and translated by Constance S. Jolly from the German edition of 1860, 1966, p. 478.
[xxii] John Crabbe, 1982, p. 101.
[xxiii] Emily Anderson, editor and translator, 1961, Vol. 3, Letter No. 1318, p. 1149.
[xxiv] *Ibid*, Letter No. 1538a, pp. 1318–9. See also the text: Beethoven House, Digital Archives, Library Document, H. C. Bodmer, HCB BMh 6/46.
[xxv] Electra Slonimsky Yourke editor, *Nicolas Slonimsky: writings on music*, 4 Vols. 2003–2005, p. 169.
[xxvi] Arthur Shepherd, 1935, p. 80.
[xxvii] As related by: Anton Felix Schindler, *Beethoven as I knew him*, edited by Donald W. MacArdle and translated by Constance S. Jolly from the German edition of 1860, 1966, pp. 337–8; and Elliot Forbes editor, *Thayer's life of Beethoven*, 1967 pp, 976–7.
[xxviii] Emily Anderson, editor and translator, 1961, Vol. 3, Letter No. 1510, p. 1301.
[xxix] For a facsimile copy of the note in question, with the German text transcribed, see Beethoven House, Digital Archives, Library Document H. C. Bodmer, HCB BBr 24.
[xxx] Barry Cooper, 2000, p. 342.
[xxxi] Joseph de Marliave, 1925 (reprint 1961), pp. 372–3.
[xxxii] See, for example, Joseph Kerman, 1967, p. 362.
[xxxiii] Paul Bekker, 1925, p. 336.
[xxxiv] Marion Scott, 1940, p. 276.
[xxxv] Anton Neumayr, 1994–97, pp. 287–8.
[xxxvi] Harold Truscott, 1968, p. 130.

[cxxxvii] Alec Harman with Anthony Milner and Wilfrid Mellers, 1988, p. 656.
[cxxxviii] Marion M. Scott, 1940, p. 277.
[cxxxix] Paul Bekker, 1925, p. 336.
[cxl] Harold Truscott, 1968, p. 131.
[cxli] Joseph Kerman, 1967, p. 200.
[cxlii] *Ibid*, p. 365.
[cxliii] Igor Stravinsky, 1972, p. 263.
[cxliv] David Wyn Jones, *Beethoven and the Viennese Legacy* in: Robin Stowell editor, *The Cambridge companion to the string quartet*, 2003, p. 227.
[cxlv] Robert Winter and Robert Martin editors, 1994, pp. 281–2.
[cxlvi] Joseph Kerman, 1967, p. 366.
[cxlvii] Alfred Einstein, 1958, p. 86.
[cxlviii] William Kinderman, 1997, p. 334.
[cxlix] Joseph de Marliave, 1925, (reprint 1961), p. 379.
[cl] Alfred Einstein, 1958, p. 86.
[cli] Martin Cooper, 1970, p. 414.
[clii] Barry Cooper, 2000, p. 342.
[cliii] Denis Matthews, 1985, pp. 146–7.
[cliv] Igor Stravinsky, 1972, pp. 263–4.
[clv] Robert Winter and Robert Martin editors, *The Beethoven quartet companion*, 1994, p. 1.
[clvi] Robert Simpson, *The chamber music for strings* in: Denis Arnold and Nigel Fortune, editors, *The Beethoven companion*, 1973, pp. 277–8.

BIBLIOGRAPHY

The author has individually consulted all the publications listed in this bibliography and can confirm that each makes reference, in some way or other, to Beethoven and his works. It will be evident from their titles which of these are publications devoted exclusively to the composer. Others that make only passing reference to Beethoven and his compositions, nevertheless unfailingly bear testimony to his genius and humanity. The diversity of the titles listed testifies to the centrality of Beethoven to western culture and beyond; the mere survey of these should be of itself a rewarding experience for a lover of so-called classical music. The entries are confined to book publications, reflecting the scope of the author's researches. The cut-off date for this was 2007; no works after this date are listed, notwithstanding the author is mindful that Beethoven musicology, and related publication, continue to be a major field of endeavour.

Abraham, Gerald. *Beethoven's second-period quartets*. London: Oxford University Press: Humphrey Milford, 1944.

Abraham, Gerald. *Essays on Russian and East European music*. Oxford: Clarendon Press: New York: Oxford University Press, 1985.

Abraham, Gerald, Editor. *The age of Beethoven, 1790-1830*. London: Oxford University Press, 1982.

Abraham, Gerald. *The tradition of Western music*. London: Oxford University Press, 1974.

Abse, Dannie and Joan. *The Music lover's literary companion*. London: Robson Books, 1988.

Adorno, Theodor W., Translator. *Alban Berg: master of the smallest link*. Cambridge: Cambridge University Press, 1991.

Adorno, Theodor W. *Beethoven: the philosophy of music; fragments and texts*. Cambridge: Polity Press, 1998.

Albrecht, Daniel, Editor. *Modernism and music: an anthology of sources*. Chicago; London: University of Chicago Press, 2004.

Albrecht, Theodore, Translator and Editor. *Letters to Beethoven and other correspondence*. Lincoln, New England: University of Nebraska Press, 3 vols., 1996.

Allsobrook, David Ian. *Liszt: my travelling circus life*. London: Macmillan, 1991.

Anderson, Christopher, Editor and Translator. *Selected writings of Max Reger*. New York; London: Routledge, 2006.

Anderson, Emily, Editor and Translator. *The letters of Beethoven*. London: Macmillan, 3 vols.,1961.

Anderson, Martin, Editor. *Klemperer on music: shavings from a musician's workbench*. London: Toccata Press, 1986.

Antheil, George. *Bad boy of music*. London; New York: Hurst & Blackett Ltd., 1945.

Appleby, David P. *Heitor Villa-Lobos: a bio-bibliography*. New York: Greenwood Press, 1988.

Aprahamian, Felix, Editor. *Essays on music: an anthology from The Listener*. London, Cassell, 1967.

Armero, Gonzalo and Jorge de Persia. *Manuel de Falla : his life & works*. London: Omnibus Press, 1999.

Arnold, Ben, Editor. *The Liszt companion*. Westport, Connecticut; London: Greenwood Press, 2002.

Arnold, Denis and Nigel Fortune, Editors. *The Beethoven companion*. London: Faber and Faber, 1973.

Ashbrook, William. *Donizetti*. London: Cassell, 1965.

Auner, Joseph Henry. *A Schoenberg reader: documents of a life*. New Haven Connecticut; London: Yale University Press, 2003.

Avins, Styra, Editor. *Johannes Brahms: life and letters*. Oxford: Oxford University Press, 1997.

Azoury, Pierre H. *Chopin through his contemporaries: friends, lovers, and rivals*. Westport, Connecticut: Greenwood Press, 1999.

Badura-Skoda, Paul. *Carl Czerny: On the Proper Performance of all Beethoven's Works for the Piano*. Universal Edition: A. G. Wien, 1970.

Bailey, Cyril. *Hugh Percy Allen*. London: Oxford University

Press, 1948.

Bailey, Kathryn. *The life of Webern.* Cambridge: Cambridge University Press, 1998.

Barenboim, Daniel. *A life in music.* London: Weidenfeld & Nicolson, 1991.

Barlow, Michael. *Whom the gods love: the life and music of George Butterworth.* London: Toccata Press, 1997.

Barrett-Ayres, Reginald. *Joseph Haydn and the string quartet.* New York: Schirmer Books, 1974.

Bartos, Frantisek. *Bedrich Smetana: Letters and reminiscences.* Prague: Artia, 1953.

Barzun, Jacques. *Pleasures of music: an anthology of writing about music and musicians.* London: Cassell, 1977.

Bauer-Lechner, Natalie. *Recollections of Gustav Mahler.* London: Faber Music, 1980.

Bazhanov, N. Nikolai. *Rakhmaninov.* Moscow: Raduga, 1983.

Beaumont, Antony, Editor. *Ferruccio Busoni: Selected letters.* London: Faber and Faber, 1987.

Beaumont, Antony, Editor. *Gustav Mahler, letters to his wife.* London: Faber and Faber, 2004.

Beecham, Thomas. *A mingled chime: an autobiography.* New York: Da Capo Press, 1976.

Bekker, Paul. *Beethoven.* London: J. M. Dent & Sons, 1925.

Bellasis, Edward. *Cherubini: memorials illustrative of his life.* London: Burns and Oates, 1874.

Bennett, James R. Sterndale. *The life of William Sterndale Bennett.* Cambridge: University Press, 1907.

Benser, Caroline Cepin. *Egon Wellesz (1885–1974): chronicle of twentieth-century musician.* New York: P. Lang, 1985.

Berlioz, Hector. *Evenings in the orchestra.* Harmondsworth: Penguin Books, 1963.

Berlioz, Hector. *The musical madhouse (Les grotesques de la musique).* Rochester, New York: University of Rochester Press, 2003.

Bernard, Jonathan W., Editor. *Elliott Carter: collected essays and lectures, 1937-1995.* Rochester, New York; Woodbridge: University of Rochester Press, 1998.

Bernstein, Leonard. *The joy of music.* New York: Simon and Schuster, 1959.

Bertensson, Sergei. *Sergei Rachmaninoff: a lifetime in music.* London: G. Allen & Unwin, 1965.

Biancolli, Louis. *The Flagstad manuscript.* New York: Putnam, 1952.

Bickley, Nora, Editor. *Letters from and to Joseph Joachim.* London: Macmillan, 1914.

Bie, Oskar. *A history of the pianoforte and pianoforte players.* New York: Da Capo Press, 1966.

Blaukopf, Herta. *Mahler's unknown letters.* London: Gollancz, 1986.

Blaukopf, Kurt and Herta. *Mahler: his life, work and world.* London: Thames and Hudson, 1991.

Bliss, Arthur. *As I remember.* London: Thames Publishing, 1989.

Block, Adrienne Fried. *Amy Beach, passionate Victorian: the life and work of an American composer, 1867–1944.* New York: Oxford University Press, 1998.

Bloch, Ernst. *Essays on the philoso-*

phy of music. Cambridge: Cambridge University Press, 1985.

Blocker, Robert. *The Robert Shaw reader.* New Haven; London: Yale University Press, 2004.

Blom, Eric. *A musical postbag.* London: J. M. Dent, 1945.

Blom, Eric. *Beethoven's pianoforte sonatas discussed.* London: J. M. Dent, 1938.

Blom, Eric. *Classics major and minor: with some other musical ruminations.* London: J. M. Dent, 1958.

Blum, David. *The art of quartet playing: the Guarneri Quartet in conversation with David Blum.* London: Gollancz, 1986.

Blume, Friedrich. *Classic and Romantic music: a comprehensive survey.* London: Faber and Faber, 1972.

Boden, Anthony. *The Parrys of the Golden Vale: background to genius.* London: Thames Publishing, 1998.

Bonavia, Ferruccio. *Musicians on music.* London: Routledge & Kegan Paul, 1956.

Bonds, Mark Evan *After Beethoven: imperatives of originality in the symphony.* Cambridge, Massachusetts; London: Harvard University Press, 1996.

Bonis, Ferenc, Editor. *The selected writings of Zoltán Kodály.* London; New York: Boosey & Hawkes, 1974.

Bookspan, Martin. *André Previn: a biography.* London: Hamilton, 1981.

Boros, James and Richard Toop, Editors. *Brian Ferneyhough: Collected writings.* Amsterdam: Harwood Academic, 1995.

Boulez, Pierre. *Stocktakings from an apprenticeship.* Oxford: Clarendon Press, 1991.

Boult, Adrian. *Boult on music: words from a lifetime's communication.* London: Toccata Press, 1983.

Boult, Adrian. *My own trumpet.* London, Hamish Hamilton, 1973.

Boult, Adrian with Jerrold Northrop Moore. *Music and friends: seven decades of letters to Adrian Boult from Elgar, Vaughan Williams, Holst, Bruno Walter, Yehudi Menuhin and other friends.* London: Hamish Hamilton, 1979.

Bovet, Marie Anne de. *Charles Gounod: his life and his works.* London: S. Low, Marston, Searle & Rivington, Ltd., 1891.

Bowen, Catherine Drinker. *Beloved friend: the story of Tchaikowsky and Nadejda von Meck.* London: Hutchinson & Co., 1937.

Bowen, Meiron, Editor. *Gerhard on music: selected writings.* Brookfield, Vermont: Ashgate, 2000.

Bowen, Meirion. *Michael Tippett.* London: Robson Books, 1982.

Bowen, Meiron, Editor. *Music of the angels: essays and sketchbooks of Michael Tippett.* London: Eulenburg, 1980.

Bowen, Meiron, Editor. *Tippett on music.* Oxford: Clarendon Press, 1995.

Bowers, Faubion. *Scriabin: a biography.* Mineola: Dover; London: Constable, 1996.

Boyden, Matthew. *Richard Strauss.* London: Weidenfeld & Nicolson, 1999.

Bozarth, George S., Editor. *Brahms studies: analytical and historical perspectives; papers delivered at the International Brahms Conference, Washington, DC, 5-8 May 1983.* Oxford: Clarendon Press, 1990.

Brand, Juliane, Christopher Hailey and Donald Harris, Editors. *The Berg-Schoenberg correspondence: selected letters.* Basingstoke: Macmillan, 1987.

Brandenbugh, Sieghard, Editor. *Haydn, Mozart, & Beethoven: studies in the music of the classical period: essays in honor of Alan Tyson.* Oxford: Clarendon Press, 1998.

Braunstein, Joseph. *Musica Æterna, program notes for 1961-1971.* New York: Musica Æterna, 1972.

Braunstein, Joseph. *Musica Æterna, program notes for 1971-1976.* New York: Musica Æterna, 1978.

Brendel, Alfred. *Alfred Brendel on music: collected essays.* Chicago, Iliinois: A Cappella Books, 2001.

Brendel, Alfred. *The veil of order: Alfred Brendel in conversation with Martin Meyer.* London: Faber and Faber, 2002.

Breuning, Gerhard von. *Memories of Beethoven: from the house of the black-robed Spaniards.* Cambridge: Cambridge University Press, 1992.

Briscoe, James R., Editor. (Brief Description): *Debussy in performance.* New Haven: Yale University Press, 1999.

Brott, Alexander Betty Nygaard King. *Alexander Brott: my lives in music.* Oakville, Ontario; Niagara Falls, New York: Mosaic Press, 2005.

Brown, Alfred Peter. *The symphonic repertoire. Vol. 2, The first golden age of the Viennese symphony: Haydn, Mozart, Beethoven, and Schubert.* Bloomington, Indiana: Indiana University Press, 2002.

Brown, Maurice John Edwin. *Schubert: a critical biography.* London: Macmillan; New York: St. Martin's Press, 1958.

Broyles, Michael. *Beethoven: the emergence and evolution of Beethoven's heroic style.* New York: Excelsior Music Publishing Co., 1987.

Brubaker, Bruce and Jane Gottlieb, Editors. *Pianist, scholar, connoisseur: essays in honor of Jacob Lateiner.* Stuyvesant, N.Y., Pendragon Press, 2000.

Buch, Esteban. *Beethoven's Ninth: a political history.* Chicago; London: University of Chicago Press, 2003.

Burk, John N., Editor. *Letters of Richard Wagner: the Burrell collection.* London: Gollancz, 1951.

Burnham, Scott G. *Beethoven hero.* Princeton, New Jersey: Princeton University Press, 1995.

Burnham, Scott G and Michael P. Steinberg, Editors. *Beethoven and his world.* Princeton, New Jersey; Oxford: Princeton University Press, 2000.

Burton, William Westbrook, Editor. *Conversations about Bernstein.* New York; Oxford: Oxford University Press, 1995.

Busch, Fritz. *Pages from a musician's life.* London: Hogarth Press, 1953.

Busch, Hans, Editor. *Verdi's Aida: the history of an opera in letters and documents.* Minneapolis:

University of Minnesota Press, 1978.

Busch, Hans, Editor. *Verdi's Falstaff in letters and contemporary reviews*. Bloomington: Indiana University Press, 1997.

Busch, Marie, Translator. *Memoirs of Eugenie Schumann*. London: W. Heinemann, 1927.

Bush, Alan Dudley. *In my eighth decade and other essays*. London: Kahn & Averill, 1980.

Busoni, Ferruccio. *Letters to his wife*. Translated by Rosamond Ley. New York: Da Capo Press, 1975.

Byron, Reginald. *Music, culture, & experience: selected papers of John Blacking*. Chicago: University of Chicago Press, 1995.

Cairns, David. *Responses: musical essays and reviews*. New York: Da Capo Press, 1980.

Cardus, Neville. *Talking of music*. London: Collins, 1957.

Carley, Lionel. *Delius: a life in letters*. London: Scolar Press in association with the Delius Trust, 1988.

Carley, Lionel. *Grieg and Delius: a chronicle of their friendship in letters*. London: Marion Boyars, 1993.

Carner, Mosco. *Major and minor*. London: Duckworth, 1980

Carner, Mosco. *Puccini: a critical biography*. London: Duckworth, 1958.

Carroll, Brendan G. *The last prodigy: a biography of Erich Wolfgang Korngold*. Portland, Oregon: Amadeus Press, 1997.

Carse, Adam von Ahn. *The life of Jullien: adventurer, showman-conductor and establisher of the Promenade Concerts in England, together with a history of those concerts up to 1895*. Cambridge England: Heffer, 1951.

Carse, Adam von Ahn. *The orchestra from Beethoven to Berlioz: a history of the orchestra in the first half of the 19th century, and of the development of orchestral baton-conducting*. Cambridge: W. Heffer, 1948.

Casals, Pablo. *Joys and sorrows: reflections by Pablo Casals as told to Albert E. Kahn*. London: Macdonald, 1970.

Casals, Pablo. *The memoirs of Pablo Casals as told to Thomas Dozier*. London: Life en Español, 1959.

Chappell, Paul. *Dr. S. S. Wesley, 1810-1876: portrait of a Victorian musician*. Great Wakering: Mayhew-McCrimmon, 1977.

Chasins, Abram. *Leopold Stokowski, a profile*. New York: Hawthorn Books, 1979.

Charlton, Davi, Editor and Martyn Clarke Translator. *E.T.A. Hoffmann's musical writings: Kreisleriana, The Poet and the Composer*. Cambridge: Cambridge University Press, 1989.

Chávez, Carlos. *Musical thought*. Cambridge: Harvard University Press, 1961.

Chesterman, Robert, Editor. *Conversations with conductors: Bruno Walter, Sir Adrian Boult, Leonard Bernstein, Ernest Ansermet, Otto Klemperer, Leopold Stokowski*. Totowa, New Jersey: Rowman and Littlefield, 1976.

Chissell, Joan. *Clara Schumann: a dedicated spirit; a study of her life and work*. London: Hamilton, 1983.

Chua, Daniel K. L. *The "Galitzin" quartets of Beethoven: Opp.127, 132, 130*. Princeton: Princeton

University Press, 1995.

Citron, Marcia, Editor. *The letters of Fanny Hensel to Felix Mendelssohn*. Stuyvesant, New York: Pendragon Press, 1987.

Clark, Walter Aaron. *Enrique Granados: poet of the piano*. Oxford, England; New York, N.Y.: Oxford University Press, 2006.

Clark, Walter Aaron. *Isaac Albéniz: portrait of a romantic*. Oxford; New York: Oxford University Press, 1999.

Clive, Peter. *Beethoven and his world*. Oxford University Press, 2001.

Closson, Ernest. *History of the piano*. Translated by Delano Ames and edited by Robin Golding. London: Paul Elek, 1947.

Cockshoot, John V. *The fugue in Beethoven's piano music*. London: Routledge & Kegan Paul, 1959.

Coe, Richard N, Translator. *Life of Rossini by Stendhal*. London: Calder & Boyars, 1970.

Coleman, Alexander, Editor. *Diversions & animadversions: essays from The new criterion*. New Brunswick, New Jersey; London: Transaction Publishers, 2005.

Colerick, George. *From the Italian girl to Cabaret: musical humour, parody and burlesque*. London: Juventus, 1998.

Coleridige, A. D. *Life of Moscheles, with selections from his diaries and correspondence by his wife*. London: Hurst & Blackett, 1873.

Colles, Henry Cope. *Essays and lectures*. London: Humphrey Milford, Oxford University Press, 1945.

Cone, Edward T., Editor. *Roger Sessions on music: collected essays*. Princeton, New Jersey: Princeton University Press, 1979.

Cone, Edward T. *The composer's voice*. Berkeley; London: University of California Press, 1974.

Cook, Susan and Judy S. Tsou, Editors. *Cecilia reclaimed: feminist perspectives on gender and music*. Urbana: University of Illinois Press, 1994.

Cooper, Barry. *Beethoven: The master musicians series*. Oxford: Oxford University Press, 2000.

Cooper, Barry. *Beethoven and the creative process*. Oxford: Clarendon Press, 1990.

Cooper, Barry. *Beethoven's folksong settings: chronology, sources, style*. Cambridge: Cambridge University Press, 1991.

Cooper, Barry. *The Beethoven compendium: a guide to Beethoven's life and music*. London: Thames and Hudson, 1991.

Cooper, Martin. *Beethoven: the last decade, 1817–1827*. London: Oxford University Press, 1970.

Cooper, Martin. *Judgements of value: selected writings on music*. Oxford; New York: Oxford University Press, 1988.

Cooper, Martin. *Ideas and music*. London: Barrie and Rockliff, 1965.

Cooper, Victoria L. *The house of Novello: the practice and policy of a Victorian music publisher, 1829–1866*. Aldershot, Hants: Ashgate, 2003.

Coover, James. *Music at auction: Puttick and Simpson (of London), 1794–1971: being an annotated, chronological list of sales of musical materials*. Warren, Michigan: Harmonie Park Press, 1988.

Copland, Aaron. *Copland on music.* London: Deutsch, 1961.

Corredor, J. Ma. *Conversations with Casals.* London: Hutchinson, 1956.

Cott, Jonathan. *Stockhausen: conversations with the composer.* London: Picador, 1974.

Cottrell, Stephen. *Professional music making in London: ethnography and experience.* Aldershot: Ashgate, 2004.

Cowell, Henry. *Charles Ives and his music.* New York: Oxford University Press, 1955.

Cowling, Elizabeth. *The cello.* London: Batsford, 1983.

Crabbe, John. *Beethoven's empire of the mind.* Newbury: Lovell Baines, 1982.

Craft, Robert. *An improbable life: memoirs.* Nashville: Vanderbilt University Press, 2002.

Craft, Robert, Editor. *Stravinsky: selected correspondence.* London: Faber and Faber, 3 Vols. 1982–1985.

Craw, Howard Allen. *A biography and thematic catalog of the works of J. L. Dussek: 1760–1812.* Ann Arbor: Michigan, 1965.

Crawford, Richard, R. Allen Lott and Carol J. Oja, Editors. *A Celebration of American music: words and music in honor of H. Wiley Hitchcock.* Ann Arbor: University of Michigan Press, 1990.

Craxton, Harold and Tovey, Donald Francis. *Beethoven: Sonatas for Pianoforte.* London: The Associated Board, [1931].

Crichton, Ronald: Editor. *The memoirs of Ethel Smyth.* New York: Viking, 1987.

Crist, Stephen A. and Roberta M. Marvin, Editors. *Historical musicology: sources, methods, interpretations.* Rochester, New York: University of Rochester Press, 2004.

Crofton, Ian and Donald Fraser, Editors. *A dictionary of musical quotations.* London: Croom Helm, 1985.

Crompton, Louis, Editor. *Shaw, Bernard: The great composers: reviews and bombardments.* Berkeley; London: University of California Press, 1978.

Csicserry-Ronay, Elizabeth, Translator and Editor. *Hector Berlioz: The art of music and other essays: (A travers chants).* Bloomington: Indiana University Press, 1994.

Curtiss, Mina Kirstein. *Bizet and his world.* London: Secker & Warburg, 1959.

Cuyler, Louise Elvira. *The symphony.* New York: Harcourt Brace Jovanovich, 1973.

Dahlhaus, Carl. *Ludwig van Beethoven: approaches to his music.* Oxford: Clarendon Press, 1991.

Dahlhaus, Carl. *Nineteenth-century music.* Translated by J. Bradford Robinson. Berkeley; London: University of California Press, 1989.

Daniels, Robin. *Conversations with Cardus.* London: Gollancz, 1976.

Daniels, Robin. Conversations with Menuhin. London: Macdonald General Books, 1979.

Day, James. *Vaughan Williams.* London: Dent, 1961.

Davies, Peter Maxwell. *Studies from two decades.* Selected and introduced by Stephen Pruslin.

London: Boosey & Hawkes, 1979.

Dean, Winton. *Georges Bizet: his life and work*. London: J.M. Dent, 1965.

Deas, Stewart. *In defence of Hanslick*. London: Williams and Norgate, 1940.

Debussy, Claude. *Debussy on music*. London: Secker & Warburg, 1977.

Delbanco, Nicholas. *The Beaux Arts Trio*. London: Gollancz, 1985.

Demény, Janos, Editor. *Béla Bartók: letters*. London: Faber and Faber, 1971.

Dent, Edward Joseph. *Selected essays*. Edited by Hugh Taylor. Cambridge; New York: Cambridge University Press, 1979.

Deutsch, Otto Erich. *Mozart: a documentary biography*. London: Adam & Charles Black, 1965.

Deutsch, Otto Erich. *Schubert: a documentary biography*. London: J.M. Dent, 1946

Deutsch, Otto Erich. *Schubert: memoirs by his friends*. London: Adam & Charles Black, 1958.

Dibble, Jeremy. *C. Hubert H. Parry: his life and music*. Oxford: Clarendon Press, 1992.

Dibble, Jeremy. *Charles Villiers Stanford: man and musician*. Oxford: Oxford University Press, 2002.

Donakowski, Conrad L. *A muse for the masses: ritual and music in an age of democratic revolution, 1770–1870*. Chicago: University of Chicago Press, 1977.

Dower, Catherine. *Alfred Einstein on music: selected music criticisms*. New York: Greenwood Press, 1991.

Downs, Philip G. *Classical music: the era of Haydn, Mozart, and Beethoven*. New York: W.W. Norton, 1992.

Drabkin, William. *Beethoven: Missa Solemnis*. Cambridge: Cambridge University Press, 1991.

Dreyfus, Kay. *The farthest north of humanness: letters of Percy Grainger, 1901–1914*. South Melbourne; Basingstoke: Macmillan, 1985.

Dubal, David, Editor. *Remembering Horowitz: 125 pianists recall a legend*. New York: Schirmer Books, 1993.

Dubal, David. *The world of the concert pianist*. London: Victor Gollancz, 1985.

Dvořák, Otakar. *Antonín Dvořák, my father*. Spillville, Iowa: Czech Historical Research Center, 1993.

Dyson, George. *The progress of music*. London: Oxford University Press, Humphrey Milford, 1932.

Eastaugh, Kenneth. *Havergal Brian: the making of a composer*. London: Harrap, 1976.

Edwards, Allen. *Flawed words and stubborn sounds: a conversation with Elliott Carter*. New York: Norton & Company, 1971.

Edwards, Frederick George. *Musical haunts in London*. London: J. Curwen & Sons, 1895.

Ehrlich, Cyril. *First philharmonic: a history of the Royal Philharmonic Society*. Oxford: Clarendon Press, 1995.

Einstein, Alfred. *A short history of music*. London: Cassell and Company Ltd., 1948.

Einstein, Alfred. *Essays on music*. London: Faber and Faber, 1958.

Einstein, Alfred. *Mozart: his character, his work*. London: Cassell and Company Ltd., 1946.

Einstein, Alfred. *Music in the Romantic era.* London: J.M. Dent Ltd., 1947.

Ekman, Karl. *Jean Sibelius, his life and personality.* New York: Tudor Publishing. Co., 1945.

Elgar, Edward. *A future for English music: and other lectures*, Edited by Percy M. Young. London: Dobson, 1968.

Elkin, Robert. *Queen's Hall, 1893–1941.* London: Rider, 1944.

Ella, John. *Musical sketches, abroad and at home: with original music by Mozart, Czerny, Graun, etc., vocal cadenzas and other musical illustrations.* London: Ridgway, Vol. 1., 1869.

Ellis, William Ashton. *The family letters of Richard Wagner.* Edited and translated by William Ashton Ellis and enlarged with introduction and notes by John Deathridge. Basingstoke: Macmillan, 1991.

Ellis, William Ashton. *Richard Wagner's prose works: Vol. 1, The art-work of the future.* Edited and translated by William Ashton Ellis. London: Kegan Paul, Trench, Trübner, 1895.

Ellis, William Ashton. *Richard Wagner's prose works: Vol. 2, Opera and drama.* Edited and translated by William Ashton Ellis. London: Kegan Paul, Trench, Trübner, 1900.

Ellis, William Ashton. *Richard Wagner's prose works: Vol. 3, The theatre.* Edited and translated by William Ashton Ellis. London: Kegan Paul, Trench, Trübner, 1907.

Ellis, William Ashton. *Richard Wagner's prose works: Vol. 4, Art and politics.* Edited and translated by William Ashton Ellis. London: Kegan Paul, Trench, Trübner, 1895.

Ellis, William Ashton. *Richard Wagner's prose works: Vol. 5, Actors and singers.* Edited and translated by William Ashton Ellis. London: Kegan Paul, Trench, Trübner, 1896.

Ellis, William Ashton. *Richard Wagner's prose works: Vol. 6, Religion and art.* Edited and translated by William Ashton Ellis. London: Kegan Paul, Trench, Trübner, 1897.

Ellis, William Ashton. *Richard Wagner's prose works: Vol. 7, In Paris and Dresden.* Edited and translated by William Ashton Ellis. London: Kegan Paul, Trench, Trübner, 1898.

Ellis, William Ashton. *Richard Wagner's prose works: Vol. 8, Posthumous.* Edited and translated by William Ashton Ellis. London: Kegan Paul, Trench, Trübner, 1899.

Elterlein, Ernst von. *Beethoven's pianoforte sonatas: explained for the lovers of the musical art.* London: W. Reeves, 1898.

Engel, Carl. *Musical myths and facts.* London: Novello, Ewer & Co.; New York: J.L. Peters, 1876.

Eosze, László. *Zoltán Kodály: his life and work.* London: Collet's, 1962.

Etter, Brian K. *From classicism to modernism: Western musical culture and the metaphysics of order.* Aldershot: Ashgate, 2001.

Ewen, David. *From Bach to Stravinsky: the history of music by its foremost critics.* New York, Greenwood Press, 1968.

Ewen, David. *Romain Rolland's Essays on music.* New York: Dover Publications, 1959.

Fay, Amy. *Music-study in Germany: from the home correspondence of Amy Fay.* New York: Dover Publications, 1965.

Fenby, Eric. *Delius as I knew him.* London: Quality Press, 1936.

Ferguson, Donald Nivison. *Masterworks of the orchestral repertoire: a guide for listeners.* Minneapolis: University of Minnesota Press, 1954.

Fétis, François-Joseph. *Curiosités historiques de la musique: complément nécessaire de la Musique mise à la portée de tout le monde.* Paris: Janet et Cotelle, 1830.

Fifield, Christopher. *Max Bruch: his life and works.* London: Gollancz, 1988.

Fifield, Christopher. *True artist and true friend: a biography of Hans Richter.* Oxford: Clarendon Press, 1993.

Finson, Jon and R. Larry Todd, Editors. *Mendelssohn and Schumann: essays on their music and its context.* Durham, N.C.: Duke University Press, 1984.

Fischer, Edwin. *Beethoven's pianoforte sonatas: a guide for students & amateurs.* London: Faber and Faber, 1959.

Fischer, Edwin. *Reflections on music.* London: Williams and Norgate, 1951.

Fischer, Hans Conrad and Erich Kock. *Ludwig van Beethoven: a study in text and pictures.* London: Macmillan; New York, St. Martin's Press, 1972.

Fischmann, Zdenka E. *Janáček-Newmarch correspondence. 1st limited and numbered edition.* Rockville, MD: Kabel Publishers, 1986.

Fitzlyon, April. *Maria Malibran: diva of the romantic age.* London: Souvenir Press, 1987.

FitzLyon, April. *The price of genius: a life of Pauline Viardot.* London: John Calder, 1964.

Forbes, Elliot, Editor. *Thayer's life of Beethoven.* Princeton, New Jersey: Princeton University Press, 1967.

Foreman, Lewis. *Bax: a composer and his times.* London: Scolar Press, 1983.

Foreman, Lewis, Editor. *Farewell, my youth, and other writings by Arnold Bax.* Aldershot: Scolar Press, 1992.

Foster, Myles Birket. *History of the Philharmonic Society of London, 1813–1912: a record of a hundred years' work in the cause of music.* London: Bodley Head, 1912.

Foulds, John. *Music today: its heritage from the past, and legacy to the future.* London: I. Nicholson and Watson, limited, 1934.

Frank, Mortimer H. *Arturo Toscanini: the NBC years.* Portland, Oregon: Amadeus Press, 2002.

Fraser, Andrew Alastair. *Essays on music.* London: Oxford University Press, H. Milford, 1930.

Frohlich, Martha. *Beethoven's Appassionata' sonata.* Oxford: Clarendon Press, 1991.

Gal, Hans. *The golden age of Vienna.* London: Max Parrish & Co. Limited, 1948.

Gal, Hans. *The musician's world: great composers in their letters.* London: Thames and Hudson,

1965.

Galatopoulos, Stelios. *Bellini: life, times, music.* London: Sanctuary, 2002.

Garden, Edward and Nigel Gottrei, Editors. *'To my best friend': correspondence between Tchaikovsky and Nadezhda von Meck, 1876–1878.* Oxford: Clarendon Press, 1993.

Geck, Martin. Beethoven. London: Haus, 2003.

Gerig, Reginald. *Famous pianists & their technique.* Washington: R. B. Luce, 1974.

Gilliam, Bryan. *The life of Richard Strauss.* Cambridge: Cambridge University Press, 1999.

Gilliam, Bryan, Editor. *Richard Strauss and his world.* Princeton, New Jersey: Princeton University Press, 1992.

Gillies, Malcolm and Bruce Clunies Ross, Editors. *Grainger on music.* Oxford; New York: Oxford University Press, 1999.

Gillies, Malcolm and David Pear, Editors. *The all-round man: selected letters of Percy Grainger, 1914–1961.* Oxford: Clarendon Press, 1994.

Gillies, Malcolm, Editor. *The Bartók companion.* London: Faber and Faber, 1993.

Gillmor, Alan M. *Erik Satie.* Basingstoke: Macmillan Press, 1988.

Glehn, M. E. *Goethe and Mendelssohn : (1821–1831).* London: Macmillan, 1874.

Glowacki, John, Editor. *Paul A. Pisk: Essays in his honor.* Austin, Texas: University of Texas, 1966

Gollancz, Victor. *Journey towards music: a memoir.* London: Victor Gollancz Ltd., 1964.

Good, Edwin Marshall. *Giraffes, black dragons, and other pianos: a technological history from Cristofori to the modern concert grand.* Stanford, California: Stanford University Press, 1982.

Gordon, David. *Musical visitors to Britain.* London: Routledge, 2005.

Gordon, Stewart. *A history of keyboard literature: music for the piano and its forerunners.* Schirmer Books: New York: London : Prentice Hall International, 1996.

Gorrell, Lorraine. *The nineteenth-century German lied.* Portland, Oregon: Amadeus Press, 1993.

Goss, Glenda D. *Jean Sibelius: the Hämeenlinna letters: scenes from a musical life, 1875–1895.* Esbo, Finland: Schildts, 1997.

Goss, Madeleine. *Bolero: the life of Maurice Ravel.* New York: Tudor, 1945.

Gotch, Rosamund Brunel, Editor. *Mendelssohn and his friends in Kensington: letters from Fanny and Sophy Horsley, written 1833–36.* London: Oxford University Press, 1938.

Gounod, Charles. *Charles Gounod; autobiographical reminiscences: with family letters and notes on music; from the French.* London: William Heinemann, 1896.

Grabs, Manfred, Editor. *Hanns Eisler: a rebel in music; selected writings.* Berlin: Seven Seas Publishers, 1978.

Grace, Harvey. *A musician at large.* London: Oxford University Press, H. Milford, 1928.

(La) Grange, Henry-Louis de. *Gustav Mahler.* Oxford: Oxford University Press, 1995.

Graves, Charles L. *Hubert Parry: his life and works.* London: Macmillan, 1926.

Graves, Charles L. *Post-Victorian music: with other studies and sketches.* London: Macmillan and Co., limited, 1911.

Graves, Charles L. *The life & letters of Sir George Grove, Hon. D.C.L. (Durham), Hon. LL.D. (Glasgow), formerly director of the Royal college of music.* London: Macmillan and Co., Ltd.; New York: The Macmillan Co., 1903.

Gray, Cecil. *Musical chairs, or, between two stools: being the life and memoirs of Cecil Gray.* London: Home & Van Thal, 1948.

Gregor-Dellin and Dietrich Mack, Editors. *Cosima Wagner's diaries.: Vol. 1, 1869 - 1877.* London: Collins, 1978-1980.

Griffiths, Paul. *Modern music: the avant-garde since 1945.* London: J. M. Dent & Sons Ltd., 1981.

Griffiths, Paul. *Olivier Messiaen and the music of time.* London: Faber and Faber, 1985.

Griffiths, Paul. *Peter Maxwell Davies.* London: Robson Books, 1988.

Griffiths, Paul. *The sea on fire: Jean Barraqué.* Rochester, New York: Woodbridge: University of Rochester Press, 2003.

Griffiths, Paul. *The string quartet.* London: Thames and Hudson, 1983.

Grout, Donald Jay and Claude V. Palisca, Editors. *A history of Western music.* London: J. M. Dent, 1988.

Grove, George. *Beethoven and his nine symphonies.* London: Novello, Ewer, 1896.

Grover, Ralph Scott. *Ernest Chausson: the man and his music.* London: The Athlone Press, 1980.

Grover, Ralph Scott. *The music of Edmund Rubbra.* Aldershot: Scolar Press, 1993.

Grun, Bernard. *Alban Berg: letters to his wife.* Edited and translated by Bernard Grun. London: Faber and Faber, 1971.

Gutman, David. *Prokofiev.* London: Omnibus Press, 1990.

Hadow, William Henry. *Collected essays.* London: H. Milford at the Oxford University Press, 1928.

Hadow, William Henry. *Beethoven's Op. 18 Quartets.* London: H. Milford at the Oxford University Press, 1926.

Haggin, Bernard H. *Music observed.* New York: Oxford University Press, 1964.

Hailey, Christopher. *Franz Schreker, 1878–1934: a cultural biography.* Cambridge: Cambridge University Press, 1993.

Hall, Michael. *Leaving home: a conducted tour of twentieth-century music with Simon Rattle.* London: Faber and Faber, 1996.

Hall, Patricia and Friedemann Sallis, Editors. (Brief Description): *A handbook to twentieth-century musical sketches.* Cambridge: Cambridge University Press, 2004.

Hallé, C. E. *Life and letters of Sir Charles Hallé: being an autobiography (1819–1860) with correspondence and diaries.* London: Smith, Elder & Co., 1896.

Halstead, Jill. *The woman composer: creativity and the gendered politics of musical composition. Aldershot: Ashgate, 1997.

Hamburger, Michael, Editor and Translator. *Beethoven letters, journals, and conversations.* New York: Thames and Hudson, 1951.

Hammelmann, Hanns A. and Ewald Osers. *The correspondence between Richard Strauss and Hugo von Hofmannsthal.* London: Collins, 1961.

Hanson, Lawrence and Elisabeth Hanson. *Tchaikovsky: the man behind the music.* New York: Dodd, Mead & Co, 1967.

Harding, James. *Massenet.* London: J. M. Dent & Sons Ltd., 1970.

Harding, James. *Saint-Saëns and his circle.* London: Chapman & Hall, 1965.

Harding, Rosamond E. M. *Origins of musical time and expression.* London: Oxford University Press, 1938.

Harman, Alec with Anthony Milner and Wilfrid Mellers. *Man and his music: the story of musical experience in the West.* London: Barrie & Jenkins, 1988.

Harper, Nancy Lee. *Manuel de Falla: his life and music.* Lanham, Maryland; London: The Scarecrow Press, 2005.

Hartmann, Arthur. *'Claude Debussy as I knew him' and other writings of Arthur Hartmann.* Edited by Samuel Hsu, Sidney Grolnic, and Mark Peters. Rochester, New York; Woodbridge: University of Rochester Press, 2003.

Haugen, Einar and Camilla Cai. *Ole Bull: Norway's romantic musician and cosmopolitan patriot.* Madison: The University of Wisconsin Press, 1993.

Headington, Christopher. *The Bodley Head history of Western music.* London: The Bodley Head, 1974.

Heartz, Daniel. *Music in European capitals: the galant style, 1720–1780.* New York; London: W. W. Norton, 2003.

Hedley, Arthur, Editor. *Selected correspondence of Fryderyk Chopin: abridged from Fryderyk Chopin's correspondence.* London: Heinemann, 1962.

Heiles, Anne Mischakoff. *Mischa Mischakoff: journeys of a concertmaster.* Sterling Heights, Michigan: Harmonie Park Press, 2006.

Henderson, Sanya Shoilevska. *Alex North, film composer: a biography, with musical analyses of a Streetcar named desire, Spartacus, The misfits, Under the volcano, and Prizzi's honor.* Jefferson, N.C.; London: McFarland, 2003.

Henschel, George. *Personal recollections of Johannes Brahms: some of his letters to and pages from a journal kept by George Henschel.* Boston: R G. Badger, 1907.

Henze, Hans Werner. *Bohemian fifths: an autobiography.* London: Faber and Faber, 1998.

Henze, Hans Werner. *Music and politics: collected writings 1953–81.* London: Faber and Faber, 1982.

Herbert, May, Translator. *Early letters of Robert Schumann.* London: George Bell and Sons, 1888.

Heyman, Barbara B. *Samuel Barber: the composer and his music.* New York: Oxford University

Press, 1992.

Heyworth, Peter. *Otto Klemperer, his life and times.* Cambridge: Cambridge University Press, 2 Vols. 1983–1996.

Hildebrandt, Dieter. *Pianoforte: a social history of the piano.* London: Hutchinson, 1988.

Hill, Peter. *The Messiaen companion.* London: Faber and Faber, 1995.

Hill, Peter and Nigel Simeone. Messiaen. New Haven Connecticut; London: Yale University Press, 2005.

Hiller, Ferdinand. *Mendelssohn: Letters and recollections.* New York: Vienna House, 1972.

Hines, Robert Stephan. *The orchestral composer's point of view: essays on twentieth-century music by those who wrote it.* Norman: University of Oklahoma Press, 1970.

Ho, Allan B. *Shostakovich reconsidered.* London: Toccata Press, 1998.

Hodeir, André. *Since Debussy: a view of contemporary music.* New York: Da Capo Press, 1975.

Holmes, Edward. *The life of Mozart: including his correspondence.* London: Chapman and Hall, 1845.

Holmes, John L. *Composers on composers.* New York: Greenwood Press, 1990.

Hopkins, Antony. *The concertgoer's companion.* London: J.M. Dent & Sons Ltd., 1984.

Hopkins, Antony. *The seven concertos of Beethoven.* Aldershot: Scolar Press, 1996.

Holt, Richard. *Nicolas Medtner (1879–1951): a tribute to his art and personality.* London: D. Dobson, 1955.

Honegger, Arthur. *I am a composer.* London: Faber and Faber, 1966.

Hoover, Kathleen and John Cage. *Virgil Thomson: his life and music.* New York; London: T. Yoseloff, 1959.

Horgan, Paul. *Encounters with Stravinsky: a personal record.* London: The Bodley Head, 1972.

Horowitz, Joseph. *Conversations with Arrau.* London: Collins, 1982.

Horowitz, Joseph. Understanding Toscanini. London: Faber and Faber, 1987.

Horwood, Wally. *Adolphe Sax, 1814–1894: his life and legacy.* Bramley: Bramley Books, 1980.

Howie, Crawford. *Anton Bruckner: a documentary biography.* Lewiston, N.Y.; Lampeter: Edwin Mellen Press, 2002.

Hueffer, Francis. *Correspondence of Wagner and Liszt.* New York: Greenwood Press, 2 Vols.1969.

Hughes, Spike. *The Toscanini legacy: a critical study of Arturo Toscanini's performances of Beethoven, Verdi, and other composers.* London: Putnam, 1959.

Hullah, Annette. *Theodor Leschetizky.* London and New York: J. Land & Co., 1906.

Le Huray, Peter and James Day, Editors. *Music and aesthetics in the eighteenth and early-nineteenth centuries.* Cambridge: Cambridge University Press, 1988.

D'Indy, Vincent. *César Franck.* New York: Dover Publications, 1965.

Jacobs, Arthur. *Arthur Sullivan: A Victorian musician.* Aldershot: Scolar Press, 1992.

Jahn, Otto. *Life of Mozart*. London: Novello, Ewer & Co., 1882.

Jefferson, Alan. *Sir Thomas Beecham: a centenary tribute*. London: World Records Ltd., 1979.

Jezic, Diane. *The musical migration and Ernst Toch*. Ames: Iowa State University Press, 1989.

Johnson, Douglas Porter, Editor. *The Beethoven sketchbooks: history, reconstruction, inventory*. Oxford: Clarendon, 1985.

Johnson, Stephen. *Bruckner remembered*. London: Faber and Faber, 1998.

Jones, David, Wyn. *Beethoven: Pastoral symphony*. Cambridge: Cambridge University Press, 1995.

Jones, David Wyn. *The life of Beethoven*. Cambridge: Cambridge University Press, 1998.

Jones, David Wyn. *The symphony in Beethoven's Vienna*. Cambridge: Cambridge University Press, 2006.

Jones, J. Barrie, Editor. *Gabriel Fauré: a life in letters*. London: Batsford, 1989.

Jones, Peter Ward, Editor and Translator. *The Mendelssohns on honeymoon: the 1837 diary of Felix and Cécile Mendelssohn Bartholdy, together with letters to their families*. Oxford: Clarendon Press, 1997.

Jones, Timothy. *Beethoven, the Moonlight and other sonatas, Op. 27 and Op. 31*. Cambridge; New York, N.Y.: Cambridge University Press, 1999.

Kalischer, A. C., Editor. *Beethoven's letters: a critical edition*. London: J. M. Dent, 1909.

Kárpáti, János. *Bartók's chamber music*. Stuyvesant, New York: Pendragon Press, 1994.

Keefe, Simon P. *The Cambridge companion to the concerto*. Cambridge, New York, N.Y.: Cambridge University Press, 2005.

Keller, Hans. *The great Haydn quartets: their interpretation*. London: J. M. Dent, 1986.

Keller, Hans, Editor. *The memoirs of Carl Flesch*. New York: Macmillan, 1958.

Keller, Hans, and Christopher Wintle. *Beethoven's string quartets in F minor, Op. 95 and C minor, Op. 131: two studies*. Nottingham: Department of Music, University of Nottingham, 1995.

Kelly, Thomas Forrest. *First nights at the opera: five musical premiers*. New Haven: Yale University Press, 2004.

Kennedy, Michael. *Adrian Boult*. London: Hamish Hamilton, 1987.

Kennedy, Michael. *Barbirolli, conductor laureate: the authorised biography*. London: Hart-Davis, MacGibbon, 1973.

Kennedy, Michael, Editor. *The autobiography of Charles Hallé; with correspondence and diaries*. London: Paul Elek, 1972.

Kennedy, Michael. *Hallé tradition: a century of music*. Manchester: Manchester University Press, 1960.

Kennedy, Michael. *The works of Ralph Vaughan Williams*. London: Oxford University Press, 1964.

Kemp, Ian. *Tippett: the composer and his music*. London; New York: Eulenburg Books, 1984.

Kerman, Joseph. *The Beethoven quartets.* London: Oxford University Press, 1967, c1966.

Kerman, Joseph. *Write all these down: essays on music.* Berkeley, California; London: University of California Press, 1994.

Kildea, Paul, Editor. *Britten on music.* Oxford: Oxford University Press, 2003.

Kinderman, William. *Beethoven.* Oxford: Oxford University Press, 1997.

Kinderman, William. *Beethoven's Diabelli variations.* Oxford: Clarendon Press; New York: Oxford University Press, 1987.

Kinderman, William, Editor. *The string quartets of Beethoven.* Urbana, Ilinois: University of Illinois Press, 2005.

King, Alec Hyatt. *Musical pursuits: selected essays.* London: British Library, 1987.

Kirby, F. E. *Music for piano: a short history.* Amadeus Press: Portland, 1995.

Kirkpatrick, John, Editor. *Charles E. Ives: Memos.* New York: W.W. Norton, 1972.

Knapp, Raymond. *Brahms and the challenge of the symphony.* Stuyvesant, N.Y.: Pendragon Press, c.1997.

Knight, Frida. *Cambridge music: from the Middle Ages to modern times.* Cambridge, England.: New York: Oleander Press, 1980.

Knight, Max, Translator. *A confidential matter: the letters of Richard Strauss and Stefan Zweig, 1931–1935.* Berkeley; London: University of California Press, 1977.

Kok, Alexander. *A voice in the dark: the philharmonia years.* Ampleforth: Emerson Edition, 2002.

Kopelson, Kevin. *Beethoven's kiss: pianism, perversion, and the mastery of desire.* Stanford, California: Stanford University Press, 1996.

Kostelanetz, Richard, Editor. *Aaron Copland: a reader; selected writings 1923–1972.* New York; London: Routledge, 2003.

Kostelanetz, Richard. *Conversing with Cage.* New York; London: Routledge, 2003.

Kostelanetz, Richard. *On innovative musicians.* New York: Limelight Editions, 1989.

Kostelanetz, Richard, Editor. *Virgil Thomson: a reader ; selected writings, 1924–1984.* New York; London: Routledge, 2002.

Kowalke, Kim H. *Kurt Weill in Europe.* Ann Arbor, Michigan: UMI Research Press, 1979.

Krehbiel, Henry Edward. *The pianoforte and its music.* New York: Cooper Square Publishers, 1971.

Kruseman, Philip, Editor. *Beethoven's own words.* London: Hinrichsen Edition, 1948.

Kurtz, Michael. *Stockhausen: a biography.* London: Faber and Faber, 1992.

Lam, Basil. *Beethoven string quartets.* Seattle: University of Washington Press, 1975.

Lambert, Constant. *Music ho!: a study of music in decline.* London: Faber and Faber, Ltd. 1934.

Landon, H. C. Robbins. *Beethoven: a documentary study.* London: Thames and Hudson, 1970.

Landon, H. C. Robbins. *Beethoven: his life, work and world.* London: Thames and Hudson,

1992.

Landon, H. C. Robbins. *Essays on the Viennese classical style: Gluck, Haydn, Mozart, Beethoven.* London: Barrie & Rockliff The Cresset Press, 1970.

Landon, H. C. Robbins. *Haydn: chronicle and works/Haydn, the late years, 1801–1809.* Bloomington: Indiana University Press, 1977.

Landon, H. C. Robbins. *Haydn: his life and music.* London: Thames and Hudson, 1988.

Landon, H. C. Robbins. *Haydn in England, 1791–1795.* London: Thames and Hudson, 1976.

Landon, H. C. Robbins. *Haydn: the years of 'The creation', 1796–800.* London: Thames and Hudson, 1977.

Landon, H. C. Robbins. *Mozart: the golden years, 1781–1791.* New York: Schirmer Books, 1989.

Landon, H. C. Robbins. *1791, Mozart's last year.* London: Thames and Hudson, 1988.

Landon, H. C. Robbins *The collected correspondence and London notebooks of Joseph Haydn.* London: Barrie and Rockliff, 1959.

Landon, H. C. Robbins: Editor. *The Mozart companion.* London: Faber, 1956.

Landowska, Wanda. *Music of the past.* London: Geoffrey Bles, 1926.

Lang, Paul Henry. *Musicology and performance.* New Haven: Yale University Press, 1997.

Lang, Paul Henry. *The creative world of Beethoven.* New York: W. W. Norton 1971.

Laurence, Dan H., Editor. *Shaw's music: the complete musical criticism in three volumes.* London: Max Reinhardt, the Bodley Head, 1981.

Lawford-Hinrichsen, Irene. *Music publishing and patronage: C. F. Peters, 1800 to the Holocaust.* Kenton: Edition Press, 2000.

Layton, Robert, Editor. *A guide to the concerto.* Oxford: Oxford University Press, 1996.

Layton, Robert, Editor. *A guide to the symphony.* Oxford: Oxford University Press, 1995.

Lebrecht, Norman. *The maestro myth: great conductors in pursuit of power.* London: Simon & Schuster, 1991.

Lee, Ernest Markham. *The story of the symphony.* London: Scott Publishing Co., 1916.

Leibowitz, Herbert A., Editor. *Musical impressions: selections from Paul Rosenfeld's criticism.* London: G. Allen & Unwin, 1970.

Lenrow, Elbert, Editor and Translator. *The letters of Richard Wagner to Anton Pusinelli.* New York: Vienna House, 1972.

Leonard, Maurice. *Kathleen: the life of Kathleen Ferrier: 1912–1953.* London: Hutchinson, 1988.

Lesure, François and Roger Nichols, Editors. *Debussy, letters.* London: Faber and Faber, 1987.

Letellier, Robert Ignatius, Editor and Translator. *The diaries of Giacomo Meyerbeer.* Madison: Fairleigh Dickinson University Press; London: Associated University Presses, 4 Vols., 1999–2004.

Levas, Santeri. *Sibelius: a personal portrait.* London: J. M. Dent, 1972.

Levy, Alan Howard. *Edward Mac-

Dowell, an American master. Lanham, Md. & London: Scarecrow Press, 1998.

Levy, David Benjamin. *Beethoven: the Ninth Symphony.* New Haven, Connecticut; London: Yale University Press, 2003.

Leyda, Jay and Sergi Bertensson. *The Musorgsky reader: a life of Modeste Petrovich Musorgsky in letters and documents.* New York: W.W. Norton, 1947.

Lewis, Thomas P., Editor. *Raymond Leppard on music: an anthology of critical and personal writings.* White Plains, N.Y.: Pro/Am Music Resources, 1993.

Liébert, Georges. *Nietzsche and music.* Chicago: University of Chicago Press, 2004.

Liszt, Franz. *An artist's journey: lettres d'un bachelier ès musique, 1835–1841.* Chicago: University of Chicago Press, 1989.

Litzmann, Berthold, Editor. *Clara Schumann: an artist's life, based on material found in diaries and letters.* London: Macmillan; Leipzig: Breitkopf & Härtel, 2 Vols. 1913.

Litzmann, Berthold, Editor. *Letters of Clara Schumann and Johannes Brahms, 1853–1896.* New York, Vienna House. 2 Vols. 1971.

Lloyd, Stephen. *William Walton: muse of fire.* Woodbridge, Suffolk: The Boydell Press, 2001.

Locke, Ralph P. and Cyrilla Barr, Editors. *Cultivating music in America: women patrons and activists since 1860.* Berkeley: University of California Press, 1997.

Lockspeiser, Edward. *Debussy: his life and mind.* London: Cassell. 2 Vols. 1962–1965.

Lockspeiser, Edward. *The literary clef: an anthology of letters and writings by French composers.* London: J. Calder. 1958.

Lockwood, Lewis, Editor. *Beethoven essays: studies in honor of Elliot Forbes.* Cambridge, Massachusetts: Harvard University Department of Music: Distributed by Harvard University Press, 1984.

Lockwood, Lewis and Mark Kroll, Editors. *The Beethoven violin sonatas: history, criticism, performance.* Urbana: University of Illinois Press, 2004.

Loft, Abram. *Violin and keyboard: the duo repertoire.* New York: Grossman Publishers. 2 Vols. 1973.

Longyear, Rey Morgan. *Nineteenth-century romanticism in music.* Englewood Cliffs: Prentice-Hall, 1969.

Lowe, C. Egerton. *Beethoven's pianoforte sonatas: hints on their rendering, form, etc., with appendices on definition of sonata, music forms, ornaments, pianoforte pedals, and how to discover keys.* London: Novello, 1929.

Macdonald, Hugh, Editor. *Berlioz: Selected letters.* London: Faber and Faber, 1995.

Macdonald, Malcolm, Editor. *Havergal Brian on music: selections from his journalism: Volume One, British music.* London: Toccata Press, 1986.

MacDonald, Malcolm. *Varèse: astronomer in sound.* London: Kahn & Averill, 2003.

MacDowell, Edward. *Critical and historical essays: lectures deliv-*

ered at *Columbia University*. Edited by W. J. Baltzell. London: Elkin; Boston: A.P. Schmidt, 1912.

MacFarren, Walter. Memories: an autobiography. London: Walter Scott Publishing Co.,1905.

Mackenzie, Alexander Campbell. *A musician's narrative*. London: Cassell and company, Ltd, 1927.

McCarthy, Margaret William, Editor. *More letters of Amy Fay: the American years, 1879–1916*. Detroit: Information Coordinators, 1986.

McClary, Susan. *Feminine endings: music, gender, and sexuality*. Minneapolis: University of Minnesota Press, 1991.

McClatchie, Stephen, Editor and Translator. *The Mahler family letters*. Oxford: Oxford University Press, 2006.

McVeigh, Simon. *Concert life in London from Mozart to Haydn*. Cambridge: Cambridge University Press, 1993.

Mahler, Alma. *Gustav Mahler: memories and letters*. Enlarged edition revised and edited and with and introduction by Donald Mitchell. London: John Murray, 1968.

Mai, François Martin. *Diagnosing genius: the life and death of Beethoven*. Montreal; London: McGill-Queen's University Press, 2007.

Del Mar, Norman. *Orchestral variations: confusion and error in the orchestral repertoire*. London: Eulenburg, 1981.

Del Mar, Norman. *Richard Strauss: a critical commentary on his life and works*. London: Barrie & Jenkins. 3 Vols. 1978.

(La) Mara [pseudonym]. *Letters of Franz Liszt*. London: H. Grevel & Co., 2 Vols. 1894.

Marek, George Richard. *Puccini*. London: Cassell & Co., 1952.

Marek, George Richard. *Toscanini*. London: Vision, 1976.

(De) Marliave, Joseph. *Beethoven's quartets*. New York: Dover Publications (reprint), 1961.

Martin, George Whitney. *Verdi: his music, life and times*. London: Macmillan, 1965.

Martner, Knud, Editor. *Selected letters of Gustav Mahler*. London; Boston: Faber and Faber, 1979.

Martyn, Barrie. *Nicolas Medtner: his life and music*. Aldershot: Scolar Press, 1995.

Martyn, Barrie. *Rachmaninoff: composer, pianist, conductor*. Aldershot: Scolar, 1990.

Massenet, Jules. *My recollections*. Westport, Connecticut: Greenwood Press.1970.

Matheopoulos, Helena. *Maestro: encounters with conductors of today*. London: Hutchinson, 1982.

Matthews, Denis. *Beethoven*. London: J. M. Dent, 1985.

Matthews, Denis. *Beethoven piano sonatas*. London: British Broadcasting Corporation, 1967.

Matthews, Dennis. *In pursuit of music*. London: Victor Gollancz Ltd., 1968.

Matthews, Denis. *Keyboard music*. Newton Abbot: London David & Charles, 1972.

Mellers, Wilfrid Howard. *Caliban reborn: renewal in twentieth-century music*. London: Victor Gollancz, 1967.

Mellers, Wilfrid Howard. *The sonata

principle (from c. 1750). London: Rockliff, 1957.

Mendelssohn Bartholdy. *Letters from Italy and Switzerland.* London: Longman, Green, Longman, and Roberts, 1862.

Mendelssohn Bartholdy, Paul. *Letters of Felix Mendelssohn Bartholdy, from 1833 to 1847.* London: Longman, Green, Longman, Roberts, & Green, 1864.

Menuhin, Yehudi and Curtis W. Davis. *The music of man.* London: Macdonald and Jane's, 1979.

Menuhin, Yehudi. *Theme and variations.* London: Heinemann Educational Books Ltd., 1972.

Menuhin, Yehudi. *Unfinished journey.* London: Macdonald and Jane's, 1977.

Messian, Olivier. *Music and color: conversations with Claude Samuel.* Portland, Oregon: Amadeus, 1994.

Miall, Antony. *Musical bumps.* London: J.M. Dent & Sons Ltd, 1981.

Michotte, Edmond. *Richard Wagner's visit to Rossini (Paris 1860): and, An evening at Rossini's in Beau-Sejour (Passy), 1858.* Chicago; London: University of Chicago Press, 1982.

Mies, Paul. *Beethoven's sketches: an analysis of his style based on a study of his sketchbooks.* New York: Johnson Reprint, 1969.

Milhaud, Darius. *My happy life.* London: Boyars, 1995.

Miller, Mina. *The Nielsen companion.* London: Faber and Faber, 1994.

Milsom, David. *Theory and practice in late nineteenth-century violin performance: an examination of style in performance, 1850–1900.* Aldershot: Ashgate, 2003.

Mitchell, Donald, Editor. *Letters from a life: the selected letters and diaries of Benjamin Britten 1913–1976.* London: Faber and Faber. 3 Vols., 1991.

Mitchell, Donald and Hans Keller, Editors. *Music survey: new series 1949–1952.* London: Faber Music in association with Faber & Faber, 1981.

Mitchell, Jon C. *A comprehensive biography of composer Gustav Holst, with correspondence and diary excerpts: including his American years.* Lewiston, New York: Edwin Mellen Press, 2001.

Moldenhauer, Hans. *Anton von Webern: a chronicle of his life and work.* London: Victor Gollancz, 1978.

Monrad-Johansen. Edvard Grieg. New York: Tudor Publishing Co., 1945.

Moore, Gerald. *Am I too loud?: memoirs of an accompanist.* London: Hamish Hamilton, 1962.

Moore, Gerald. *Farewell recital: further memoirs.* Harmondsworth: Penguin Books, 1979.

Moore, Gerald. *Furthermoore: interludes in an accompanist's life.* London: Hamish Hamilton, 1983.

Moore, Jerrold Northrop. *Edward Elgar: a creative life.* Oxford: Oxford University Press, 1984.

Moore, Jerrold Northrop. *Elgar, Edward. The windflower letters: correspondence with Alice Caroline Stuart Wortley and her family.* Oxford: Clarendon Press; New York: Oxford University Press, 1989.

Moore, Jerrold Northrop. *Elgar, Edward. Edward Elgar: letters of a lifetime.* Oxford: Clarendon Press; New York: Oxford University Press, 1990.

Moore, Jerrold Northrop. *Elgar, Edward. Elgar and his publishers: letters of a creative life.* Oxford: Clarendon, 1987.

Moreux, Serge. *Béla Bartók.* London: Harvill Press, 1953.

Morgan, Kenneth. *Fritz Reiner, maestro and martinet.* Urbana: University of Illinois Press, 2005.

Cone, Edward T., Editor. *Music, a view from Delft: selected essays.* Chicago: University of Chicago Press, 1989.

Morgan, Robert P. *Twentieth-century music: a history of musical style in modern Europe and America.* New York: Norton, 1991.

Morgenstern, Sam., Editor. *Composers on music: an anthology of composers' writings.* London: Faber & Faber, 1956.

Morrow, Mary Sue. *Concert life in Haydn's Vienna: aspects of a developing musical and social institution.* Stuyvesant, New York: Pendragon Press, 1989.

Moscheles, Felix, Editor and Translator. *Letters from Felix Mendelssohn-Bartholdy to Ignaz and Charlotte Moscheles.* London: Trübner and Co., 1888.

Mudge, Richard B., Translator. *Glinka, Mikhail Ivanovich: Memoirs.* Norman: University of Oklahoma Press, 1963.

Munch, Charles. *I am a conductor.* New York: Oxford University Press, 1955.

Mundy, Simon. *Bernard Haitink: a working life.* London: Robson Books, 1987.

Musgrave, Michael. *The musical life of the Crystal Palace.* Cambridge: Cambridge University Press, 1995.

Music & Letters. *Beethoven: special number.* London: Music & Letters, 1927.

Musical Times. *Special Issue.* John A. Fuller-Maitland London: Vol. VIII, No. 2, 1927.

Myers, Rollo H., Editor. *Twentieth-century music.* London: Calder and Boyars, 1960.

National Gallery (Great Britain). *Music performed at the National Gallery concerts, 10th October 1939 to 10th April 1946.* London: Privately printed, 1948.

Nattiez, Jean-Jacques, Editor. *Orientations: collected writings — Pierre Boulez.* London: Faber and Faber, 1986.

Nauhaus, Gerd, Editor. *The marriage diaries of Robert & Clara Schumann.* London: Robson Books, 1994.

Nectoux, Jean Michel. *Gabriel Fauré: a musical life.* Translated by Roger Nichols. Cambridge: Cambridge University Press, 1991.

Nettl, Paul. *Beethoven handbook.* Westport, Connecticut: Greenwood Press, 1975.

Neumayr, Anton. *Music and medicine.* Bloomington, Illinois: Medi-Ed Press, 1994–1997

Newbould, Brian. *Schubert and the symphony: a new perspective.* Surbiton: Toccata Press, 1992.

Newlin, Dika. *Schoenberg remembered: diaries and recollections (1938–76).* New York: Pendragon Press, 1980.

Newman, Ernest. *From the world of*

music: essays from 'The Sunday Times'. London: J. Calder, 1956.

Newman, Ernest. Hugo Wolf. New York: Dover Publications, 1966.

Newman, Ernest, Annotated and Translated. *Memoirs of Hector Berlioz from 1803 to 1865, comprising his travels in Germany, Italy, Russia, and England.* New York: Knopf, 1932.

Newman, Ernest. *More essays from the world of music: essays from the 'Sunday Times'.* London: John Calder, 1958.

Newman, Ernest. *Musical studies.* London; New York: John Lane, 1910.

Newman, Ernest. *Testament of music: essays and papers.* London: Putnam, 1962.

Newman, Richard. *Alma Rosé: Vienna to Auschwitz.* Portland, Oregon: Amadeus Press, 2000.

Newman, William S. *The sonata in the classic era.* Chapel Hill: University of North Carolina Press 1963.

Newman, William S. *The sonata in the Classic era.* New York; London: W.W. Norton, 1983.

Newmarch, Rosa Harriet. *Henry J. Wood.* London & New York: John Lane, 1904.

Nicholas, Jeremy. *Godowsky: the pianists' pianist; a biography of Leopold Godowsky.* Hexham: Appian Publications & Recordings, 1989.

Nichols, Roger. *Debussy remembered.* London: Faber and Faber, 1992.

Nichols, Roger. *Mendelssohn remembered.* London: Faber and Faber, 1997.

Nichols, Roger. *Ravel remembered.* London: Faber and Faber, 1987.

Niecks, Frederick. *Robert Schumann.* London: J. M. Dent, 1925.

Nielsen, Carl. *Living music.* Copenhagen, Wilhelm Hansen, 1968.

Nielsen, Carl. *My childhood.* Copenhagen, Wilhelm Hansen, 1972.

Nikolska, Irina. *Conversations with Witold Lutoslawski, (1987–92).* Stockholm: Melos, 1994.

Nohl, Ludwig. *Beethoven depicted by his contemporaries.* London: Reeves, 1880.

De Nora, Tia. *Beethoven and the construction of genius: musical politics in Vienna, 1792–1803.* Berkeley: University of California Press, 1997.

Norton, Spencer, Editor and Translator. *Music in my time: the memoirs of Alfredo Casella.* Norman: University of Oklahoma Press, 1955.

Nottebohm, Gustav. *Two Beethoven sketchbooks: a description with musical extracts.* London: Gollancz, 1979.

Oakeley, Edward Murray. *The life of Sir Herbert Stanley Oakeley.* London: George Allen, 1904.

Lucas, Brenda and Michael Kerr. *Virtuoso: the story of John Ogdon.* London: H. Hamilton, 1981.

Oliver, Michael, Editor. *Settling the score: a journey through the music of the twentieth century.* London: Faber and Faber, 1999.

Olleson, Philip. *Samuel Wesley: the man and his music.* Woodbridge: Boydell Press, 2003.

Olleson, Philip, Editor. *The letters of Samuel Wesley: professional and social correspondence, 1797–1837.* Oxford; New York: Oxford University Press, 2001.

Olmstead, Andrea. *Conversations with Roger Sessions.* Boston: Northeastern University Press, 1987.

Orenstein, Arbie, Editor. *A Ravel reader: correspondence, articles, interviews.* New York: Columbia University Press, 1990.

Orenstein, Arbie. *Ravel: man and musician.* New York: Columbia University Press, 1975.

Orledge, Robert. *Charles Koechlin (1867–1950): his life and works.* New York: Harwood Academic Publishers, 1989.

Orledge, Robert. *Gabriel Fauré.* London: Eulenburg Books, 1979.

Orledge, Robert. *Satie remembered.* London: Faber and Faber, 1995.

Orledge, Robert. *Satie the composer.* Cambridge: Cambridge University Press, 1990.

Orlova, Alexandra. *Glinka's life in music: a chronicle.* Ann Arbor: UMI Research Press, 1988.

Orlova, Alexandra. *Musorgsky's days and works: a biography in documents.* Ann Arbor: UMI Research Press, 1983.

Orlova, Alexandra. *Tchaikovsky: a self-portrait.* Oxford: Oxford University Press, 1990.

Osborne, Charles, Editor and Translator. *Letters of Giuseppe Verdi.* London: Victor Gollancz, 1971.

Osmond-Smith David, Editor and Translator. *Luciano Berio: Two interviews with Rossana Dalmonte and Bálint András Varga.* New York; London: Boyars, 1985.

Ouellette, Fernand. *Edgard Varèse.* London: Calder & Boyars, 1973.

Paderewski, Ignacy Jan and Mary Lawton. *The Paderewski memoirs.* London: Collins, 1939.

Page, Tim: Editor. *The Glenn Gould reader.* London: Faber and Faber, 1987.

Page, Tim. *Music from the road: views and reviews, 1978–1992.* New York; Oxford: Oxford University Press, 1992.

Page, Tim and Vanessa Weeks, Editors. *Selected letters of Virgil Thomson.* New York: Summit Books, 1988.

Page, Tim. *Tim Page on music: views and reviews.* Portland, Oregon: Amadeus Press, 2002.

Palmer, Christopher. *Herbert Howells, (1892–1983): a celebration.* London: Thames, 1996.

Palmer, Christopher, Editor. *Sergei Prokofiev: Soviet diary 1927 and other writings.* London: Faber and Faber, 1991.

Palmer, Fiona M. *Domenico Dragonetti in England (1794–1846): the career of a double bass virtuoso.* Oxford: Clarendon, 1997.

Palmieri, Robert, Editor. *Encyclopedia of the piano.* New York: Garland, 1996.

Panufnik, Andrzej. *Composing myself.* London: Methuen, 1987.

Parsons, James, Editor. *The Cambridge companion to the Lied.* Cambridge: Cambridge University Press, 2004.

Paynter, John, Editor. *Between old worlds and new: occasional writings on music by Wilfrid Mellers.* London: Cygnus Arts, 1997.

Pestelli, Giorgio. *The age of Mozart and Beethoven.* Cambridge: Cambridge University Press, 1984.

Peyser, Joan. *Bernstein: a biography: revised & updated.* New York: Billboard Books, 1998.

Phillips-Matz, Mary Jane. *Verdi: a biography.* Oxford: Oxford University Press, 1993.

Piggott, Patrick. *The life and music of John Field, 1782–1837: creator of the nocturne.* London: Faber and Faber, 1973.

Plantinga, Leon. *Beethoven's concertos: history, style, performance.* New York: Norton, 1999.

Plantinga, Leon. *Clementi: his life and music.* London: Oxford University Press, 1977.

Plantinga, Leon. *Romantic music: a history of musical style in nineteenth-century Europe.* New York; London: Norton, 1984.

Plaskin, Glenn. *Horowitz: a biography of Vladimir Horowitz.* London: Macdonald, 1983.

Pleasants, Henry, Editor and Translator. *Hanslick, Eduard: Music criticisms, 1846–99.* Baltimore: Penguin Books, 1963.

Pleasants, Henry, Editor and Translator. *Hanslick's music criticisms.* New York: Dover Publications, 1988.

Pleasants, Henry, Editor and Translator. *The music criticism of Hugo Wolf.* New York: Holmes & Meier Publishers, 1978.

Pleasants, Henry, Editor and Translator. *The musical journeys of Louis Spohr.* Norman: University of Oklahoma Press, 1961.

Pollack, Howard. *Aaron Copland: the life and work of an uncommon man.* New York: Henry Holt, 1999.

Poulenc, Francis. *My friends and myself.* London: Dennis Dobson, 1978.

Powell, Richard, Mrs. *Edward Elgar: memories of a variation.* Aldershot, Hants, England: Scolar Press; Brookfield, Vermont, USA: Ashgate Publishing. Co., 1994.

Poznansky, Alexander, Editor. *Tchaikovsky through others' eyes.* Bloomington: Indiana University Press, 1999.

Praeger, Ferdinand. *Wagner as I knew him.* London; New York: Longmans, Green, 1892.

Previn, Andre. *Antony Hopkins. Music face to face.* London, Hamish Hamilton, 1971.

Prieberg, Fred K. *Trial of strength: Wilhelm Furtwängler and the Third Reich.* London: Quartet, 1991.

Procter-Gregg, Humphrey. *Beecham remembered.* London: Duckworth, 1976.

Prokofiev, Sergey. *Prokofiev by Prokofiev: a composer's memoir.* London: Macdonald and Jane's, 1979.

Rachmaninoff, Sergei. *Rachmaninoff's recollections told to Oskar von Riesemann.* London: George Allen & Unwin, 1934.

Radcliffe, Philip. *Beethoven's string quartets.* Cambridge: Cambridge University Press, 1978.

Radcliffe, Philip. *Piano Music in: The Age of Beethoven, The New Oxford History of Music, Vol. VIII.* Gerald Abraham, (Editor), 1988, p. 340.

Ratner, Leonard G. *Romantic music: sound and syntax.* New York: Schirmer Books, 1992.

Raynor, Henry. *A social history of music: from the middle ages to Beethoven.* London: Barrie & Jenkins, 1972.

Rees, Brian. *Camille Saint-Saëns: a life.* London: Chatto & Windus, 1999.

Reich, Willi, Editor. *Anton Webern: The path to the new music.* London; Bryn Mawr: Theodore Presser in association with Universal Edition, 1963.

Reid, Charles. *John Barbirolli: a biography.* London, Hamish Hamilton, 1971.

Reid, Charles. *Malcolm Sargent: a biography.* London: Hamilton, 1968.

Rennert, Jonathan. *William Crotch (1775–1847): composer, artist, teacher.* Lavenham: Terence Dalton, 1975.

Rice, John A. *Antonio Salieri and Viennese Opera.* Chicago, Illinois: University of Chicago Press, 1998.

Rice, John A. *Empress Marie Therese and music at the Viennese court, 1792–1807.* Cambridge: Cambridge University Press, 2003.

Richards, Fiona. *The Music of John Ireland.* Aldershot: Ashgate, 2000.

Rigby, Charles. *Sir Charles Hallé: a portrait for today.* Manchester: Dolphin Press, 1952.

Ringer, Alexander, Editor. *The early Romantic era: between Revolutions; 1789 and 1848.* Basingstoke: Macmillan, 1990.

Roberts, John P.L. and Ghyslaine Guertin, Editors. *Glenn Gould: Selected letters.* Toronto; Oxford: Oxford University Press, 1992.

Robertson, Alec. *More than music.* London: Collins, 1961.

Robinson, Harlow, Editor and Translator. *Selected letters of Sergei Prokofiev.* Boston: Northeastern University Press, 1998.

Robinson, Harlow. *Sergei Prokofiev: a biography.* London: Hale, 1987.

Robinson, Paul A. *Ludwig van Beethoven, Fidelio.* Cambridge: Cambridge University Press, 1996.

Robinson, Suzanne, Editor. *Michael Tippett: music and literature.* Aldershot: Ashgate, 2002.

Rochberg, George. *The aesthetics of survival: a composer's view of twentieth-century music.* Ann Arbor, Michigan: University of Michigan Press, 2004.

Rodmell, Paul. *Charles Villiers Stanford.* Aldershot: Ashgate, 2002.

Roeder, Michael Thomas. *A history of the concerto.* Portland, Oregon: Amadeus Press, 1994.

Rohr, Deborah Adams. *The careers of British musicians, 1750–1850: a profession of artisans.* Cambridge: Cambridge University Press, 2001.

Rolland, Romain. *Goethe and Beethoven.* New York; London: Blom, 1968.

Rolland, Romain. *Beethoven and Handel.* London: Waverley Book Co., 1917.

Rolland, Romain. *Beethoven the creator.* Garden City, New York: Garden City Pub., 1937.

Roscow, Gregory, Editor. *Bliss on music: selected writings of Arthur Bliss, 1920–1975.* Oxford: Oxford University Press, 1991.

Rosen, Charles. *Beethoven's piano sonatas: a short companion.* New Haven, Connecticut: London: Yale University Press, 2002.

Rosen, Charles. *Critical entertainments: music old and new.* Cambridge, Massachusetts; London: Harvard University Press, 2000.

Rosen, Charles. *The classical style: Haydn, Mozart, Beethoven.* London: Faber and Faber, 1976.

Rosen, Charles. *The romantic generation.* Cambridge, Massachusetts: Harvard University Press, 1995.

Rosenthal, Albi. *Obiter scripta: essays, lectures, articles, interviews and reviews on music, and other subjects.* Oxford: Offox Press; Lanham: Scarecrow Press, 2000.

Rostal, Max. *Beethoven: the sonatas for piano and violin; thoughts on their interpretation.* London: Toccata Press, 1985.

Rostropovich, Mstislav and Galina Vishnevskaya. *Russia, music, and liberty.* Portland, Oregan: Amadeus Press, 1995.

Rubinstein, Arthur. *My many years.* London: Jonathan Cape, 1980.

Rubinstein, Arthur. *My young years.* London: Jonathan Cape, 1973.

Rumph, Stephen C. *Beethoven after Napoleon: political romanticism in the late works.* Berkeley; London: University of California Press, 2004.

Rye, Matthew Rye. *Notes to the BBC Radio Three Beethoven Experience, Friday 10 June 2005,* www.bbc.co.uk/radio3/Beethoven.

Sachs, Harvey. *Toscanini.* London: Weidenfeld and Nicholson, 1978.

Sachs, Joel. *Kapellmeister Hummel in England and France.* Detroit: Information Coordinators, 1977.

Saffle, Michael, Editor. *Liszt and his world: proceedings of the International Liszt Conference held at Virginia Polytechnic Institute and State University, 20–23 May 1993.* Stuyvesant, New York: Pendragon Press, 1998.

Safránek, Milos. *Bohuslav Martinu, his life and works.* London: Allan Wingate, 1962.

Saint-Saëns, Camille. *Outspoken essays on music.* Westport, Connecticut: Greenwood Press, 1970.

Saussine, Renée de. *Paganini.* Westport, Connecticut: Greenwood Press, 1976.

Sayers, W. C. Berwick. *Samuel Coleridge-Taylor, musician: his life and letters.* London; New York: Cassell and Co., 1915.

Schaarwächter, Jürgen. *HB: aspects of Havergal Brian.* Aldershot: Ashgate, 1997.

Schafer, R. Murray. *E.T.A. Hoffmann and music.* Toronto: University of Toronto Press, 1975.

Schafer, R. Murray, Editor. *Ezra Pound and music: the complete criticism.* London: Faber and Faber, 1978.

Schat, Peter. *The tone clock.* Chur, Switzerland; Langhorne, Pa.: Harwood Academic Publishers, 1993.

Schenk, Erich. *Mozart and his times.* Edited and Translated by Richard and Clara Winstin. London: Secker & Warburg, 1960.

Schindler, Anton Felix. *Beethoven as I knew him.* Edited by Donald W. MacArdle and Translated by Constance S. Jolly from the German edition of 1860 London: Faber and Faber, 1966.

Schlosser, Johann. *Beethoven: the first biography, 1827.* Edited by Barry Cooper. Portland, Oregon: Amadeus Press, 1996.

Schnabel, Artur. *My life and music.*

London: Longmans, 1961.

Schnittke, Alfred. *A Schnittke reader.* Bloomington: Indiana University Press, 2002.

Scholes, Percy Alfred. *Crotchets: a few short musical notes.* London: John Lane, 1924.

Schonberg, Harold C. *The great pianists.* London: Victor Gollancz, 1964.

Schrade, Leo. *Beethoven in France: the growth of an idea.* New Haven; London: Yale University Press, H. Milford, Oxford University Press, 1942.

Schrade, Leo. *Tragedy in the art of music.* Cambridge, Massachusetts: Harvard University Press, 1964.

Schuh, Willi. *Richard Strauss: a chronicle of the early years 1864–1898.* Cambridge: Cambridge University Press, 1982.

Schuh, Willi, Editor. *Richard Strauss: Recollections and reflections.* London; New York: Boosey & Hawkes, 1953.

Schuller, Gunther. *Musings: the musical worlds of Gunther Schuller.* New York: Oxford University Press, 1986.

Schumann, Robert. *Music and musicians: essays and criticisms.* London: William Reeves, 1877.

Schuttenhelm, Editor. *Selected letters of Michael Tippett.* London: Faber and Faber, 2005.

Schwartz, Elliott. *Music since 1945: issues, materials, and literature.* New York: Schirmer Books, 1993.

Scott, Marion M. *Beethoven: (The master musicians).* London: Dent, 1940.

Scott-Sutherland, Colin. *Arnold Bax.* London: J. M. Dent, 1973.

Searle, Muriel V. *John Ireland: the man and his music.* Tunbridge Wells: Midas Books, 1979.

Secrest, Meryle. *Leonard Bernstein: a life.* London: Bloomsbury, 1995.

Seeger, Charles. *Studies in musicology II, 1929–1979.* Edited by Anne M. Pescatello. Berkeley; London: University of California Press, 1994.

Selden-Goth, Gisela, Editor. *Felix Mendelssohn: letters.* London: Paul Elek Publishers Ltd, 1946.

Senner, Wayne M., Robin Wallace and William Meredith, Editors. *The critical reception of Beethoven's compositions by his German contemporaries.* Lincoln: University of Nebraska Press, in association with the American Beethoven Society and the Ira F. Brilliant Center for Beethoven Studies, San José State University, 1999.

Seroff, Victor I. *Rachmaninoff.* London: Cassell & Company, 1951.

Sessions, Roger. *Questions about music.* Cambridge, Massachusetts: Harvard University Press, 1970.

Sessions, Roger. *The musical experience of composer, performer, listener.* New York: Atheneum, 1966, 1950.

Seyfried, Ignaz von. *Louis van Beethoven's Studies in thoroughbass, counterpoint and the art of scientific composition.* Leipzig; New-York: Schuberth and Company, 1853.

Sharma, Bhesham R. *Music and culture in the age of mechanical reproduction.* New York: Peter Lang, 2000.

Shaw, Bernard. *How to become a musical critic.* London: R. Hart Davis, 1960.

Shaw, Bernard. *London music in 1888–89 as heard by Corno di Bassetto (later known as Bernard Shaw): with some further autobiographical particulars.* London: Constable and Company, 1937.

Shaw, Bernard. *Music in London, 1890–1894.* London: Constable and Company Limited, 3 Vols., 1932.

Shedlock, John South. *Beethoven's pianoforte sonatas: the origin and respective values of various readings.* London: Augener Ltd., 1918.

Shedlock, John South. *The pianoforte sonata: its origin and development.* London: Methuen, 1895.

Shepherd, Arthur. *The string quartets of Ludwig van Beethoven.* Cleveland: H. Carr, The Printing Press, 1935.

Sheppard, Leslie and Herbert R. Axelrod. *Paganini: containing a portfolio of drawings by Vido Polikarpus.* Neptune City, New Jersey: Paganiniana Publications, 1979.

Short, Michael. *Gustav Holst: the man and his music.* Oxford: Oxford University Press, 1990.

Shostakovich, Dmitry. *Dmitry Shostakovich: about himself and his times.* Moscow: Progress Publishers, 1981.

Simpson, John Palgrave. *Carl Maria von Weber: the life of an artist, from the German of his son Baron, Max Maria von Weber.* London: Chapman and Hall, 1865.

Simpson, Robert. *Beethoven symphonies.* London: British Broadcasting Corporation, 1970.

Sipe, Thomas. *Beethoven: Eroica symphony.* Cambridge: Cambridge University Press, 1998.

Sitwell, Sacheverell. *Mozart.* Edinburgh: Peter Davies Limited, 1932.

Skelton, Geoffrey. *Paul Hindemith: the man behind the music; a biography.* London: Victor Gollancz, 1975.

Smallman, Basil. *The piano trio: its history, technique, and repertoire.* Oxford: Clarendon Press; Oxford; New York: Oxford University Press, 1990.

Smidak, Emil. *Isaak-Ignaz Moscheles: the life of the composer and his encounters with Beethoven, Liszt, Chopin, and Mendelssohn.* Aldershot, Hampshire, England: Scolar Press; Brookfield, Vermont, USA: Gower Publishing Co., 1989.

Smith, Barry. *Peter Warlock: the life of Philip Heseltine.* Oxford: Oxford University Press, 1994.

Smith, Joan Allen. *Schoenberg and his circle: a Viennese portrait.* New York: Schirmer Books, London: Collier Macmillan, 1986.

Smith, Richard Langham, Editor. *Debussy on music: the critical writings of the great French composer Claude Debussy.* London: Secker & Warburg, 1977.

Smith, Ronald. *Alkan.* London: Kahn and Averill, 1976.

Snowman, Daniel. *The Amadeus Quartet: the men and the music.* London: Robson Books, 1981.

Solomon, Maynard. *Beethoven.* New York: Schirmer, 1977.

Solomon, Maynard. *Beethoven*

essays. Cambridge, Massachusetts; London: Harvard University Press, 1988.

Solomon, Maynard. *Late Beethoven: music, thought, imagination*. Berkeley; London: University of California Press, 2003.

Solomon, Maynard. *Mozart: a life*. London: Hutchinson, 1995.

Sonneck, Oscar George Theodore. *Beethoven: impressions of contemporaries*. London: Oxford University Press, 1927.

Spalding, Albert. *Rise to follow: an autobiography*. London: Frederick Muller Ltd., 1946.

Spohr, Louis. *Louis Spohr's autobiography*. London: Longman, Green, Longman, Roberts, & Green, 1865.

Stafford, William. *Mozart myths: a critical reassessment*. Stanford, California: Stanford University Press, 1991.

Stanford, Charles Villiers. *Interludes: records and reflections*. London: John Murray, 1922.

Stanley, Glenn, Editor. *The Cambridge companion to Beethoven*. Cambridge; New York: Cambridge University Press, 2000

Stedman, Preston. *The symphony*. Englewood Cliffs, New Jersey; London: Prentice-Hall, 1979.

Stedron, Bohumír, Editor and Translator. *Leos Janácek: letters and reminiscences*. Prague: Artia, 1955.

Stein, Erwin, Editor. *Arnold Schoenberg: letters*. London: Faber and Faber, 1964.

Stein, Erwin. *Orpheus in new guises*. London: Rockliff, 1953.

Stein, Jack Madison. *Poem and music in the German lied from Gluck to Hugo Wolf*. Cambridge, Massachusetts: Harvard University Press, 1971.

Stein, Leonard, Editor. *Style and idea: selected writings of Arnold Schoenberg*. London: Faber and Faber, 1975.

Steinberg, Michael P. *Listening to reason: culture, subjectivity, and nineteenth-century music*. Princeton, New Jersey: Princeton University Press, 2004.

Steinberg, Michael. *The concerto: a listener's guide*. New York: Oxford University Press, 1998.

Steinberg, Michael. *The symphony: a listener's guide*. Oxford; New York: Oxford University Press, 1995.

Sternfeld, Frederick William. *Goethe and music: a list of parodies and Goethe's relationship to music; a list of references*. New York: Da Capo Press, 1979.

Stivender, David. *Mascagni: an autobiography compiled, edited and translated from original sources*. New York: Pro/Am Music Resources; London: Kahn & Averill, 1988.

Stone, Else and Kurt Stone, Editors. *The writings of Elliott Carter: an American composer looks at modern music*. Bloomington: Indiana University Press, 1977.

Stowell, Robin. *Beethoven: violin concerto*. Cambridge: Cambridge University Press, 1998.

Stowell, Robin: Editor. *The Cambridge companion to the cello*. Cambridge: Cambridge University Press, 1999.

Stowell, Robin: Editor. *The Cambridge companion to the string quartet*. Cambridge: Cambridge University Press, 2003.

Stratton, Stephen Samuel. *Men-

delssohn. London: J.M. Dent & Co.; New York: E.P. Dutton & Co., 1901.

Straus, Joseph N. *Remaking the past: musical modernism and the influence of the tonal tradition.* Cambridge, Massachusetts: Harvard University Press, 1990.

Stravinsky, Igor. *An autobiography.* London: Calder and Boyars, 1975.

Stravinsky, Igor. *Themes and conclusions.* London: Faber and Faber, 1972.

Stravinsky, Igor and Robert Craft. *Conversations with Igor Stravinsky.* London: Faber and Faber, 1959.

Stravinsky, Igor and Robert Craft. *Dialogues and a diary.* London: Faber and Faber 1968.

Stravinsky, Igor and Robert Craft. *Memories and commentaries.* London: Faber and Faber, 2002.

Strunk, Oliver. *Source readings in music history, 4: The Classic era.* London: Faber and Faber 1981.

Sullivan, Blair, Editor. *The echo of music: essays in honor of Marie Louise Göllner.* Warren, Michigan: Harmonie Park Press, 2004.

Sullivan, Jack, Editor. *Words on music: from Addison to Barzun.* Athens: Ohio University Press, 1990.

Symonette, Lys and Kim H. Kowalke, Editors and Translators. *Speak low (when you speak love): the letters of Kurt Weill and Lotte Lenya.* London: Hamish Hamilton, 1996.

Swalin, Benjamin F. *The violin concerto: a study in German romanticism.* New York, Da Capo Press, 1973.

Szigeti, Joseph. *With strings attached: reminiscences and reflections.* London: Cassell & Co. Ltd, 1949.

Tanner, Michael, Editor. *Notebooks, 1924–1954: Wilhelm Furtwängler.* London: Quartet Books, 1989.

Taylor, Robert, Editor. *Furtwängler on music: essays and addresses.* Aldershot: Scolar, 1991.

Taylor, Ronald. *Kurt Weill: composer in a divided world.* London: Simon & Schuster, 1991.

Tchaikovsky, Peter Ilich. *Letters to his family: an autobiography.* Translated by Galina von Meck. London: Dennis Dobson, 1981.

Tertis, Lionel. *My viola and I: a complete autobiography; with, 'Beauty of tone in string playing', and other essays.* London: Paul Elek, 1974.

Thayer, Alexander Wheelock. *Salieri: rival of Mozart.* Edited by Theodore Albrecht. Kansas City, Missouri: Philharmonia of Greater Kansas City, 1989.

Thomas, Michael Tilson. *Viva voce: conversations with Edward Seckerson.* London: Faber and Faber 1994.

Thomson, Andrew. *Vincent d'Indy and his world.* Oxford: Clarendon Press, 1996.

Thomson, Virgil. *The musical scene.* New York: Greenwood Press, 1968.

Thomson, Virgil. *Virgil Thomson.* London: Weidenfeld & Nicolson, 1967.

Tillard, Françoise. *Fanny Mendelssohn.* Amadeus Press: Portland, 1996.

Tilmouth, Michael, Editor. *Donald Francis Tovey: The classics of* music: talks, essays, and other writings previously uncollected. Oxford: Oxford University Press, 2001

Tippett, Michael. *Moving into Aquarius*. London: Routledge and Kegan Paul, 1959.

Tippett, Michael. *Those twentieth century blues: an autobiography*. London: Hutchinson, 1991.

Todd, R. Larry, Editor. *Nineteenth-century piano music*. New York; London: Routledge, 2004.

Todd, R. Larry, Editor. *Schumann and his world*. Princeton: Princeton University Press, 1994.

Tommasini, Anthony. *Virgil Thomson: composer on the aisle*. New York: W.W. Norton, 1997.

Tortelier, Paul. *A self-portrait: in conversation with David Blum*. London: Heinemann, 1984.

Tovey, Donald Francis. *A Companion to Beethoven's Pianoforte Sonatas*. Revised by Barry Cooper. London: The Associated Board, [1931], 1998.

Tovey, Donald Francis. *Beethoven*. London: Oxford University Press, 1944.

Tovey, Donald Francis. *Essays and lectures on music*. London: Oxford University Press, 1949.

Tovey, Donald Francis. *Essays in musical analysis*. London: Oxford University Press, H. Milford, 7 Vols., 1935–41.

Tovey, Donald Francis. *The forms of music: musical articles from The Encyclopaedia Britannica*. London: Oxford University Press, 1944.

Toye, Francis. *Giuseppe Verdi: his life and works*. London: William Heinemann Ltd., 1931.

Truscott, Harold. *Beethoven's late string quartets*. London: Dobson, 1968.

Tyler, William R. *The letters of Franz Liszt to Olga von Meyendorff, 1871–1886, in the Mildred Bliss Collection at Dumbarton Oaks*. Translated by William R. Tyler. Washington: Dumbarton Oaks, Trustees for Harvard University; Cambridge, Massachusetts: distributed by Harvard University Press, 1979.

Tyrrell, John. *Janácek: years of a life. Vol. 1, (1854–1914) The lonely blackbird*. London: Faber and Faber, 2006.

Tyrrell, John, Editor and Translator. *My life with Janácek: the memoirs of Zdenka Janácková*. London: Faber and Faber, 1998.

Tyson, Alan, Editor. *Beethoven studies 2*. Cambridge: Cambridge University Press, 1977.

Tyson, Alan, Editor. *Beethoven studies 3*. Cambridge: Cambridge University Press, 1982.

Tyson, Alan. *Mozart: studies of the autograph scores*. Cambridge, Massachusetts; London: Harvard University Press, 1987.

Tyson, Alan. *The authentic English editions of Beethoven*. London: Faber and Faber, 1963.

Underwood, J. A., Editor. *Gabriel Fauré: his life through his letters*. London: Marion Boyars, 1984.

Vechten, Carl van, Editor. *Nikolay, Rimsky-Korsakov: My musical life*. London: Martin Secker & Warburg Ltd., 1942.

Vinton, John. *Essays after a dictionary: music and culture at the close of Western civilization*. Lewisburg: Bucknell University Press, 1977.

Volkov, Solomon, Editor. *Testimony: the memoirs of Dmitri Shostakovich. London: Faber and Faber, 1981.

Volta, Ornella, Editor. *A mammal's notebook: collected writings of Erik Satie.* London: Atlas Press, 1996.

Wagner, Richard. Beethoven: *With [a] supplement from the philosophical works of A. Schopenhauer.* Translated by E. Dannreuther. London: Reeves, 1893.

Wagner, Richard. *My life.* London: Constable and Company Ltd., 1911.

Walden, Valerie. *One hundred years of violoncello: a history of technique and performance practice, 1740–1840.* Cambridge: Cambridge University Press, 1998.

Walker, Alan. *Franz Liszt. Volume 1, The virtuoso years: 1811–1847.* New York: Alfred A. Knopf, 1983.

Walker, Alan. *Franz Liszt. Volume 2, The Weimar years: 1848–1861.* London: Faber and Faber, 1989.

Walker, Alan. *Franz Liszt. Volume 3, The final years, 1861–1886.* London: Faber and Faber, 1997.

Walker, Bettina. *My musical experiences.* London: Richard Bentley and Son, 1890.

Walker, Ernest. *Free thought and the musician, and other essays.* London; New York: Oxford University Press, 1946.

Walker, Frank. *Hugo Wolf: a biography.* London: J. M. Dent, 1951.

Walker, Frank. *The man Verdi.* London: Dent, 1962.

Wallace, Grace, *[Lady Wallace].* Beethoven's letters (1790–1826): from the collection of Dr. Ludwig Nohl. Also his letters to the Archduke Rudolph, Cardinal-Archbishop of Olmutz, K.W., from the collection of Dr. Ludwig Ritter Von Koĺchel. London: Longmans, Green, 2 Vols., 1866.

Wallace, Robin. *Beethoven's critics: aesthetic dilemmas and resolutions during the composer's lifetime.* Cambridge; New York: Cambridge University Press, 1986.

Walter, Bruno. *Theme and variations: an autobiography.* London: H. Hamilton, 1948.

Warrack, John Hamilton. *Writings on music.* Cambridge: Cambridge University Press, 1981.

Wasielewski, Wilhelm Joseph von. *Life of Robert Schumann: with letters, 1833–1852.* London: William Reeves, 1878.

Watkins, Glenn. *Proof through the night: music and the Great War.* Berkeley: University of California Press, 2003.

Watkins, Glenn. *Pyramids at the Louvre: music, culture, and collage from Stravinsky to the postmodernists.* Cambridge, Massachusetts; London: Belknap Press of Harvard University Press, 1994.

Watkins, Glenn. *Soundings: music in the twentieth century.* New York: Schirmer Books London: Collier Macmillan, 1988.

Watson, Derek. *Liszt.* London: J. M. Dent, 1989.

Weaver, William, Editor. *The Verdi-Boito correspondence.* Chicago; London: University of Chicago Press, 1994.

Wegeler, Franz. *Remembering Beethoven: the biographical*

notes of Franz Wegeler and Ferdinand Ries. London: Andre Deutsch, 1988.

Weingartner, Felix. *Buffets and rewards: a musician's reminiscences.* London: Hutchinson & Co., 1937.

Weinstock, Herbert. *Rossini: a biography.* New York: Limelight, 1987.

Weiss, Piero and Richard Taruskin. *Music in the Western World: a history in documents.* New York: Schirmer; London: Collier Macmillan, 1984.

Weissweiler, Eva *The complete correspondence of Clara and Robert Schumann.* New York: Peter Lang, 2 Vols., 1994.

Whittaker, William Gillies. *Collected essays.* London: Oxford University Press, 1940.

Whittall, Arnold. *Exploring twentieth-century music: tradition and innovation.* Cambridge; New York: Cambridge University Press, 2003.

Whittall, Arnold. *Music since the First World War.* London: J. M. Dent, 1977.

Whitton, Kenneth S. *Lieder: an introduction to German song.* London: Julia MacRae, 1984.

Wightman, Alistair, Editor. *Szymanowski on music: selected writings of Karol Szymanowski.* London: Toccata Press, 1999.

Wilhelm, Kurt. *Richard Strauss: an intimate portrait.* London: Thames and Hudson, 1999.

Will, Richard James. *The characteristic symphony in the age of Haydn and Beethoven.* Cambridge: Cambridge University Press, 2002.

Willetts, Pamela J. *Beethoven and England: an account of sources in the British Museum.* London: British Museum, 1970.

Williams, Adrian, Editor and Translator. *Liszt, Franz: Selected letters.* Oxford: Clarendon Press, 1998.

Williams, Adrian. *Portrait of Liszt: by himself and his contemporaries.* Oxford: Clarendon Press, 1990.

Williams, Ralph Vaughan. *Heirs and rebels: letters written to each other and occasional writings on music.* London; New York: Oxford University Press, 1959.

Williams, Ralph Vaughan. *Some thoughts on Beethoven's Choral symphony: with writings on other musical subjects.* London; Oxford University Press, 1953.

Williams, Ralph Vaughan. *The making of music.* Ithaca, New York: Cornell University Press, 1955.

Williams, Ursula Vaughan. *R.V.W.: a biography of Ralph Vaughan Williams.* London: Oxford University Press, 1964.

Wilson, Conrad. *Notes on Beethoven: 20 crucial works.* Edinburgh: Saint Andrew Press, 2003.

Wilson, Elizabeth. *Shostakovich: a life remembered.* Princeton, New Jersey: Princeton University Press, 1994.

Winter, Robert, Editor. *Beethoven, performers, and critics: the International Beethoven Congress, Detroit, 1977.* Detroit: Wayne State University Press, 1980.

Winter, Robert. *Compositional origins of Beethoven's opus 131.* Ann Arbor, Michigan: UMI Research Press, 1982.

Winter, Robert and Robert Martin,

Editors. *The Beethoven quartet companion*. Berkeley: University of California Press, 1994.

Wolf, Eugene K. and Edward H. Roesner, Editors. *Studies in musical sources and style: essays in honor of Jan LaRue*. Madison, Wisconsin: A-R Editions, 1990.

Wolff, Christoph and Robert Riggs. *The string quartets of Haydn, Mozart and Beethoven: studies of the autograph manuscripts: a conference at Isham Memorial Library, March 15–17, 1979*. Cambridge, Massachusetts: Department of Music, Harvard University, 1980.

Wolff, Konrad. *Masters of the keyboard: individual style elements in the piano music of Bach, Haydn, Mozart, Beethoven, Schubert, Chopin, and Brahms*. Bloomington: Indiana University Press, 1990.

Wörner, Karl Heinrich. *Stockhausen: life and work*. London: Faber, 1973.

Wright, Donald, Editor. *Cardus on music: a centenary collection*. London: Hamish Hamilton, 1988.

Wyndham, Henry Saxe. *August Manns and the Saturday concerts: a memoir and a retrospect*. London and Felling-on-Tyne, New York, The Walter Scott Publishing Co., Ltd., 1909.

Yastrebtsev, V.V. Edited and Translated by Florence Jonas. *Reminiscences of Rimsky-Korsakov*. New York: Columbia University Press, 1985.

Yates, Peter. *Twentieth century music: its evolution from the end of the harmonic era into the present era of sound*. London: Allen & Unwin Ltd., 1968.

Young, Percy M. *Beethoven: a Victorian tribute based on the papers of Sir George Smart*. London: D. Dobson, 1976.

Young, Percy M. *George Grove, 1820–1900: a biography*. London: Macmillan, 1980.

Young, Percy M. *Letters of Edward Elgar and other writings*. London: Geoffrey Bles, 1956.

Young, Percy M., Editor. *Letters to Nimrod: Edward Elgar to August Jaeger, 1897–1908*. London: Dennis Dobson, 1965.

Young, Percy M. *The concert tradition: from the middle ages to the twentieth century*. London: Routledge and Kegan Paul, 1965.

Young, Rob, Editor. *(Brief Description): Undercurrents: the hidden wiring of modern music*. London; New York, N.Y.: Continuum, 2002.

Yourke, Electra Slonimsky, Editor. *Nicolas Slonimsky: writings on music*. New York, N.Y.; London: Routledge, 4 Vols. 2003-2005.

Slonimsky, Nicolas. *The great composers and their works*. Edited by Electra Slonimsky Yourke. New York: Schirmer Books, 2 Vols. 2000.

Ysaÿe, Antoine. *Ysaÿe: his life, work and influence*. London: W. Heinemann, 1947.

Zamoyski, Adam. *Paderewski*. London: Collins, 1982.

Zegers, Mirjam, Editor. *Louis Andriessen: The art of stealing time*. Todmorden: Arc Music, 2002.

Zemanova, Mirka, Editor. *Janácek's uncollected essays on music*. London: Marion Boyars, 1989.

INDEX

Index to Grosse Fuge, Op 133, Fugue Transcription, Op. 134, String Quartet Op. 131 and String Quartet Op. 135. Incorporating a Beethoven timeline of significant musical and related events.

The order adopted for the listing of the individual entries in this index, for each of the string quartets under consideration, is chronological — according to the sequential unfolding of events under discussion. Thereby, the reader is provided with both a guide to the contents discussed in the main text and a timeline of the principal events bearing on Beethoven's life and work.

GROSSE FUGE, OP. 133 PP. 1-37
Beethoven's disposition to fugal writing
J. S. Bach, influence of
Struggle between 'body and spirit'
Christian Gottlob Neefe, counterpoint instruction
Mozart's C minor fugue, K 426, influence of
Haydn's fugal treatment, influence of
Pierre Boulez, views of
'Struggle sublimated into ecstasy'
Creation origins
Sketchbook sources

Estimations of Op. 133
Construction, Beethoven's terminology and significance of
21 March 1826, first public performance
AmZ, critical reception
Anton Schindler, views of
Anton Schindler, recollections of
Matthias Artaria, publisher
Title Page
Dedication
Pleyel & Sons, publication in France
Nineteenth-century reception
Felix Weingartner, transcription
Contemporary estimations
Fugue construction and conception, discussion of

GROSSE FUGE, TRANSCRIPTION, OP. 134 PP. 41-47

Challenges posed by fugal ending to Op. 130
AmZ, critical response
Karl Holz, Beethoven's interlocutor
Matthias Artaria, request for pianoforte arrangement — four hands
Beethoven's previous piano transcriptions
Anton Halm, first transcription
Beethoven's disaffection
Carl Czerny, potential involvement with
Beethoven's negotiations of publication rights
Autograph score, sale of
2005, rediscovery of manuscript in Palmer Theological Seminary

STRING QUARTET, OP. 131 PP. 49-128

Karl Holz, recollections of
Beethoven's creative powers, further evidence of
Expansion of four-movement design
Triptych concept: A minor, B-flat major and C-sharp minor
Denis Matthews, views of
linking consecutive movements, concept of
Transformation of role of string quartet
Ignaz Schuppanzigh, pioneering role of
C-sharp minor, choice of key
Beethoven's harmonic language
Numbering of movements, Beethoven's care with
Johann Reinhold Schultz, recollections of
Carl Maria von Weber, recollections of
Ferdinand Georg Waldmüller, portrait
Bernhard Schotts, negotiations with
Illness
Heinrich Albert Probst, putative negotiations with
Work on *Grosse Fuge*
Misunderstanding with Schotts
Metronome markings, discussion of
Illness
Johann Nepomuk Wolfmayer, intended dedicatee
Carl Gottlieb von Tucher
Schotts' solicitous conduct towards Beethoven
Completion of Op. 131
Lieutenant Field-Marshall, Baron Joseph von Stutterheim, change of dedicatee
Intelligenzblatt der Caecilla, publication announcement
Title Page
AmZ, estimation
Early performances
Hector Berlioz, recollections of
Nineteenth-century reception
Joseph Hellmesberger
Gustav Mahler
Franz Schubert, anecdote
Modern-day reception
Sketchbook sources

Quartet movements, discussion of
Summative remarks

STRING QUARTET, OP. 135 PP. 138-190

Beethoven's return to traditional models
Haydnesque world
Return to smaller construction
Four-movement design
Potential new beginning, projected works
Beethoven's personal circumstances
Ludwig Rellstab, recollections of
Karl van Beethoven
Baron von Stutterheim
Illness
Dr. Andreas Wawruch
Ignaz Schuppanzigh
Beethoven domiciled at Gneixendorf
Dr. Keller, anecdote concerning
Adolf and Maurice Schlesinger, negotiations with
Karl Holz, role of
Ess muss sein?, origins of
Illness
Title Page, Jean Wolfmayer dedicatee
23 March 1828, first performance
Adolf Bernhard Marx, recollections of
Wolfgang Goethe, recollections of
English edition
Nineteenth-century reception
Music Weekly, London
Richard Wagner's Beethoven Centennial essay, 1870
Sketch sources
Quartet movements, discussion of
Summative remarks
Beethoven's achievement in genre of string quartet

ABOUT THE AUTHOR

Terence M. Russell graduated with first class honours in architecture and was a nominee for the coveted Silver Medal of the Royal Institute of British Architects. He is a Fellow of the Royal Incorporation of Architects in Scotland (retired), was formerly Reader in the School of Arts, Culture and Environment at the University of Edinburgh, a Fellow of the British Higher Education Academy, and Senior Assessor to the Scottish Higher Education Funding Council. Alongside his professional work in the field of architecture — embracing practice, teaching and research — he has maintained a lifetime's interest in the music and musicology of Beethoven. He has an equal admiration for the work of Franz Schubert and was for many years an active member of the Schubert Institute, UK. His book writings in the field of architecture include the following:

The Built Environment: A Subject Index, Gregg Publishing (1989):
- Vol. 1: Town planning and urbanism, architecture, gardens and landscape design
- Vol. 2: Environmental technology, constructional engineering, building and materials
- Vol. 3: Decorative art and industrial design, international exhibitions and collections, recreational and performing arts
- Vol. 4: Public health, municipal services, community welfare

Architecture in the Encyclopédie of Diderot and D'Alemebert: The Letterpress Articles and Selected Engravings, Scolar Press (1993)

The Encyclopaedic Dictionary in the Eighteenth Century: Architecture, Arts and Crafts, Scolar Press (1997):
- Vol. 1: John Harris, Lexicon Technicum
- Vol. 2: Ephraim Chambers, Cyclopaedia
- Vol. 3: The Builder's Dictionary
- Vol. 4: Samuel Johnson, A Dictionary of the English Language
- Vol. 5: A Society of Gentlemen, Encyclopaedia Britannica

Gardens and Landscapes in the Encyclopédie of Diderot and D'Alemebert: The Letterpress Articles and Selected Engravings, 2 Vols., Ashgate (1999)

The Napoleonic Survey of Egypt: The Monuments and Customs of Egypt, 2 Vols., Ashgate (2001)

The Discovery of Egypt: Vivant Denon's Travels with Napoleon's Army, History Press (2005)

www.ingramcontent.com/pod-product-compliance
Lightning Source LLC
Chambersburg PA
CBHW010021130526
44590CB00047B/3754